THE
COMPLETE
DOG
BREED
BOOK

THE
COMPLETE
DOG
BREED
BOOK

Consultant Editor
DR. KIM DENNIS-BRYAN

Commissioned photography by
TRACY MORGAN

Penguin Random House

SECOND EDITION

DK UK

Senior Editor Helen Fewster
Managing Editor Angeles Gavira Guerrero
Managing Art Editor Michael Duffy
Senior Producer, Pre-Production Andy Hilliard
Senior Producer Meskerem Berhane
Jacket Design Development Manager Sophia M.T.T.
Associate Publishing Director Liz Wheeler
Art Director Karen Self
Publishing Director Jonathan Metcalf

Consultant Editor Kim Dennis-Bryan
Contributors Ann Baggaley, Adam Beral,
Candida Frith-Macdonald, James Harrison

DK INDIA

Senior Editor Arani Sinha
Assistant Editor Ankita Gupta
Art Editor Anukriti Arora
Managing Editor Soma B. Chowdhury
Senior Managing Art Editor Arunesh Talapatra
Assistant Picture Researcher Geetika Bhandari
Picture Research Manager Taiyaba Khatoon
Senior DTP Designers Vishal Bhatia, Jagtar Singh
Production Manager Pankaj Sharma
Pre-production Manager Balwant Singh
Senior Jacket Designer Suhita Dharamjit

This edition published in 2020
First published in Great Britain in 2012 by
Dorling Kindersley Limited
80 Strand, London, WC2R 0RL

Copyright © 2012, 2020 Dorling Kindersley Limited

A Penguin Random House Company

10 9 8 7 6 5 4 3 2 1

001-316671-Feb/2020

A CIP catalogue record for this book is available from the British Library.

ISBN: 978-0-2414-1273-2

Manufactured in Hong Kong

A WORLD OF IDEAS:
SEE ALL THERE IS TO KNOW

www.dk.com

CONTENTS

1 INTRODUCTION TO DOGS

2 GUIDE TO BREEDS

3 CARE AND TRAINING

INTRODUCTION TO DOGS

WHAT IS A DOG?

The evolution of the dog from wild predator to domestic companion has been greatly influenced by human intervention. It has taken just a few hundred years to produce seemingly endless variations on the canine theme – but planned breeding has not removed the basic characteristics of the dog's ancestor, the wolf.

Dogs are social animals

Evolution of the dog

All dogs share a common ancestor: the grey wolf. While this relationship is fairly apparent in breeds such as the German Shepherd or Spitz-type dogs, with their wolf-like heads and pricked ears, it is hard to see the connection between wolves and Toy Poodles or St. Bernards. Genetically, however, any dog of any breed is virtually identical to the wolf. The transition from wolf to the huge diversity of domestic dogs known today happened relatively quickly. The process began gradually, with random changes in size and shape, but accelerated when humans began to selectively breed those dogs that exhibited characteristics they desired.

In from the wild

Grey wolves and dogs diverged between 15,000 to 40,000 years ago, but when and where they developed a close relationship with humans is unclear. DNA evidence for domesticated dogs has been found in several locations in Asia and Europe; the timing varies from 20,000 to 40,000 years ago, which suggests that domestication events may have occurred more than once, and in different areas. The oldest remains known to be domesticated dogs date back to around 14,000 years ago, and comprise human-dog burials from the Middle East and Germany. Older dog fossils from Europe and Asia also exist, but whether these are fossils of domesticated dogs remains uncertain.

There are alternative theories about how dogs became domesticated. Some scholars believe that wolves scavenging around early human encampments were killed for their meat and skin; their orphan pups were taken in and reared in captivity, and were found to be valuable as hunters and protectors, beginning the process of domestication. Others question why humans would want to domesticate a large predator that would compete with them for food. They suggest

RELATIONSHIPS OF THE DOG FAMILY

This diagram shows the relationship between the dog and some of the other canids (members of the dog family), based on genetic evidence. The dog and the grey wolf are more closely related to one another than to any other canids.

Foxes   Ethiopian Wolf   Golden Jackal   Coyote   Grey Wolf   Dog

THE SHAPE OF A PREDATOR
The canid family are shaped to be efficient hunters. This Weimaraner remains true to his ancestral body plan and can move with speed and grace.

that wolves were more trusting of humans, and could learn and adapt to human behaviour, and so in part may have domesticated themselves. Over subsequent generations, this led to physical developments such as drop ears, and behavioural changes, such as increased friendliness, to encourage humans to fulfil their needs.

Hundreds of years passed before deliberate breeding became more sophisticated, selecting for coat type, colour, temperament, and specialized skills, eventually creating hundreds of different breeds. The selection processes have altered over the years, and while certain characteristics fall out of favour, others become embedded in the breed standard.

Information from dog DNA

In the past, the history of a dog breed was pieced together from written records, pictures, and information handed down from past breeders and owners. Today, the analysis of DNA (the hereditary template found in body cells) has also made it possible to track the inheritance of features such as size and coat colour, and to look at the differences and similarities between one breed and another. Most importantly, looking at DNA has made it possible to identify which breeds are at risk of specific genetic diseases and conditions (see pp.338–39). Scientists sequenced the first complete dog genome (the complete set of genetic information possessed by an organism) in 2005 using the DNA of a Boxer.

Even with the use of genetic analysis, unravelling the history of a particular breed is not easy. Some breeds are commonly said to be very ancient, but genetic evidence suggests that the majority are, in fact, modern re-creations. With few exceptions, most breeds known today were developed no earlier than the 19th century.

Dog anatomy

The physical characteristics of a dog are typical of a predator whose survival relies on efficiency in locating and catching prey. Humans have done much to adapt canine design, but the basic anatomy of all breeds of dog is the same.

The skeleton of the dog evolved to provide speed, strength, and manoeuvrability. A highly flexible spine and freely moving forelimbs allow a dog to move with a long, swinging stride. The most important characteristics of a dog's skeleton are seen in the legs. The two large forearm bones, the radius and the ulna, are locked together in such a way that a dog can make rapid changes of direction without the bones rotating and breaking. In a further adaptation, two of the wrist bones are fused together – unlike the separate bones seen in humans – to give a dog strength and stability when moving in a straight line. Combined with long, powerful toes, with claws like studs on running shoes, this limb arrangement gives a dog a high degree of control whether it is running, jumping, or turning.

Classified as carnivores, dogs are anatomically adapted to eat primarily meat, although, given the opportunity, domestic dogs will eat almost anything. A dog's teeth are designed to deal with tough foods such as hide, flesh, and

PACK MENTALITY
Doing things cooperatively is an inbuilt canine characteristic, but domestic dogs now look to humans, rather than other dogs, when they need help.

bone. Four large canine teeth at the front of a dog's mouth are used for grabbing and biting prey, while the sides of the jaw include specially modified teeth, the carnassials, which the dog uses for shearing off meat. Dogs have a capacious stomach for the storage of large quantities of food and, as meat can be digested rapidly, a short intestinal tract.

Dogs have a wide-angled field of vision that functions best at long distance and they are extremely sensitive to movement. Out of the corner of an eye, a dog can pick up the flicker of a rabbit a hundred metres away, but at close range, canine vision is less efficient, which is why a dog may fail to spot a toy on the ground in front of his nose. Dogs have little use for sophisticated colour vision and their eyes have far fewer colour-receptive cells than those of humans.

Sharp hearing and the ability to pinpoint the direction of sounds is essential to wild hunting dogs. Breeds with erect ears shaped like those of the wolf are likely to have more acute hearing than breeds with drop ears, which rely more on sight or scent when hunting. A dog's highly sensitive ears allow it to pick up sounds at a far higher frequency than can be heard by humans. Smell is the most important of all canine senses. Sniffing is the way a dog

TALL AND SHORT
The extreme diversity of dog breeds is illustrated by the differences in leg length between an Irish Wolfhound and a Wire-haired Dachshund.

reads its surroundings and the area of the brain that interprets smells is around 40 times larger than the corresponding area in a human brain. Dogs' noses are packed with far more scent receptive cells than humans: while a person has an estimated 5 million scent receptors, a small dog may have closer to 130 million. In breeds renowned for their scenting ability, such as hounds, the number of scent receptors may be as many as 200–300 million.

Unlike humans, dogs do not have sweat glands in their skin, except on the bottoms of their paws. To cool down, dogs must pant, tongue hanging out. The tongue produces copious saliva, some of which evaporates and so helps to reduce body temperature.

A DOG'S BODY PLAN
All dogs have the same basic body design, handed down from their wolf ancestor, although centuries of selective breeding have produced dramatic variations.

Occiput

Stop

Cheek

Withers

Shoulder   Loins   Hip   Croup

Muzzle

Flews

Tail

Sternum

Upper thigh

Chest   Belly   Lower thigh

Foreleg   Elbow   Stifle

Hock

Pastern

Wrist   Carpal pad

Claws

Toes

Head shapes

All canine heads are variations of three basic shapes. The majority of dogs have a mesaticephalic head, in which length and width are of medium proportions. A dolichocephalic head is long and narrow, with a barely noticeable stop. Brachycephalic heads are broad based and short in length.

**Dolichocephalic head
(Saluki)**

**Mesaticephalic head
(German Pointer)**

**Brachycephalic head
(Bulldog)**

Ear types

Pricked, sensitive, wolf-like ears – the original canine shape – occur in many breeds of dog, but centuries of planned selection have created a large variety of other ear shapes. There are three main types: erect, semi-erect, and drop. Within these categories are many variations, such as the type of erect ear known as candle flame. Ear types are often the defining characteristic of a dog group; for example, scent hounds usually have long, pendant ears. Ears strongly influence a dog's overall appearance. The correct set, shape, and carriage of the ears are considered very important in recognized breeds, and are described precisely in official breed standards.

**Erect
(Alaskan Malamute)**

**Candle flame
(Russian Toy)**

**Button
(Pug)**

**Drop
(Broholmer)**

**Rose
(Greyhound)**

**Pendant
(Bloodhound)**

Coat varieties

The majority of dog breeds have a double coat like their wolf ancestor. This usually consists of an insulating layer of soft, dense hair covered by a harsher outer coat of varying length and texture. A few thinner-coated breeds, such as greyhounds, have just a single layer of hair (no undercoat). In some breeds, chance genetic mutation has produced dogs that are either completely hairless or have just a few strands of hair on the head and legs.

**Hairless
(Chinese Crested)**

**Short
(Dalmatian)**

**Curly
(Poodle)**

**Corded
(Komondor)**

**Long, straight
(Maltese)**

**Long, fluffy
(Pekingese)**

Breeds and breed groups

Although many distinct varieties of dog were recognized earlier, until the early 20th century their breeding was not necessarily strictly controlled. When dog breeders started to cooperate with one another and form clubs they were able to produce dogs of consistent type. This led to the writing of breed standards that describe the ideal appearance (with permissible variations) and temperament of a breed, and its suitability for function. Dogs were also registered in stud books to enable their pedigrees to be reviewed for future breeding.

Despite the detailed dog breed standards that exist, there are as yet no universally recognized criteria for classifying dog breeds in groups. The main regulatory bodies are the Kennel Club (KC) in the UK; the Fédération Cynologique Internationale (FCI) – the World Canine Organization, which includes 86 member countries; and the American Kennel Club (AKC). These all group breeds together based loosely on function, but no two systems are exactly the same. Both the UK and American Kennel Clubs recognize seven groups, while the FCI has ten. The number of individual breeds recognized by these organizations also varies.

This book places breeds together in eight major groups: primitive dogs; working dogs; spitz-type dogs; sight hounds; scent hounds; terriers; gundogs; and companion dogs; plus a section on crossbreeds and random bred dogs. The groupings of the so-called primitive dogs, sight hounds, and the spitz-type dogs in this book have been made on the basis of well-established genetic relationships. In some cases, this results in a breed appearing in a different group from the one that might be expected. The Basenji, for example, is often grouped functionally with hounds but genetic evidence places it among the primitive breeds, which is where this book, and the FCI, place it. For the remainder of the groups, more traditional, functional groupings are used.

HOW DOGS ARE GROUPED IN THIS BOOK

The dog groupings used in this book are illustrated below with an example of a dog that appears in each category.

Primitive dogs
pp.22-31
Basenji

Working dogs
pp.32-95
Broholmer

Spitz-type dogs
pp.96-123
Finnish Spitz

Sight Hounds
pp.124-135
Greyhound

Scent Hounds
pp.136-185
Basset Hound

Terriers
pp.186-219
Parson Russell Terrier

Gundogs
pp.220-259
Bourbonnais Pointing Dog

Companion dogs
pp.260-281
Russian Toy

Crossbreeds
pp.282-291
Labradoodle

HOW TO USE THE BREED CATALOGUE

 Amount of exercise required: from up to 30 minutes a day (1 bar) to more than 2 hours a day (3 bars).

Amount of grooming required: from once a week (1 bar) to every day (3 bars).

Ease of training: from easy (1 bar) to time consuming (3 bars).

Level of sociability: from dogs that need early socialization (1 bar) to naturally lively and amenable dogs (3 bars).

Height of dog in relation to human adult male. The dog's height is measured from its feet to the highest point of the withers

Group to which dog belongs

WORKING DOGS 95

GREAT DANE

GENTLE AND EASY TO MAINTAIN, THIS DOG TAKES UP A LOT OF ROOM

KC

Kennel club recognized

Height range
71-76cm (28-30in)

Weight range
46-54kg (101-119lb)

Life span Under 10 years

Origin Germany

Other colours

Blue

Black

Brindle

Elegance and dignity combined with gigantic size make the Great Dane one of the most impressive of all dogs. Once a hunting dog in Germany, the easy-going Great Dane is content to be a house dog, provided there is enough room for it to flop comfortably. As well as space, the breed needs plenty of exercise.

Long, arched neck with no loose skin

Dark shading on head and ears

Short, harlequin coat

Deep, long, fawn body

 Data scale

1 bar

2 bars

3 bars

Swatches show permissible colour variations for the breed

Information on coat colour

COAT COLOURS

Some dog breeds have just one coat colour or only one colour combination, but many have two or three colour variations, or more. Where applicable, the breed descriptions in this book include colour swatches that match as closely as possible the coat colours recognized in a breed. These are in addition to the colours that can be seen in the photographs of the dog.

A swatch may represent a range of colours. The swatches listed in the key below are as specified in various breed standards but different names may be given for the same colour: for example, while red is used to describe a red coat for many breeds, ruby is used for King Charles Spaniels and Cavalier King Charles Spaniels. A final generic swatch is used to represent a variety of colours.

Cream; white; white-beige; blonde; yellow

Grey; ashen-grey; slate-grey; steel-grey; grey brindle; wolf-grey; silver

Gold; russet gold; apricot; biscuit; wheaten; sandy; mustard; straw; straw bracken; isabella; all shades of fawn; yellow-red; sable

 Red; red merle; ruby; stag-red; deep red ginger; sandy-red; red-fawn; red-brown; chestnut-brown; orange; orange roan

 Liver; bronze

 Blue; blue merle (blue-grey); ash

 Dark brown; bos (brown); chocolate; dead leaf

 Black; nearly black; dark grey

 Black and tan; vieräugl; karamis; King Charles; black grizzle and tan; black and brown

 Blue, mottled with tan; blue and tan

 Liver and tan

 Gold and white (either colour may predominate); white and chestnut; yellow and white; white with orange, sable, and white; orange belton; lemon belton

 Chestnut, red and white; red and white; red and white spotted

 Liver and white; liver belton; brown and white (either colour may predominate); red roan; roan

 Tan and white (either colour may predominate)

 Black and white (either colour may predominate); piebald; black and white spotted; sesame; black sesame; black and silver

 Black, tan and white; grey, black, and tan; white, chocolate, and tan; Prince Charles; (all also known as tricolour)

 Brindle; black brindle; dark brindle; fawn brindle; pepper and salt; range of red brindles

Variety of colours or any colour

CHOOSING THE RIGHT DOG

The dog you choose will probably be your companion for the next 10 or 12 years, so making the right decision is important. Being faced with more than 400 different breeds with a variety of exercise, training, and grooming needs can be bewildering. This section provides advice and flowcharts to help you narrow down your choice.

A puppy can grow into a big dog, so know what you are buying

The perfect match

You may be attracted to a particular breed because of its looks, or have fallen in love with a beguiling puppy, but before going any further consider carefully whether you and the dog are a good match. To avoid difficulties and disappointments later on, take a look at your lifestyle and ask yourself the following questions.

What type of home do you live in, and are you a town or country dweller? A small apartment is obviously no place for a very large breed if both owner and dog are to cohabit comfortably. Remember, though, that a small dog with exceptionally high energy levels can also seem to take up a lot of room. Whether or not you have a garden, you will need access to open spaces where your dog can safely let off steam and meet other dogs. How house-proud are you? Can you tolerate loose hairs, slobber, and muddy pawprints? Keeping the place tidy can be harder with a dog around.

Can you give a dog the exercise he needs to stay physically and mentally fit? Some owners want an undemanding companion who is content with a short daily walk followed by a long snooze. If you enjoy an active lifestyle yourself, you may want a lively running mate to help set the pace for jogging or on long hikes. Large dogs do not necessarily need

more exercise than small ones. Some of the bigger breeds have a very laid-back attitude to life, while many small dogs, such as terriers, have boundless energy.

How much effort are you willing to put into grooming your dog? Long-coated breeds look beautiful but they are high maintenance and may need daily brushing and detangling. You should also consider the likely cost of professional grooming: some dogs have coats that are easy to care for in day-to-day terms but may need regular trimming.

Is your dog to be part of a family that includes children or other pets? Be wary of picking a breed that is large or exuberant enough to knock over a small child or an older person, or a dog with a natural chasing instinct that might put a beloved cat or guinea pig at risk.

Do you have enough room in your life for a dog? Exercise will take up time every day, but what dogs need as much as walks is company; any dog left alone for too long is likely to become bored, morose, and destructive. If you work away from the house all week, then unless you can make adequate care arrangements, a dog may not be a suitable pet for you.

Owning a dog is a long-term commitment in financial and practical terms. Make it a joy by choosing the breed that is as near as possible the perfect one for you.

HOW TO USE THE FLOWCHARTS

The following flowcharts will help you to choose a dog. They are based on three criteria: exercise, grooming, and training. Decide if you want a dog with high, medium, or low exercise requirements, and follow the paths to find suggestions for suitable breeds. Also look at the breed catalogue data to find further dogs not listed here.

HOW MUCH EXERCISE?

HIGH More than 2 hours per day

MEDIUM 1–2 hours per day

LOW Up to 30 minutes per day

HOW MUCH GROOMING?

HIGH Every day

MEDIUM More than once a week

LOW Once a week

HOW MUCH TRAINING?

HIGH Not so easy to train – time consuming

MEDIUM Quite easy to train – needs patience

LOW Easy to train

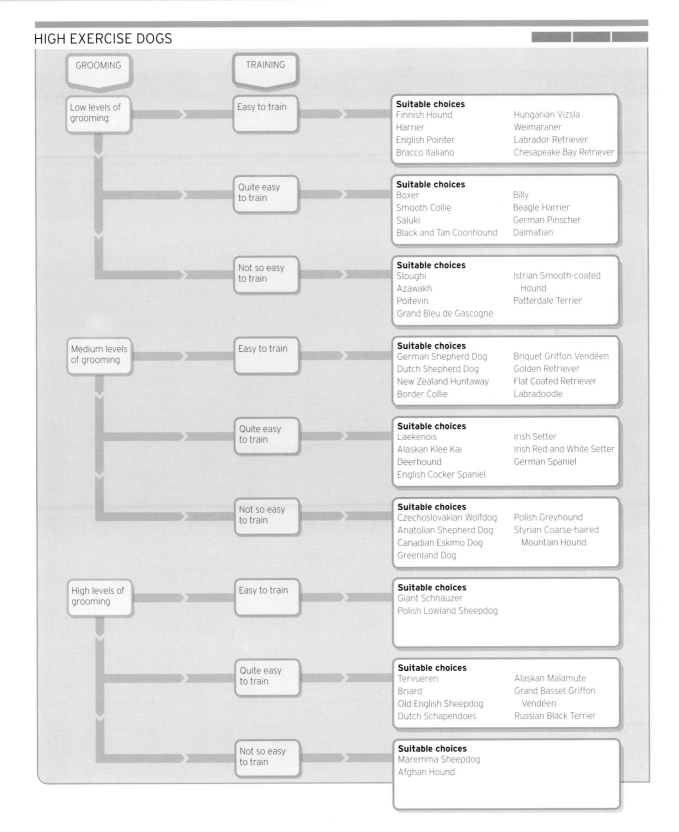

HIGH EXERCISE DOGS

GROOMING

TRAINING

Low levels of grooming

Easy to train

Suitable choices
Finnish Hound	Hungarian Vizsla
Harrier	Weimaraner
English Pointer	Labrador Retriever
Bracco Italiano	Chesapeake Bay Retriever

Quite easy to train

Suitable choices
Boxer	Billy
Smooth Collie	Beagle Harrier
Saluki	German Pinscher
Black and Tan Coonhound	Dalmatian

Not so easy to train

Suitable choices
Sloughi	Istrian Smooth-coated
Azawakh	Hound
Poitevin	Patterdale Terrier
Grand Bleu de Gascogne	

Medium levels of grooming

Easy to train

Suitable choices
German Shepherd Dog	Briquet Griffon Vendéen
Dutch Shepherd Dog	Golden Retriever
New Zealand Huntaway	Flat Coated Retriever
Border Collie	Labradoodle

Quite easy to train

Suitable choices
Laekenois	Irish Setter
Alaskan Klee Kai	Irish Red and White Setter
Deerhound	German Spaniel
English Cocker Spaniel	

Not so easy to train

Suitable choices
Czechoslovakian Wolfdog	Polish Greyhound
Anatolian Shepherd Dog	Styrian Coarse-haired
Canadian Eskimo Dog	Mountain Hound
Greenland Dog	

High levels of grooming

Easy to train

Suitable choices
Giant Schnauzer	
Polish Lowland Sheepdog	

Quite easy to train

Suitable choices
Tervueren	Alaskan Malamute
Briard	Grand Basset Griffon
Old English Sheepdog	Vendéen
Dutch Schapendoes	Russian Black Terrier

Not so easy to train

Suitable choices
Maremma Sheepdog	
Afghan Hound	

MEDIUM EXERCISE DOGS

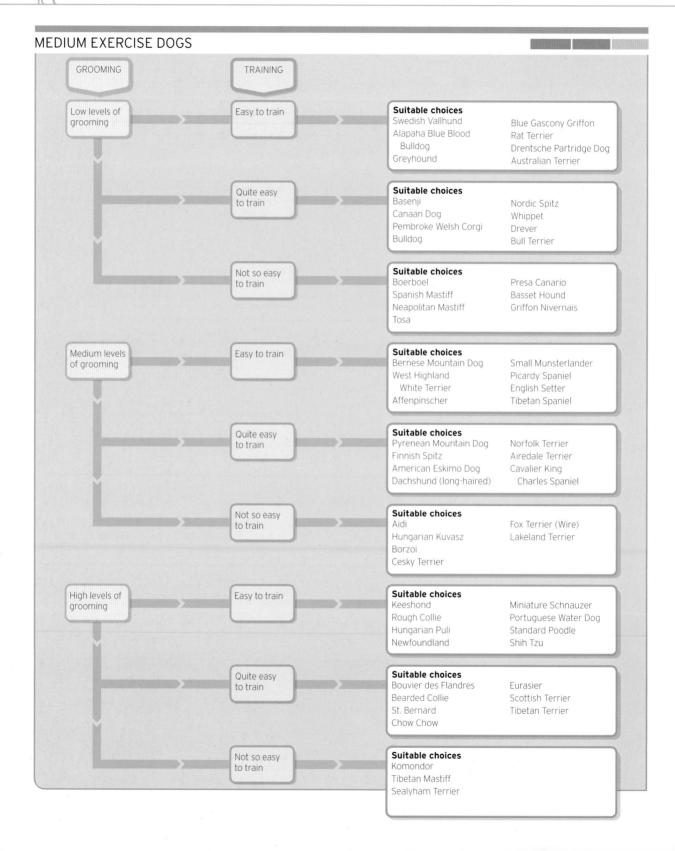

GROOMING

TRAINING

Low levels of grooming

Easy to train

Suitable choices
Swedish Vallhund
Alapaha Blue Blood Bulldog
Greyhound

Blue Gascony Griffon
Rat Terrier
Drentsche Partridge Dog
Australian Terrier

Quite easy to train

Suitable choices
Basenji
Canaan Dog
Pembroke Welsh Corgi
Bulldog

Nordic Spitz
Whippet
Drever
Bull Terrier

Not so easy to train

Suitable choices
Boerboel
Spanish Mastiff
Neapolitan Mastiff
Tosa

Presa Canario
Basset Hound
Griffon Nivernais

Medium levels of grooming

Easy to train

Suitable choices
Bernese Mountain Dog
West Highland White Terrier
Affenpinscher

Small Munsterlander
Picardy Spaniel
English Setter
Tibetan Spaniel

Quite easy to train

Suitable choices
Pyrenean Mountain Dog
Finnish Spitz
American Eskimo Dog
Dachshund (long-haired)

Norfolk Terrier
Airedale Terrier
Cavalier King Charles Spaniel

Not so easy to train

Suitable choices
Aidi
Hungarian Kuvasz
Borzoi
Cesky Terrier

Fox Terrier (Wire)
Lakeland Terrier

High levels of grooming

Easy to train

Suitable choices
Keeshond
Rough Collie
Hungarian Puli
Newfoundland

Miniature Schnauzer
Portuguese Water Dog
Standard Poodle
Shih Tzu

Quite easy to train

Suitable choices
Bouvier des Flandres
Bearded Collie
St. Bernard
Chow Chow

Eurasier
Scottish Terrier
Tibetan Terrier

Not so easy to train

Suitable choices
Komondor
Tibetan Mastiff
Sealyham Terrier

LOW EXERCISE DOGS

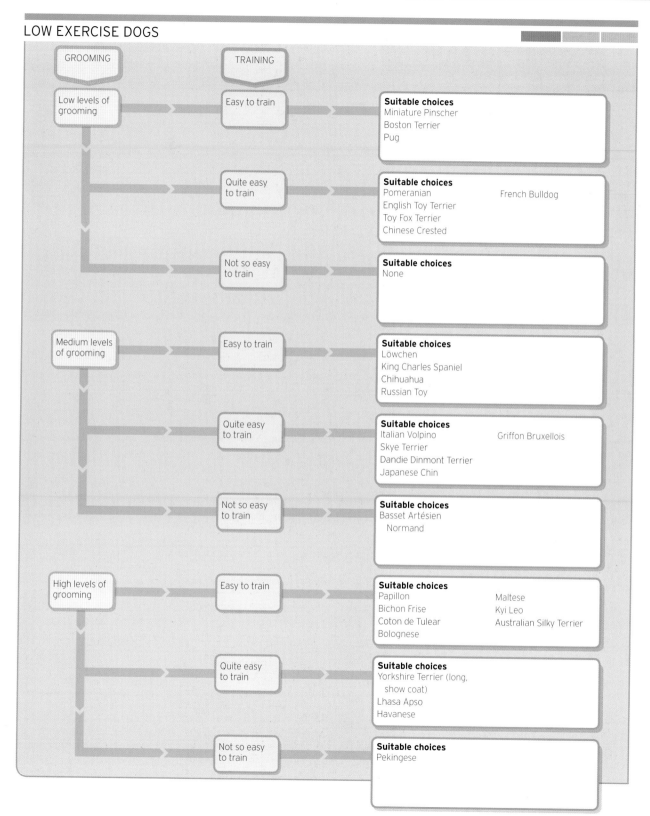

GROOMING

TRAINING

Low levels of grooming

Easy to train

Suitable choices
Miniature Pinscher
Boston Terrier
Pug

Quite easy to train

Suitable choices
Pomeranian — French Bulldog
English Toy Terrier
Toy Fox Terrier
Chinese Crested

Not so easy to train

Suitable choices
None

Medium levels of grooming

Easy to train

Suitable choices
Löwchen
King Charles Spaniel
Chihuahua
Russian Toy

Quite easy to train

Suitable choices
Italian Volpino — Griffon Bruxellois
Skye Terrier
Dandie Dinmont Terrier
Japanese Chin

Not so easy to train

Suitable choices
Basset Artésien
  Normand

High levels of grooming

Easy to train

Suitable choices
Papillon — Maltese
Bichon Frise — Kyi Leo
Coton de Tulear — Australian Silky Terrier
Bolognese

Quite easy to train

Suitable choices
Yorkshire Terrier (long,
  show coat)
Lhasa Apso
Havanese

Not so easy to train

Suitable choices
Pekingese

Finding a breeder

If you decide to buy a pedigree dog, you need to find a reputable breeder. A recommendation from your vet or a friend is ideal, and some kennel clubs provide lists of breeders; otherwise, the best way to choose a breeder is to visit several armed with a list of questions (see box opposite for the most important ones to ask).

Good breeders will be happy to give you plenty of time to observe the litter. It is particularly important to see puppies with their litter mates and their mother. Young puppies should never be kept in isolation, and if this is the case at any kennels you visit, then do not consider buying from them. The sire may not be at the same breeders, but if he is, ask if you can see him too. The appearance, behaviour, and temperament of the adult dogs will enable you to make a judgement on the likely future development of your puppy.

Watch how the puppies interact with each other and with people. Some puppies are boisterous and outgoing from the start, showing no reservations about approaching strangers, while others hang back from rough play and are nervous or shy. A confident puppy is usually a good choice, but a quieter dog may appeal to you more. However, check that a seemingly subdued puppy does not have health problems and is failing to thrive.

Expect breeders to ask you some questions too. They will want to know what sort of home and lifestyle you are offering, whether you are an experienced or a first-time

PICK OF THE LITTER
Even very young puppies have distinct personalities. Whether you favour a shy one or the boss of the litter, make sure that he has bright eyes, a clean coat, and appears used to a home environment.

owner, and if you are fully aware of the time and cost that keeping a dog entails. Do some homework before you pay your visit, and be honest with your answers.

A breeder should be able to supply vet's references and provide other credentials such as membership of a breed association. Also find out if your chosen breeder offers "after-sales" service, such as advice on feeding or health. Once you have come to an agreement, expect to collect your new puppy when he is about eight weeks of age.

Puppy farms

Never buy a dog from one of the many so-called "puppy farms". Such establishments are usually little more than canine battery farms, where dogs are kept in inhumane conditions, bred to exhaustion, and given little or nothing in the way of health care. Avoid buying from petshops too, as the puppies they sell do not usually have a history and may come from puppy farms. Also beware of advertisements offering a selection of different breeds, as these are often placed by dealers who trade in farmed puppies.

Buying a rescue dog

Unless you are set on buying a young puppy from a recognized breeder, you may find just what you want at a dog rescue centre. These centres occasionally have litters of puppies but in most cases their dogs are either fully mature or at least a few months old. Many rescue dogs are of mixed breeding, although some purebreds do turn up. If you prefer a pedigree dog, you could also try one of the numerous rescue societies that specialize in rehousing particular breeds, such as greyhounds.

Not all rescue dogs come from a background of neglect or cruelty. Some need rehousing because of an owner's death or change in family circumstances. However, many have an unknown or traumatic history, and may display behavioural

FAMILY GROUP
Never consider buying a puppy unless you can see the litter with their mother. No reputable breeder will keep young puppies in separate accommodation.

problems and anxieties that can be difficult to overcome. Think carefully before being tempted to take on such a dog in the hope of rehabilitating him, as you could end up with more than you bargained for. A good, loving home goes a long way, but traumatized dogs need experienced handling, an above-average amount of patience, and possibly professional retraining. Most rescue centres will offer you back-up advice and support.

When buying a dog from a rescue home, use the same approach as you would if buying from a breeder. Observe the dogs closely and ask, and expect to be asked, questions. Rescue homes screen prospective owners very carefully and will probably want to visit your home.

MAKING A GOOD MATCH

Adopting a rescue dog is a two-way process. While you are deciding which dog you want, a good rescue centre will assess your suitability as an owner. It will want to know as much as possible about you, your home, and your family.

10 IMPORTANT QUESTIONS TO ASK A BREEDER

- Will the puppy have received his first vaccinations and been wormed before I collect him?
- Are your dogs screened for inherited diseases, and may I take a look at the screening certificates?
- Can you provide a written guarantee of the puppy's health?
- Will you provide a written contract of sale and does it specify what I should do if I can no longer care for my puppy?
- Can you provide references from, for example, a vet or previous customers?
- Have you registered the puppy with a kennel club?
- Can you provide a printed pedigree for the puppy?
- What do you consider the most important characteristics of this breed?
- How long have you been working with this breed?
- Have your puppies been well socialized in your home as well as in the outside environment?

GUIDE TO BREEDS

PRIMITIVE DOGS

Most modern dog breeds are the result of many years of selective breeding for particular characteristics, but a few, commonly regarded as primitive dogs, have remained close to the original "blueprint" of their wolf ancestors. As a group, primitive dogs are not clearly defined, and not all authorities agree that such a category should be recognized.

Hairless dogs are depicted in ancient Pre-Incan artefacts

As variously listed, primitive dogs are a diverse group but many of them share typically wolf-like characteristics. These include erect ears, a wedge-shaped head with a pointed muzzle, and a tendency to howl rather than bark. Their coats are usually short but vary in colour and density according to the region from which the dog originates. Most primitive dogs come into season only once a year, unlike other domestic dogs, which have two cycles of oestrus a year.

Canine specialists are now taking an interest in dogs that have had little to do with humans and nothing to do with breed development programmes. These primitive dogs, which come from various parts of the world, include the Carolina Dog of North America and the rare New Guinea Singing Dog, which is genetically close to the dingo of Australia. Such dogs have evolved naturally rather than through breeding

for temperament or appearance and cannot be considered completely domesticated. The New Guinea Singing Dog, which is highly endangered in the wild, is more likely to be seen in zoos than in homes.

Several dogs are included in the primitive group because they are believed to be uninfluenced by any other types over thousands of years. Among them is the Basenji from Africa, long used for hunting in its native country before becoming a popular pet. Other examples are hairless dogs from Mexico and South America, genetic mutations of coated breeds, which resemble dogs depicted in the art and artefacts of ancient civilizations.

Recent genetic investigations suggest that two dogs included in this section – the Pharaoh Hound and the Ibizan Hound – should no longer be considered primitive. These breeds are popularly supposed to be the direct descendants of big-eared Egyptian hounds pictured in drawings dating back 5,000 years. However, there is genetic evidence that the line

of descent may not have remained unbroken down the centuries. It is probable that the Pharaoh and Ibizan Hounds are in fact modern recreations of a primitive dog type.

MAGICAL DOG
The Aztecs believed that hairless dogs were sent by the gods and had magical properties.

STILL WILD
The dingo-like New Guinea Singing Dog does not adapt well to domestic life. It may have inhabited New Guinea from prehistoric times.

NEW GUINEA SINGING DOG

IN TOUCH WITH ITS WILD SIDE, THIS DOG HAS A UNIQUE VOCAL RANGE

Height range
40–45cm (16–18in)

Weight range
8–14kg (18–31lb)

Life span 15–20 years

Origin New Guinea

Other colours

Sable

Black and tan

White markings are common with all colour types.

This rare dingo-like breed is a native of New Guinea, where it lives feral or in semi-domestication. The Singing Dog is kept as a curiosity in zoos worldwide but has become a challenging pet for a few dedicated owners. It has the extraordinary ability to vary the notes of its howl, hence the name.

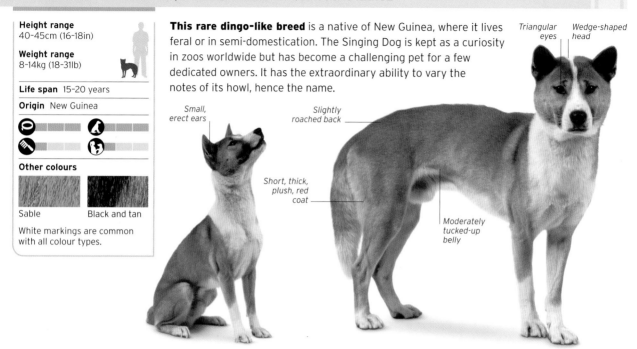

Triangular eyes

Wedge-shaped head

Small, erect ears

Slightly roached back

Short, thick, plush, red coat

Moderately tucked-up belly

BASENJI

THIS NEAT AND GRACEFUL DOG IS SOMETIMES SHY WITH STRANGERS, BUT DOES NOT BARK

KC

Height range
40–43cm (16–17in)

Weight range
10–11kg (22–24lb)

Life span Over 10 years

Origin Central Africa

Other colours

Variety of colours

White markings may appear on chest, feet, and tail tip.

A hunting dog from Africa, the Basenji was used for driving big game, locating its prey by both sight and scent. Sleek and beautifully built with an immaculate appearance, the Basenji is affectionate and fun-loving, and is a popular house dog. Unable to bark, it can, however, make yodelling noises.

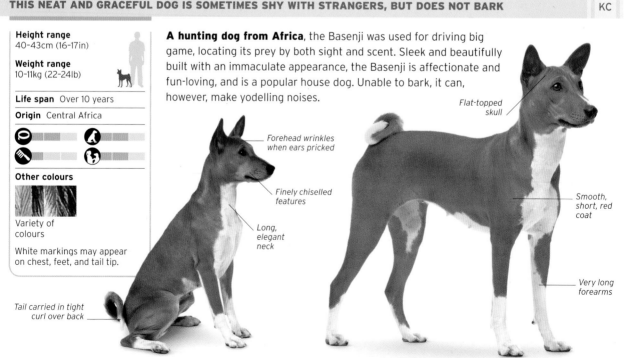

Flat-topped skull

Forehead wrinkles when ears pricked

Finely chiselled features

Long, elegant neck

Smooth, short, red coat

Very long forearms

Tail carried in tight curl over back

CANAAN DOG

THIS STURDY AND STEADFAST DOG IS ALWAYS ON THE ALERT AND READY TO PROTECT

KC

Height range
50-60cm (20-24in)

Weight range
18-25kg (40-55lb)

Life span Over 10 years

Origin Israel

Other colours

White

Black

Red and white spotted

Black and white spotted

Grey, brindle, black and tan, or tricolour undesirable.

Bred in Israel as a watchdog and herder, the Canaan Dog has strong protective instincts that do not usually turn into aggression. It is highly intelligent, and with steady training makes a reliable and affectionate companion. Not a common breed, it has yet to achieve widespread popularity.

Dark, slightly slanting eyes

Brush-like, thick tail, carried high and curled

Low-set, broad ears

White chest marking

Tucked-up belly

Dense, harsh, sandy coat

PHARAOH HOUND

THIS STREAMLINED, ELEGANT DOG IS GOOD IN THE HOUSE BUT WILL CHASE ANYTHING SMALL OUTDOORS

KC

Height range
53-63cm (21-25in)

Weight range
20-25kg (44-55lb)

Life span Over 10 years

Origin Malta

Although the modern Pharaoh Hound was developed in Malta, this graceful breed bears a strong resemblance to the prick-eared hunting dogs illustrated in the art and artefacts of ancient Egypt. The Pharaoh Hound is calm-tempered but needs a lot of exercise and, unless restrained outdoors, will fly off in pursuit of small animals, including other pets.

Large, erect ears

Amber-coloured eyes

Whippy tail, carried in a high curve when active

Slender, elegant body

Toes often marked white

Well-arched, long neck

White marks on chest common

Short, glossy, slightly harsh, rich tan coat

CANARIAN WARREN HOUND

THIS HIGHLY STRUNG DOG IS BRED TO HUNT, AND NEEDS AN OUTDOOR LIFE

FCI

Height range
53–64cm (21–25in)

Weight range
16–22kg (35–49lb)

Life span 12–13 years

Origin Spain

Also known as the Podenco Canario, this hound – found on all the Canary Islands – has Egyptian roots dating back thousands of years. The breed has long been used as a rabbit-hunter and is highly valued for its speed, keen sight, and excellent nose. Sensitive and restless, the Canarian Warren Hound is unable to adapt to a quiet life indoors.

Flesh-coloured nose

Sleek, smooth, red coat

White markings on chest

Fine-boned but strong legs

Slender, athletic body

Low-set, slightly tapered tail

Large ears, erect when alert

Small, amber-coloured eyes

CIRNECO DELL'ETNA

GENTLE BUT LIVELY, THIS IS A HUNTER RATHER THAN A HOUSE DOG

KC

Height range
42–52cm (17–20in)

Weight range
8–12kg (18–26lb)

Life span 12–14 years

Origin Italy

Other colours

White

White with orange

This Sicilian breed, which may well have originated in the area immediately around Mount Etna, is rare outside its native country. Lithe and strong, the Cirneco dell'Etna is built to run and hunt. Although good-natured, this dog is not an ideal option for owners who want a placid house pet.

Narrow, almost flat skull

Short, glossy, fawn coat

Strong, arched neck

White markings on chest

Erect, rigid ears set high on head

Low-set tail

Powerful, muscular hind quarters

IBIZAN HOUND

THIS FAST RUNNER WITH AN OUTSTANDING ABILITY TO JUMP NEEDS SPACE AND EXERCISE

KC

Height range
56-74cm (22-29in)

Weight range
20-23kg (44-51lb)

Life span 10-12 years

Origin Spain

Other colours

Red

Used in Spain as a pack dog for hunting rabbits, the Ibizan Hound can cover the roughest ground at a "raking trot" characteristic of the breed. This dog also has an enormous jump and can easily leap over a garden fence. As long as an owner bears security in mind, the Ibizan Hound is not difficult to keep, but it is an all-action dog that needs relentless exercise. The breed has a charming temperament and fits in well with family life. There are two coat types, smooth and rough, both of which are easy to maintain.

Short, fawn coat

Flat skull

Long, slender muzzle

Smooth-coated

Narrow head

Large, pointed ears

Clear, amber eyes

Lean, muscular, white body

Long forearms

Slender, strong toes

Rough-coated

PORTUGUESE PODENGO

AN ALERT WATCHDOG THAT MAKES A GOOD COMPANION

KC

Height range
Pequeno:
20–30cm (8–12in)
Medio:
40–53cm (16–21in)
Grande:
55–70cm (22–28in)

Weight range
Pequeno:
4–5kg (9–11lb)
Medio:
16–20kg (35–44lb)
Grande:
20–30kg (44–66lb)

Life span Over 12 years

Origin Portugal

Other colours

White, yellow | Black

White dogs have patches of yellow, black, or fawn. Pequeno dogs may be brown.

Commonly known as the Portuguese Warren Hound, this breed has developed into several varieties with distinct differences in size and coat. Today's dogs may be small (pequeno), medium (medio), or large (grande), and some are smooth-haired while others have moderately long, wiry coats. All were traditionally used for hunting, and in Portugal some are still kept for that purpose, working either in a pack or alone. Regardless of size, their intelligence and alertness make them excellent watchdogs.

Fawn coat

Bearded muzzle

Wire-haired pequeno

Short, fawn coat

Large, triangular, erect ears

Smooth-haired pequeno

White blaze on face

Short, fawn coat

White markings on legs

Smooth-haired medio

CAROLINA DOG

THIS DOG RESPONDS TO TRAINING BUT CAN BE SHY

Height range 45–50cm (18–20in)	
Weight range 15–20kg (33–44lb)	

Life span 12–14 years

Origin USA

Other colours

Deep red-ginger

Black and tan

Also known as the "American Dingo", this dog's ancestors are thought to have been domesticated and brought into North America by early settlers from Asia. In America's south-eastern states, some still live semi-wild. Naturally wary, this dog needs early socializing to make it an acceptable pet.

Triangular, erect ears

Longer hairs on neck

Lighter-coloured chest

Short, dense, wheaten coat

Tail carried in distinctive hook when alert

PERUVIAN INCA ORCHID

A HAIRLESS, STRIKINGLY PATTERNED DOG WHOSE SKIN NEEDS PROTECTION FROM THE ELEMENTS

Height range 50–65cm (20–26in)	
Weight range 12–23kg (26–51lb)	

Life span 11–12 years

Origin Peru

Other colours

Any colour

Hairless dogs always have pink skin but the colour of mottling can vary.

The true origins of the Peruvian Inca Orchid are lost in time, but dogs of this type are known to have been important in Inca civilizations. There are two varieties of this breed: hairless and coated. The hairless Inca Orchid is better suited to indoor rather than outdoor life because of its delicate skin.

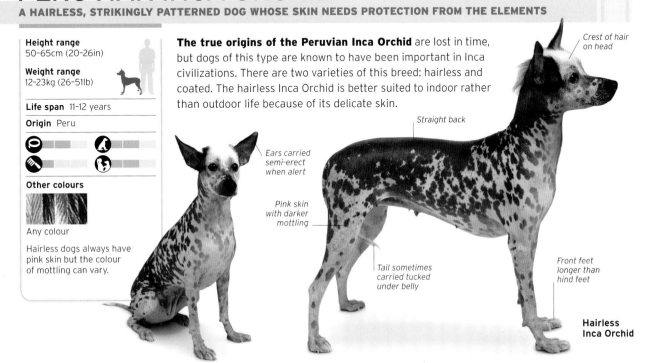

Crest of hair on head

Straight back

Ears carried semi-erect when alert

Pink skin with darker mottling

Tail sometimes carried tucked under belly

Front feet longer than hind feet

Hairless Inca Orchid

PERUVIAN HAIRLESS

THIS BRIGHT AND AGILE DOG IS AFFECTIONATE WITH OWNERS BUT SHY WITH STRANGERS

FCI

Height range
Miniature:
25-40cm (10-16in)
Medio:
40-50cm (16-20in)
Grande:
50-65cm (20-26in)

Weight range
Miniature:
4-8kg (9-18lb)
Medio:
8-12kg (18-26lb)
Grande:
12-25kg (26-55lb)

Life span 11-12 years

Origin Peru

Other colours

Blonde

Dark brown

Black

Records of hairless dogs in South America date back to pre-Inca times. It has been suggested that this lively and graceful breed may have originated in China or Africa before it was introduced in Peru. Hairlessness, often accompanied by the absence of certain teeth, is produced by a particular recessive gene, but occasionally, coated dogs do occur in litters. The Peruvian Hairless breeds come in three sizes – miniature, medio, and grande. The fine skin needs some protection as these dogs are susceptible to the cold and easily sunburned.

Distinct stop

Grande

Crest of hairs

Rose ear

Eyes match skin colour

Long feet

Miniature

Fine, elastic, elephant-grey skin

Tucked-up belly

Pink patches on legs

Medio

XOLOITZCUINTLE

THIS CALM-NATURED, ALERT DOG IS EASY TO CARE FOR AND MAKES A DELIGHTFUL COMPANION

KC

Height range
Miniature:
25–35cm (10–14in)
Intermediate:
36–45cm (14–18in)
Standard:
46–60cm (18–24in)

Weight range
Miniature:
2–7kg (10–15lb)
Intermediate:
7–14kg (15–31lb)
Standard:
14–25kg (31–55lb)

Life span Over 10 years

Origin Mexico

Other colours

Red   Liver

In pre-Conquest Mexico hairless dogs were believed to have sacred significance and were often used as a sacrifice or ritually eaten in religious ceremonies. Because of these practices, hairless dogs barely escaped extinction and it was not until the mid-20th century that breeders began to work towards its recovery. Three different sizes are now recognized. Like all hairless dogs, this breed has limited general appeal and remains something of a rarity. Nonetheless, the Xoloitzcuintle, also known as the Mexican Hairless, is charming, good-tempered, and intelligent, and is likely to reward its owner with loyalty and affection.

Black skin

Standard

Tufts of hair on forehead

Large, long ears, erect when alert

Bronze skin

Miniature (puppy)

Head has slight stop and tapering muzzle

Firm, slender neck

Traces of dark hair on tail

Dark grey skin

Intermediate

RESCUE WORK
A German Shepherd Dog working for a search-and-rescue team hunts for survivors in a collapsed building following an earthquake.

WORKING DOGS

The list of jobs that humans ask dogs to perform is almost endless. In the thousands of years since dogs were domesticated, canine helpers have guarded homes, rescued people in danger, gone to war, and looked after the sick and disabled — to give only a few examples. In this book the working group is represented by breeds traditionally developed for pastoral work and guard duties.

Shepherd dogs work as herders and guardians

In general, the dogs in this highly diverse group tend to be large, though there are a few small but nonetheless robust exceptions. Working dogs are bred for strength and stamina, and many of them are capable of living outdoors in all weathers.

A collie rounding up its flock is for most people the archetypal shepherd dog, but many other types of dog are used to work with livestock. These pastoral breeds, as they are known, are used for both herding and guarding. Herding dogs have a natural instinct for driving stock, though not all of them work in the same way. Border Collies, for example, keep their sheep in order by stalking and staring, while the traditional cattle-herders such as Welsh Corgis and the Australian Cattle Dog nip at heels, and some herders bark as they work. Guardian sheepdogs, which include mountain breeds such as the Maremma and Pyrenean Mountain Dog, are designed to protect their flocks from predators such as wolves. Usually very large, many of these dogs are white and heavy-coated, scarcely distinguishable from the sheep they spend their lives guarding.

Guard duties of another kind are often carried out by dogs of the mastiff type, recognizable as descendants of the enormous Molossus dogs seen in friezes and artefacts from the ancient world. Such breeds as the Bullmastiff, the Dogue de Bordeaux, and the Neapolitan Mastiff are used worldwide by security forces and for guarding property. Typically, these dogs are massively built and powerful, with small ears (often cropped in countries where the practice is still legal) and pendulous lips.

Many working breeds are excellent as companion dogs. Pastoral herders are extremely intelligent and generally easy to train, and often enjoy using their skills in agility trials and other canine competitions. Livestock guardian dogs, because of their sheer size and protective nature, are less likely to be suited to family life. In recent decades a number of the mastiff-type breeds have achieved great popularity as companions. Although some were produced originally for fighting, if reared in the home and socialized early they can adapt to life as a pet.

LIVESTOCK GUARDIANS
The protective instincts of breeds such as the Hungarian Kuvasz make these dogs unsuitable for the inexperienced owner.

AGILITY TRIALS
Border Collies are often seen displaying their agility and intelligence at working dog trials.

SAARLOOS WOLFDOG

THIS SELF-WILLED DOG IS RESERVED WITH STRANGERS BUT MAKES A LOYAL COMPANION

FCI

Height range
60-75cm (24-30in)

Weight range
35-40kg (77-88lb)

Life span Over 10 years

Origin The Netherlands

Other colours

Cream

Bos (brown)

The Saarloos Wolfdog is the result of selective crossbreeding to produce a German Shepherd-type dog with natural traits closer to those of its wolf ancestors. Although it was suggested that this new breed could be useful as a guide dog, the Saarloos Wolfdog has proved better suited to life as a pet and companion. However, it needs sensitive handling.

Almond-shaped eyes

Wedge-shaped, wolf-like head

Triangular ears with rounded tips

Wolf-grey coat

Body longer than leg length

Heavy-coated, broad tail

Long, arched feet

CZECHOSLOVAKIAN WOLFDOG

A WOLF-LIKE DOG WITH A DOCILE TEMPERAMENT

FCI

Height range
60-65cm (24-26in)

Weight range
20-26kg (44-57lb)

Life span 12-16 years

Origin Czech Republic

Created through breeding programs that initially crossed German Shepherd Dogs with wolves, the Czechoslovakian Wolfdog has inherited many of the traits of its wild ancestors. This breed is quick, fearless, resilient, and wary of strangers. It is also faithful and obedient with familiar handlers, qualities that make it an excellent house dog.

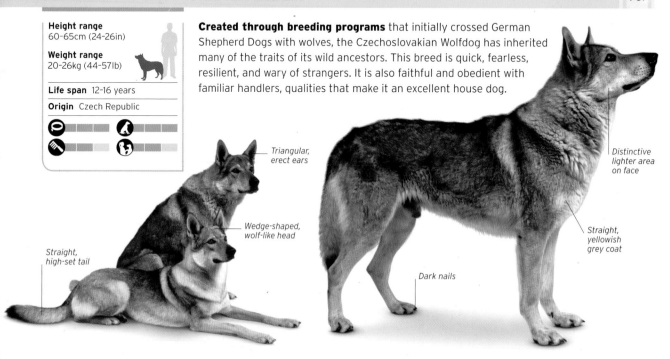

Triangular, erect ears

Distinctive lighter area on face

Wedge-shaped, wolf-like head

Straight, high-set tail

Straight, yellowish grey coat

Dark nails

GERMAN SHEPHERD DOG

THIS INTELLIGENT AND VERSATILE DOG IS ONE OF THE MOST POPULAR BREEDS WORLDWIDE

KC

Height range
58–63cm (23–25in)

Weight range
22–40kg (49–88lb)

Life span Over 10 years

Origin Germany

Other colours

Sable

Black

As the name implies, this breed (formerly known as the Alsatian) originally worked as a shepherd dog and a protector of sheep. Highly adaptable and trainable, the German Shepherd Dog has proved valuable as a guard dog, guide dog, and tracker, and is widely used by police and armed forces all over the world. Despite occasional bad publicity for aggressive behaviour, German Shepherd Dogs produced by reputable breeders usually have a steady temperament. When trained by a responsible owner and allowed to enjoy an active outdoor lifestyle, this dog can become a trusted and faithful member of the family. Coats range from short-haired to long-haired.

Bushy tail

Long-haired

Large, firm, erect ears

Head has clean-cut appearance

Strong hind quarters

Short-haired

Croup slopes slightly downwards to tail

Thick, black-with-tan coat

Dark saddle

Long forelegs straight to elbow

Short-haired

KING SHEPHERD

EASY TO TRAIN, THIS DOG IS RELIABLE WITH CHILDREN AND OTHER PETS

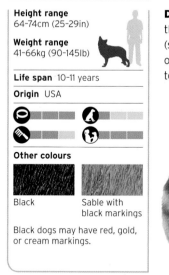

Height range
64-74cm (25-29in)

Weight range
41-66kg (90-145lb)

Life span 10-11 years

Origin USA

Other colours

Black | Sable with black markings

Black dogs may have red, gold, or cream markings.

Developed in the United States and recognized since the late 1990s, this large and handsome dog clearly shows the German Shepherd Dog (see p.35) in its breeding history. King Shepherds love to work as herders or guard dogs, but have a placid and tolerant nature that allows them to fit in well with a family. There are two coat types: smooth and rough.

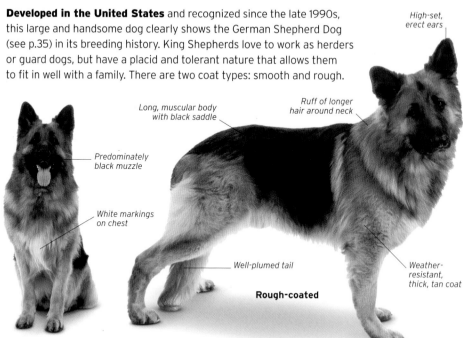

High-set, erect ears

Long, muscular body with black saddle

Ruff of longer hair around neck

Predominately black muzzle

White markings on chest

Well-plumed tail

Weather-resistant, thick, tan coat

Rough-coated

PICARDY SHEEPDOG

THIS DOG ADORES LONG WALKS AND IS GENTLE WITH CHILDREN, BUT DISLIKES BEING LEFT ALONE KC

Height range
55-65cm (22-26in)

Weight range
23-32kg (51-71lb)

Life span 13-14 years

Origin France

Other colours

Dark grey | Fawn brindle

May have white markings.

The history of the Picardy Sheepdog is uncertain, but this tough-looking breed may have originated over a century ago in the Picardy region of northeastern France. With quiet and patient training, this dog makes a sociable companion and a good playmate for children. The rugged coat is relatively easy to groom.

Finely shaped head hidden by long hair

High-set, erect ears

Long eyebrows do not obscure eyes

Hair on muzzle forms moustache and beard

Thick, fawn coat, harsh and crisp to touch

Lighter hair on chest

Long tail curves slightly at tip

DUTCH SHEPHERD DOG

Height range
55–62cm (22–24in)

Weight range
30–31kg (66–68lb)

Life span 12–14 years

Origin The Netherlands

Not often seen outside the Netherlands, and relatively uncommon even there, in the last 200 years this breed has become far more than an all-purpose farm dog. The Dutch Shepherd Dog has been used for security and police work, as a guide dog, and in obedience trials. Reliable and affectionate, the breed also makes a good family dog, though it has a natural wariness of strangers. There are three varieties of the Dutch Shepherd Dog: long-haired, short-haired, and rough-haired. The rough-haired type needs to have its coat plucked by a professional dog-groomer about twice a year.

Erect ears

Silver-brindle coat

Long-haired

Fawn-brindle coat

Short-haired

Coarse eyebrows

Harsh, wavy, silver-brindle coat

Feathering on underside of tail

Shorter hair below hock on hind legs

Light feathering on back of legs

Rough-haired

LAEKENOIS

KC

Height range
56-66cm (22-26in)

Weight range
25-29kg (55-65lb)

Life span Over 10 years

Origin Belgium

Of the four breeds of Belgian Shepherd Dog, this wiry-coated variety was the first to be developed, in the 1880s. The Laekenois is named after the Château de Laeken, near Antwerp, and was once much favoured by the Belgian royal family. Rarely seen, this delightful dog deserves to be more widely appreciated.

Area of darker shading

High-set, erect ears

Shorter hair on muzzle

Head carried high with alert expression

Body powerful but not heavy

Round feet

Wiry, reddish fawn coat

GROENENDAEL

KC

Height range
56-66cm (22-26in)

Weight range
23-34kg (51-75lb)

Life span Over 10 years

Origin Belgium

From 1893 black-coated Belgian Shepherd Dogs were selectively bred at a kennel in the village of Groenendael, near Brussels. This handsome variety is now extremely popular. Like most dogs formerly used for work, the Groenendael needs an owner who understands the importance of early socializing and firm but kindly control.

Finely shaped muzzle

Slightly sloping rump

Long, straight, black coat

Ruff of longer hair around neck

Long feathering on legs

MALINOIS

A VERY HARDY AND ENERGETIC DOG WITH STRONG GUARDING INSTINCTS | KC

Height range
56–66cm (22–26in)

Weight range
27–29kg (60–65lb)

Life span Over 10 years

Origin Belgium

Other colours

Grey   Red

All colours have
black overlay.

Believed to have originated in Malines, in Belgium, the Malinois is a short-haired variety of the Belgian Shepherd Dog. Like its fellow breeds, it is a natural guard dog. Although its behaviour may be unpredictable, with responsible training the Malinois socializes well and makes a loyal companion.

Thicker collar around neck

Triangular ears, mostly black

Almond-shaped, brown eyes

Pointed muzzle and medium stop

Distinctive black mask

Darker tip on bushy tail

Short, straight, fawn coat with black tips to the hairs

TERVUEREN

THIS DOG HAS A DOMINANT PERSONALITY AND ENJOYS A GOOD RUN, BUT SHOULD BE SUPERVISED | KC

Height range
56–66cm (22–26in)

Weight range
18–29kg (40–65lb)

Life span Over 10 years

Origin Belgium

Other colours

Grey

All colours have
black overlay.

The most popular of the Belgian Shepherd Dogs worldwide, this variety was named after the village where it was developed by a local breeder. The Tervueren has strong protective instincts and is frequently used for guarding and police work. Its beautiful, black-tipped coat sheds regularly and needs plenty of grooming.

Head carried high

Strongly muscled back

Upright, muscular neck

Abundant "breeches" on hind quarters

Black ears and mask

Rich, long, fawn coat with black overlay

Red coat

MUDI

THIS ACTIVE AND PLAYFUL FAMILY DOG ALSO MAKES A FEARLESS GUARD DOG

FCI

Height range
38–47cm (15–19in)

Weight range
8–13kg (18–29lb)

Life span 13–14 years

Origin Hungary

Other colours

Fawn

Blue merle, ash

Brown

May have white markings.

Originally used as a working dog by Hungarian sheep- and cattle-herders, this rare breed is tough, bold, and energetic. With its friendly and adaptable nature, the Mudi makes a good house dog. It needs plenty of exercise to stay fit and healthy, and responds well to sympathetic training.

Wedge-shaped head

Erect ears, covered with thick hair

Dense, shiny, wavy, black coat

Black nose

Shorter hair below hock

Feathered backs to legs

SCHNAUZER

LIVELY BUT OBEDIENT, THIS DOG IS GOOD-TEMPERED WITH CHILDREN

KC

Height range
45–50cm (18–20in)

Weight range
14–20kg (31–44lb)

Life span Over 10 years

Origin Germany

Other colours

Black

The medium-sized Schnauzer was established as a breed in the 1880s in southern Germany. Alert and agile, the Schnauzer was used primarily as a versatile farm dog with a formidable reputation for rat-hunting. Placid and affectionate, but with a lively sense of fun, the breed is now popular as a family dog.

Bushy eyebrows

Straight back

High-set, drop ears

Bristly, lighter-coloured beard

Short, wiry, pepper and salt coat

Longer hair extends over feet

Lighter-coloured hair on lower legs

GIANT SCHNAUZER

AN EVEN-TEMPERED, INTELLIGENT, AND EASY-TO-TRAIN DOG

Height range
60–70cm (24–28in)

Weight range
29–41kg (65–90lb)

Life span Over 10 years

Origin Germany

Other colours

Pepper and salt

Robust and powerfully built, the Giant Schnauzer from southern Germany was originally used for farm work and cattle-herding. By the 20th century the breed's intelligence, trainability, and impressive appearance had been recognized as ideal qualities for a guard dog. This breed is now widely used by police and security forces, but an equable temperament also makes it suitable as a home watchdog and pet. Despite its size, the Giant Schnauzer is easily manageable if given plenty of exercise. Its dense, wiry, double-layered coat needs regular maintenance, with daily grooming and an occasional trim.

Dark eyes

Deep chest

Tail carried high

Drop ears with rounded tips

Bushy eyebrows overhang eyes

Dense, wiry, black coat

Bearded muzzle

Strong, graceful neck

Slight feathering on back of legs

BOUVIER DES ARDENNES

A RARE DOG WITH A LONG-ESTABLISHED REPUTATION AS A WILLING WORKER   FCI

Height range
52–62cm (20–24in)

Weight range
22–35kg (49–77lb)

Life span Over 10 years

Origin Belgium

Other colours

Variety of colours

This hardy, active, former cattle-herder from the Belgian Ardennes is now rarely seen, either as a working dog or a house dog. A handful of enthusiasts have kept the breed in existence, and with its adaptable temperament and zest for life the Bouvier des Ardennes has the potential for future popularity.

Ears slightly darker than body

Body length equals leg length

Black-edged lips

Tousled, fawn coat, dry to touch

Rounded feet

Erect, pointed ears

Coarse moustache and beard

Black coat

BOUVIER DES FLANDRES

THIS TOWN OR COUNTRY DOG IS HAIRY BUT NOT TOO DIFFICULT TO GROOM   KC

Height range
59–68cm (23–27in)

Weight range
27–40kg (60–88lb)

Life span Over 10 years

Origin Belgium

Other colours

Variety of colours

May have small, white star on chest.

Of the various types of Bouviers once used in Belgium and France for cattle-herding and guarding, this breed from Flanders is the most commonly encountered. Despite originally being an outdoor dog – with an appropriately weatherproof coat – the Bouvier des Flandres can happily adjust to an urban home.

High-set, drop ears

Heavily feathered tail

Long, coarse beard

Very thick, silver-brindle coat, harsh to touch

Dense coat extends over feet

CROATIAN SHEPHERD DOG

THIS HERDING AND GUARDING DOG IS MORE SUITED TO WORK THAN DOMESTICITY

FCI

Height range
40–50cm (16–20in)

Weight range
13–20kg (29–44lb)

Life span 13–14 years

Origin Croatia

Relatively small and lightly built for a shepherd dog, this breed is active and alert. Easy to train for work, the Croatian Shepherd Dog may be harder to handle as a house dog because of its natural herding and guarding instincts. Its unusually wavy or curly coat is a distinctive feature.

Narrow muzzle

Erect, triangular ears, lined with long hair

Wavy, black coat

Short hair on face

Backs of legs slightly feathered

Shorter hair on lower legs

SARPLANINAC

THIS MAGNIFICENT AND VERY PROTECTIVE WORKING DOG IS HAPPY TO LIVE OUTDOORS

FCI

Height range
Over 58cm (over 23in)

Weight range
30–45kg (66–99lb)

Life span 11–13 years

Origin Macedonia

Other colours

Any solid colour

Formerly known as the Illyrian Shepherd Dog, this impressive breed is now named after the Sarplanina Mountains of Macedonia where it originated. The Sarplaninac is very much an outdoor, working dog. Although it has a sociable, though protective, temperament, its size and energy levels make it impractical as a family pet.

Drop ears

Broad, slightly rounded top to head

Longer hair forms ruff around neck

Heavily feathered, bushy tail

Long, dense, dark brown coat

Long feathering on hind quarters

Yellowish-grey lower legs

Broad chest

KARST SHEPHERD DOG

THIS RELIABLE AND DEVOTED DOG NEEDS A SPACIOUS HOME AND CORRECT HANDLING

FCI

Height range
53–63cm (21–25in)

Weight range
25–42kg (55–93lb)

Life span 11–12 years

Origin Slovenia

Formerly known as the Illyrian Shepherd, this dog was separated from another breed of the same name and renamed the Karst, or Istrian, Shepherd Dog in the 1960s. Used for herding and guarding in the alpine Karst region of Slovenia, this excellent working dog can make a good companion with careful training and early socialization.

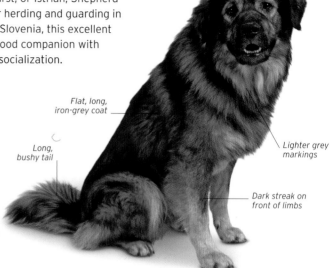

Head as wide as it is long

Flat, long, iron-grey coat

Lighter grey markings

Long, bushy tail

Dark streak on front of limbs

Hair on neck forms ruff and mane

ESTRELA MOUNTAIN DOG

THIS DOG, FOR LARGE HOMES ONLY, CAN LIVE OUTSIDE IF GIVEN SHELTER

KC

Height range
62–72cm (24–28in)

Weight range
35–60kg (77–132lb)

Life span Over 10 years

Origin Portugal

Other colours

Wolf-grey   Black brindle

May have white markings on underside and extremities.

A livestock-guardian from the Estrela Mountains of Portugal, this fearless, rugged dog was bred to protect flocks against predators such as wolves. The Estrela Mountain Dog is a loyal and friendly, but strong-willed, companion that needs consistent and patient obedience training. There are long-coated and short-coated varieties of the breed.

Long head with broad, rounded skull

Dark face mask

Thick ruff around neck and chest

Thick, slightly wavy, fawn topcoat

Black hairs intermingle with fawn hairs

Long-coated

PORTUGUESE WATCHDOG

THIS CALM-NATURED WATCHDOG MAY BE TOO BIG AND STRONG FOR MANY OWNERS

FCI

Height range
64–74cm (25–29in)

Weight range
35–60kg (77–132lb)

Life span 12 years

Origin Portugal

Other colours

Wolf-grey   Black

Coat may be brindled and will always have white markings; white coats have patches of one of the colours.

Possibly descended from the powerful mastiffs brought into Europe from Asia by nomadic herders, this breed is also known as the Rafeiro de Alentejo, named after the Alentejo region of Portugal. Traditionally used for guarding, the Portuguese Watchdog is vigilant and suspicious of strangers. Formidable in size and strength, though not aggressive, this dog is unsuitable for novice handlers.

Triangular, drop ears

Black lips

Broad chest

Tail slightly curved at tip

Straight, dense, fawn coat

White markings on chest and legs

CASTRO LABOREIRO DOG

THIS BOLD AND VIGILANT WATCHDOG IS BETTER SUITED TO WORK THAN FAMILY LIFE

FCI

Height range
55–64cm (22–25in)

Weight range
25–40kg (55–88lb)

Life span 12–13 years

Origin Portugal

Other colours

Wolf-grey

May have a small, white spot on chest.

Named after its home village in the mountains of northern Portugal, this dog, sometimes known as the Portuguese Cattle Dog, was bred to work as a livestock-guardian. Its distinctive alarm bark starts low and ends high-pitched. This dog develops a strong bond with family members but may be hostile to strangers.

Triangular, drop ears

Almond-shaped eyes

Tail long-haired on underside, usually carried low

Short, very thick, harsh-textured, "mountain" brindle coat

PORTUGUESE SHEEPDOG

THIS HIGHLY INTELLIGENT DOG LIKES TO BE ACTIVE

FCI

Height range
42–55cm (17–22in)

Weight range
17–27kg (37–60lb)

Life span 12–13 years

Origin Portugal

Other colours

Variety of colours

May have a small amount of white on chest.

In its native country this shaggy, agile dog is sometimes known as the "monkey dog". The Portuguese Sheepdog loves to be outdoors, herding. Lively and extremely intelligent, the breed has also gained popularity as a companion and sporting dog in Portugal, although it is little known elsewhere.

Large eyebrows do not obscure eyes

Fawn coat

Long beard and moustache

Black, shaggy coat resembles goat hair

Tan markings on lower legs

CATALAN SHEEPDOG

A PLEASANT-NATURED DOG, BUT PROTECTIVE OF HOME AND FAMILY

KC

Height range
45–55cm (18–22in)

Weight range
20–27kg (44–60lb)

Life span 12–14 years

Origin Spain

Other colours

Grey

Black and tan

Sable

May have white markings.

Bred in Catalonia, Spain, as a flock-herder and guard, this hardy dog has an attractive weatherproof coat that allows it to work in almost any conditions. With high intelligence, a quiet temperament, and a readiness to please, the Catalan Sheepdog is relatively easy to train and makes an excellent family companion.

Crest on top of head

Fringed ears hang close to head

Round, dark amber eyes

Rough-textured, fawn coat

Long hair extends over feet

PYRENEAN SHEEPDOG

A LIVELY COMPANION, ALMOST IMPOSSIBLE TO TIRE OUT, WITH A STRONG HERDING INSTINCT

KC

Height range
38–48cm (15–19in)

Weight range
7–14kg (15–31lb)

Life span 12–13 years

Origin France

Other colours

Grey

Blue

Black

Black and white

Blue coats may be merle, slate, or brindle. Unmixed colours are preferred.

Small and lightly built for a sheepdog, this breed has long been used for herding flocks in the French Pyrenees. It remained almost unknown beyond its native mountain regions until the beginning of the 20th century. Lithe, energetic, and ready to join in any interesting activity, the Pyrenean Sheepdog does well in canine sports such as agility trials. For an active family, the Pyrenean Sheepdog is an excellent pet. The breed comes in two coat varieties – long or semi-long – and may have a rough or smooth face.

Fawn coat with black hairs

Semi-long, rough-faced

White markings on chest

Fawn coat with black hairs

Semi-long, smooth-faced

Fawn coat woollier on hind quarters

Long, swept-back hair on face and cheeks

Long hair on legs extends over toes

Long-haired, rough-faced

BEARDED COLLIE

THIS DOG IS CALM BUT ALERT AND ACTIVE, SO BEST SUITED TO A RURAL HOME

KC

Height range
51–56cm (20–22in)

Weight range
20–25kg (44–55lb)

Life span Over 10 years

Origin UK

Other colours

Sandy

Red-brown

Blue

Black

Until the middle of the 20th century the Bearded Collie was familiar only in Scotland and the north of England, where it was valued as a sheepdog. Now widely appreciated for its attractive appearance, compact size, and gentle nature, this breed has great appeal as a pet. However, it is more likely to enjoy the space of a rural home than a compact urban environment.

Arched eyebrows do not cover eyes

Long, slate-grey outer coat

White collar

Toes hairy between pads

Large nose

Long moustache on muzzle

BRIARD

THIS LARGE AND BOISTEROUS DOG NEEDS A FIRM HAND AND PLENTY OF EXERCISE

KC

Height range
58–69cm (23–27in)

Weight range
35kg (77lb)

Life span Over 10 years

Origin France

Other colours

Slate-grey

Black

In its native country this large and lively French breed works as a herder and guarder of sheep. Bold and protective, but not aggressive, the Briard is an excellent family companion if given regular exercise and room to run and play. This is not a low-maintenance dog as the Briard's long, thick coat needs a lot of grooming.

Short, high-set, long-haired ears

Eyebrows fall over eyes

Black nose

Darker hairs blend in with main body colour

Long, flowing, slightly wavy, fawn coat

Strong, muscular legs

OLD ENGLISH SHEEPDOG

THIS GOOD-TEMPERED AND INTELLIGENT DOG NEEDS FREQUENT GROOMING

KC

Height range
56–61cm (22–24in)

Weight range
27–45kg (60–99lb)

Life span Over 10 years

Origin UK

Other colours

Grey

Any shade of grey, grizzle, or blue. Body and hind quarters of solid colour, with no white patches.

This breed is considered to be native to the UK, although it may have its earliest origins in various types of continental sheepdog. It was once the custom to completely dock the tails of Old English Sheepdogs, and the alternative name of Bobtail Sheepdog is still sometimes used. This big, strong dog requires a great deal of exercise and preferably wide open spaces to work off its energy. Its owner should be prepared to devote time and care to daily grooming, to prevent the heavy, shaggy coat from becoming tangled and matted.

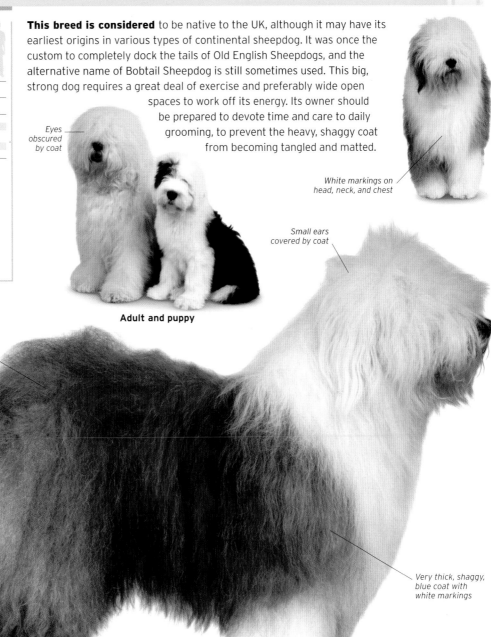

Eyes obscured by coat

Adult and puppy

White markings on head, neck, and chest

Small ears covered by coat

Deep, relatively short body

Longer coat on hind quarters

Very thick, shaggy, blue coat with white markings

Long, lean, tapering head

Smooth-haired face

Dark eyes with intelligent, inquisitive expression

Semi-erect ears

Long, very dense, harsh-textured, sable and white coat

Abundant, white mane

Profuse feathering on hind quarters

Smooth hair below hock

Well-feathered tail

ROUGH COLLIE

THIS PROUD AND BEAUTIFUL, SWEET-TEMPERED DOG MAKES A LOVELY FAMILY COMPANION   KC

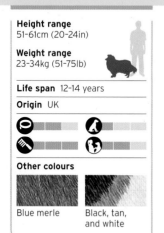

Height range
51–61cm (20–24in)

Weight range
23–34kg (51–75lb)

Life span 12–14 years

Origin UK

Other colours

Blue merle

Black, tan, and white

This rich-coated breed, a descendant of the rather less-refined Scottish working shepherd dogs, is much admired today as a pet and in the show ring. The Rough Collie's history may go back as far as Roman Britain, but dogs recognizably of this type did not attract wide attention until the 19th century. Queen Victoria is credited with popularizing the breed both in Europe and the United States. Later, "Lassie", the highly intelligent star of film and television, confirmed the Rough Collie's status as one of the best-loved dogs of all time.

This breed is mild-tempered and tolerant of other dogs and pets. It is highly responsive to training and makes an affectionate and protective companion. However, the people-loving Rough Collie readily accepts visitors to the home and therefore does not make a good guard dog. An athletic breed, it is eager for fun and will take part with brio in canine sports such as agility trials.

The herding instinct has not been entirely bred out of Rough Collies; their sharp awareness of movement may trigger an impulse to "round up" friends and family. Early socializing can prevent this trait from becoming a nuisance.

Like all breeds originally intended as working dogs, the Rough Collie becomes restless when under-exercised or left alone for long periods, and may start to bark excessively. However, given an energetic daily run, it can be kept in a modestly sized house or large apartment.

This dog's long, thick coat needs regular grooming to prevent tangles and matting. More frequent grooming sessions may be needed when the dense undercoat is being shed, which occurs twice a year.

SMOOTH COLLIE

A SLEEK, ELEGANT COLLIE WITH A FRIENDLY DISPOSITION

KC

Height range
51–61cm (20–24in)

Weight range
18–30kg (40–66lb)

Life span Over 10 years

Origin UK

Other colours

Sable and white

The Smooth Collie is recognized as a breed in its own right, rather than just a short-haired version of the Rough Collie (see p.50). This attractive collie is sometimes used as a working sheepdog but is also well liked as a house dog. The close-fitting coat is easy to maintain and gives the Smooth Collie its characteristic sleek outline.

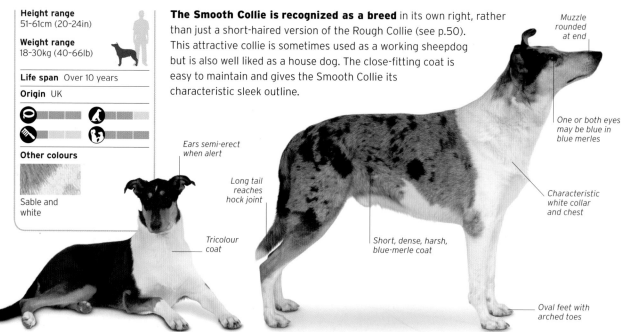

Muzzle rounded at end

One or both eyes may be blue in blue merles

Characteristic white collar and chest

Ears semi-erect when alert

Long tail reaches hock joint

Short, dense, harsh, blue-merle coat

Oval feet with arched toes

Tricolour coat

SHETLAND SHEEPDOG

A GENTLE-NATURED, FAMILY-FRIENDLY DOG THAT HAS BOUNDLESS ENERGY

KC

Height range
35–38cm (14–15in)

Weight range
7–11kg (15–24lb)

Life span Over 10 years

Origin UK

Other colours

Black and white   Blue merle

Black and tan

First bred in the rugged Shetland Islands, beyond the northern coast of mainland Scotland, this miniature collie is hardy and resilient. Bursting with energy but easily trained and affectionate, the Shetland Sheepdog adapts well to family life and is a loyal pet. Regular grooming sessions are necessary to maintain the beautiful coat.

Close-set ears

Smooth hair on face

Dense mane

Black rim around eyes

Long, thick, tricolour coat

Sable coat

BORDER COLLIE

THIS SUPER-INTELLIGENT, ACTIVE DOG NEEDS AN EXPERIENCED OWNER

KC

Height range
50–53cm (20–21in)

Weight range
12–20kg (26–44lb)

Life span Over 10 years

Origin UK

Other colours

Variety of
colours

The Border Collie's reputation for intelligence reaches far beyond the borderland counties of the UK where it originated. Its excellence as a working sheepdog is legendary, and watching it in action at competitive events has become a popular spectator sport. Tireless energy, low boredom threshold, and an independent spirit make it an unsuitable pet for owners with restricted space or a sedentary lifestyle. However, this dog is highly responsive to experienced handling, and will reward commitment to training by becoming a faithful and obedient companion. The Border Collie has two coat varieties: smooth or moderately long.

*Ears set
well apart*

*Distinct
stop*

*Muscular,
athletic body*

*Low-set tail
reaches hocks*

*Dense, black
and white coat*

*Feathering
on forelegs*

Moderately long coat

POLISH LOWLAND SHEEPDOG

EASY TO TRAIN AS A SHEEP-HERDER, GUARD DOG, OR COMPANION

KC

Height range
42–50cm (17–20in)

Weight range
14–16kg (31–35lb)

Life span 12–15 years

Origin Poland

Other colours

Any colour

Bred to work on the plainlands of Northern Europe as a herder and a guard dog, this delightfully shaggy dog is both rugged and agile. The Polish Lowland Sheepdog has brains as well as brawn and takes readily to training for a variety of purposes. Exercise and grooming should be high on its owner's agenda.

Long hair falls over eyes

Blunt muzzle

Heart-shaped drop ears hidden by hair

Oval-shaped feet

Thick, long, fluffy, black coat, fades with age

DUTCH SCHAPENDOES

THIS LITHE AND AGILE DOG WITH A JOYFUL TEMPERAMENT NEEDS TO BE FULLY OCCUPIED

FCI

Height range
40–50cm (16–20in)

Weight range
12–20kg (26–44lb)

Life span 13–14 years

Origin The Netherlands

Other colours

Any colour

Swift, tireless, and intelligent, this breed is the perfect natural sheep-herder. Moving as if on springs, a working Dutch Schapendoes can run at high speed and bound lightly over almost any obstacle in its path. The breed has the temperament to make a good companion but will not thrive without activity.

Long topknot of hair partially covers eyes

Well-feathered, long tail

Full moustache and beard

Abundant, slightly wavy, black and white coat

Well-rounded, firm, compact feet

SOUTH RUSSIAN SHEPHERD DOG

SAFE ONLY IN EXPERIENCED HANDS, THIS DOG NEEDS PLENTY OF UNDERSTANDING

FCI

Height range
62–65cm (24–26in)

Weight range
48–50kg (106–110lb)

Life span 9–11 years

Origin Russia

Other colours

Ashen-grey   Straw

Yellow and white

This big sheepdog from the Russian steppes was bred not to round up flocks but to guard them against fierce predators. Quick to react, naturally dominant, and highly protective, the South Russian Shepherd Dog, also known as the Ovtcharka ("sheep-herder" in Russian), needs an owner who can establish authority early on.

Elongated head with broad forehead

Long, dense, white coat with coarse texture

Smallish, triangular drop ears

Feet covered with long hair

CARDIGAN WELSH CORGI

A SMALL, STURDY, AND ACTIVE DOG WITH A STRONG PERSONALITY

KC

Height range
28–31cm (11–12in)

Weight range
11–17kg (24–37lb)

Life span 12–15 years

Origin UK

Other colours

Any colour

White markings, if present, should not dominate.

The two varieties of Welsh Corgi were classified as separate breeds in the 1930s. Less popular as a house dog than its relative, the Pembroke Welsh Corgi (see p.56), the Cardigan Welsh Corgi can be distinguished by its larger round ears and longer body. Full of character, it fits well into a small home.

Large, erect ears, rounded at tips

Harsh-textured, short, brindle coat

Relatively long, low-slung body

Fox-like head

Long, heavy tail

Short, sturdy legs

Large, rounded feet

PEMBROKE WELSH CORGI

A SHARP AND CONFIDENT WATCHDOG WITH A BIG BARK FOR ITS SIZE

KC

Height range
25-30cm (10-12in)

Weight range
9-12kg (20-26lb)

Life span 12-15 years

Origin UK

Other colours

Fawn and sable

The two breeds of Welsh Corgi have a long history as cattle-herders and guard dogs in Wales. The more widely known of the two breeds, the Pembroke Welsh Corgi, is distinguishable from the Cardigan Welsh Corgi (see p.55) by its slightly smaller ears and shorter tail. This alert and energetic little dog makes an excellent watchdog and enjoys family life. Their tendency to occasionally revert to their herding instincts and nip ankles can be minimized by early training. Pembroke Welsh Corgis tend to put on weight easily, so need a well-regulated regime of diet and exercise.

Erect ears, rounded at tips

Tail carried low

Red coat with white markings

Fox-like head with typical markings

Black and tan coat

Level topline

White markings on chest

Short legs

SWEDISH VALLHUND
THIS UNUSUAL BREED IS ALERT, FRIENDLY, AND WILLING TO PLEASE

KC

Height range
31–35cm (12–14in)

Weight range
12–16kg (26–35lb)

Life span 12–14 years

Origin Sweden

Other colours

Steel-grey   Red

Red and grey coats may be mixed with brown or yellow.

Like the Welsh Corgis (opposite and p.55), which at first glance it closely resembles, the Swedish Vallhund has been used for centuries as a cattle-herding dog. This tough and workman-like breed continues to make itself useful on Swedish farms. The Swedish Vallhund is uncommon as a house dog but is gradually becoming more widely known and appreciated for its happy personality. It is lively and companionable, always alert, and eager to respond to its owner's demands. Kept active and occupied, the Swedish Vallhund is likely to enjoy robust health and a long lifespan.

Thick, muscular neck

Straight back

Erect, pointed ears

Dense, harsh-textured topcoat

Wedge-shaped, long head

White markings on chest

Greyish-yellow coat

Oval-shaped feet

NEW ZEALAND HUNTAWAY

THIS INTELLIGENT AND FRIENDLY DOG BARKS READILY

Height range
56–66cm (22–26in)

Weight range
25–40kg (55–88lb)

Life span 12–14 years

Origin New Zealand

Other colours

Tricolour   Dark brindle

Currently may still appear in other colours.

The New Zealand Huntaway lacks a breed standard and is not recognized by any kennel club due to its mixed breeding, which may include German Shepherd Dog (see p.35), Border Collie (see p.53), and Rottweiler (see p.81). Developed in New Zealand to be a working sheepdog, it is an excellent worker and is also gaining popularity as a house dog.

Bright-eyed, alert expression

Short, thick, black coat

Long, strong legs

Large feet

Typical tan markings

AUSTRALIAN KELPIE

A TOUGH, HARDY, AND TIRELESS DOG WITH A STRONG NATURAL HERDING INSTINCT

FCI

Height range
43–51cm (17–20in)

Weight range
11–20kg (24–44lb)

Life span 10–14 years

Origin Australia

Other colours

Variety of colours

The Australian Kelpie was developed to work as a sheepdog in the vast open expanses of Australia. Energetic and agile, the breed has seemingly endless reserves of stamina, and a low boredom threshold. An all-action dog, it is best suited to a working life where its herding skills can be put to full use.

Pointed, erect ears

Short, thick, water-resistant, chocolate coat

Thick, brush-like, slightly curved tail

Fox-like head

Fine-boned but muscular legs

AUSTRALIAN CATTLE DOG

STRONG AND WORKMAN-LIKE, THIS TRUSTWORTHY DOG IS A LITTLE WARY OF STRANGERS

KC

Height range
43–51cm (17–20in)

Weight range
14–18kg (31–40lb)

Life span Over 10 years

Origin Australia

Other colours

Red
speckle

Once widely used for cattle-droving and guarding, this breed, also called the Australian Heeler, is little known outside Australia. It is a good family dog, being hardy, alert, companionable, and loyal and devoted to its owner. However, an ancestry that includes the wild dingo has made it naturally suspicious of strangers. This energetic dog enjoys plenty of exercise and is easy to train, as it is highly intelligent and willing to please.

Long, broad, muscular hind quarters

Tan markings on neck

Low-set tail hangs in a slight curve

Blue coat

Round feet with strong, arched toes

Tan markings on legs

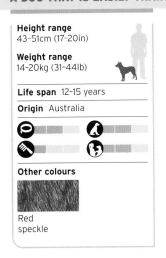

Drop ear

Blue coat

Puppy

AUSTRALIAN STUMPY TAIL CATTLE DOG

A DOG THAT IS EASILY TRAINED BUT NEEDS TO BE KEPT MENTALLY STIMULATED

FCI

Height range
43–51cm (17–20in)

Weight range
14–20kg (31–44lb)

Life span 12–15 years

Origin Australia

Other colours

Red
speckle

This short- or bobtailed breed was developed in the 19th century to herd cattle. After World War II numbers declined, and it would have disappeared but for an Australian redevelopment plan set up in 1988. The Australian Stumpy Tail Cattle Dog is easily trained but needs to be kept busy to avoid behavioural problems.

Widely set pointed ears

Broad, level back

Strong, muscular neck

Well-developed thigh

Blue coat

Closely knit toes with dark nails

LANCASHIRE HEELER

THIS EXUBERANT DOG LOVES TO PLAY AND RARELY HAS HEALTH PROBLEMS

Height range
25–30cm (10–12in)

Weight range
4–7kg (9–15lb)

Life span 15 years

Origin UK

Other colours

Liver and tan

Intelligent, tough, and workman-like, the Lancashire Heeler is well suited to its original use as a cattle-herder in the north of England. The breed may have been the result of crosses between the Pembroke Welsh Corgi (see p.56) and the Manchester Terrier (see p.211). Less inclined to be "nippy" than other heelers, this smart-looking little dog is good with families if trained carefully.

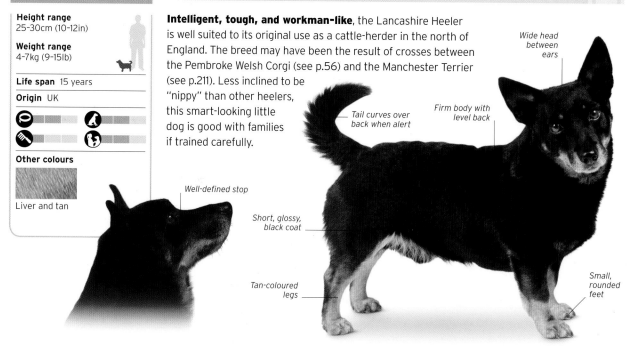

Wide head between ears

Firm body with level back

Tail curves over back when alert

Well-defined stop

Short, glossy, black coat

Tan-coloured legs

Small, rounded feet

HUNGARIAN PUMI

THIS HERDING DOG HAS ADAPTED TO HOME LIFE

Height range
38–47cm (15–19in)

Weight range
8–15kg (18–33lb)

Life span 12–13 years

Origin Hungary

Other colours

Cream   Grey

Gold

Small, white markings may occur on chest and toes.

The Hungarian Pumi was developed in Hungary during the 18th century as a cross between the Hungarian Puli (opposite) and terrier-type dogs from Germany and France. An excellent herder of livestock and a good all-round farm dog, the Hungarian Pumi has proved to be equally successful as a house dog. Bold and restless, this breed thrives on action.

Dense, wiry tufts on ears

High-set tail

Narrow, terrier-like head

Well-muscled, lean body

Thick, curly, black coat

KOMONDOR

NOT FOR NOVICES, THIS DOG NEEDS TACTFUL HANDLING AND SPECIAL GROOMING

KC

Height range
60–80cm (24–31in)

Weight range
36–61kg (79–135lb)

Life span Under 10 years

Origin Hungary

The Komondor was bred to protect livestock, and has strong natural guarding instincts. This characteristic, combined with considerable size and strength, means that ownership should be considered only by those with plenty of dog-handling experience and space. Daily grooming is essential to maintain the Komondor's extraordinary tasselled coat.

Very long, heavy, white corded coat

Long tail curved slightly at tip

Dark eyes partially obscured by coat

Drop ears hidden under coat

HUNGARIAN PULI

HIGHLY INTELLIGENT AND EAGER TO PLEASE, THIS DOG NEEDS TIME AND ATTENTION

KC

Height range
36–44cm (14–17in)

Weight range
10–15kg (22–33lb)

Life span Over 12 years

Origin Hungary

Other colours

White

Grey

Fawn

May have small, white markings on chest and feet.

Thought to have been brought into Central Europe by the nomadic Magyar tribes of Asia, the Hungarian Puli was traditionally used as a herding dog. Affectionate and quick to learn, it makes a good family pet but gets bored easily without fun and company. Its corded coat needs special attention.

Small, black nose

Straight, muscular back

Eyes covered by long-corded, black coat

Profusely coated tail curls over back

Black coat forms long cords

Short, round feet

BERGAMASCO
THIS OUTDOOR DOG NEEDS PLENTY OF SPACE AND GROOMING · KC

Height range
53–62cm (21–24in)

Weight range
26–38kg (57–84lb)

Life span Over 10 years

Origin Italy

Other colours

Light fawn and Isabella

Black

May have white markings.

A sheepdog and guard dog, the powerful Bergamasco was bred for a tough, outdoor life in the northern Italian mountains. Its weatherproof coat is thick, greasy to the touch, and easily becomes matted, but once the coat becomes flocked, grooming time is greatly reduced. The Bergamasco is companionable and loyal but needs firm control.

Broad, straight back

Pronounced stop on skull covered by hair

Tail carried low

Flocked, grey coat

AIDI
PROTECTIVE AND LOVING WITH OWNERS, THIS IS NOT AN IDEAL HOUSE DOG · FCI

Height range
53–61cm (21–24in)

Weight range
23–25kg (51–55lb)

Life span About 12 years

Origin North Africa

Other colours

Fawn

Brown

Black

Fawn, brown, and black coats may be spotted with white.

Also known as the Atlas Mountain Dog, this type of dog has been used for centuries as a guard dog by the nomadic peoples of Morocco. The Aidi is faithful, fearless, and always on the alert to protect its owners and their possessions. But its strong guarding instincts mean that this dog is not always suited to a domestic lifestyle.

Wide-set, drop ears

Black lips

Black marking

Thick, medium-length, white coat

Long, bushy, low-set tail

Feathering on back of legs

AUSTRALIAN SHEPHERD

THIS EVEN-TEMPERED, INTELLIGENT DOG ADAPTS WELL TO FAMILY LIFE

KC

Height range
46–58cm (18–23in)

Weight range
18–29kg (40–65lb)

Life span Over 10 years

Origin USA

Other colours

Red, red merle   Black

All coats may have tan markings.

Not an "Aussie" at all, this shepherd dog was bred in the United States. Its name derives from its ancestors, which were worked by Basque shepherds who emigrated to Australia in the late 19th century and then later moved on to the USA. The Australian Shepherd, still useful as a ranch dog and tracker, is becoming increasingly valued as a pet.

Pronounced stop

High-set, drop ears

Tan markings

Thick, wavy, blue-merle coat

White hairs extend across neck, chest, and legs

Bushy tail

MAREMMA SHEEPDOG

POWERFUL AND PROTECTIVE, THIS IS VERY MUCH AN OUTDOOR DOG

KC

Height range
60–73cm (24–29in)

Weight range
30–45kg (66–99lb)

Life span Over 10 years

Origin Italy

The sheep herders of the central Italian plains have long used the Maremma Sheepdog to guard their flocks. With an imposing stance and a magnificent, thick, white coat, this handsome dog has obvious attractions but needs expert handling. Like many dogs bred for outdoor work, this sheepdog is not the ideal choice for the home.

Short hair on face

Small ears hang flat at rest

Thickly haired, low-set tail

Black-rimmed eyes

Thick collar of hair on neck

Heavy, wavy, white coat

GREEK SHEPHERD DOG

THIS STRONG-WILLED BREED IS FRIENDLY WITH THOSE IT KNOWS BUT WARY OF STRANGERS

Height range
60–75cm (24–30in)

Weight range
32–50kg (71–110lb)

Life span 12 years

Origin Greece

Other colours

Variety of colours

The ancestors of this breed, which is also known as the Hellenic Shepherd Dog, may have been the sheepdogs brought into Greece many centuries ago by Turkish migrants. Tough, brave, and a natural guardian and flock leader, the Greek Shepherd Dog has excellent qualities for a working dog, but is too dominant in temperament to make a reliable family companion. There are two coat types: long-haired and short-haired.

Massive, flat-topped head

Dark brown eyes

Triangular, drop ears with darker edges

Abundant hair on tail

Dense, fawn coat with some sabling

Broad chest

Long-haired

White feet and legs

CURSINU

THIS LOYAL AND INTELLIGENT DOG IS ENERGETIC OUTDOORS BUT CALM IN THE HOUSE

Height range
46–58cm (18–23in)

Weight range
Not known

Life span Over 10 years

Origin France

Dogs of this type have existed on the island of Corsica for over a hundred years, although the Cursinu has only been recognized in France since 2003. Energetic, fast-moving, and versatile, it is used for both hunting and herding and although it can adapt to home life, it is probably at its best as a working dog.

High-set, semi-erect ears

Long tail, carried in curl when active

Short, muscular neck

Flat, wide head

Short to medium-length, fawn-brindle coat

White chest markings

White markings on feet

Long, hare-like feet

ROMANIAN SHEPHERD DOGS

THESE WATCHFUL AND COURAGEOUS DOGS NEED SPACE AND FREEDOM TO RUN

FCI

Height range
59-78cm (23-31in)

Weight range
35-70kg (77-154lb)

Life span 12-14 years

Origin Romania

Other colours

White-beige   Black

Bucovina only may appear as white, white-beige, black, or ashen-grey and may have patches of colour.

In the mountainous Carpathian region of Romania, shepherds rely on large, robust dogs to guard their flocks in all weathers. Regional breeding has resulted in several distinct types: the Carpatin, the Bucovina, and the Mioritic. All are better suited to outdoor rather than indoor life, and none is widely known as a companion dog. With strong watchdog instincts, Romanian Shepherd Dogs are highly territorial and suspicious of strangers. They need plenty of physical and mental activity, as well as early socialization and firm training.

Coat longer than other Romanian Shepherd Dogs

White coat with light fawn and grey markings

Mioritic

Carpatin

Rough, slightly wavy hair

Blaze extends to muzzle

Black nose

Wolf-grey coat

Profuse hair on tail

Slightly longer hair on neck forms ruff

Feathering on back of front legs

Carpatin

White markings on feet

APPENZELL CATTLE DOG

THIS VERSATILE DOG IS WILLING TO WORK BUT ALSO ENJOYS FAMILY LIFE

FCI

Height range
50–56cm (20–22in)

Weight range
22–32kg (49–71lb)

Life span 12–13 years

Origin Switzerland

Other colours

Havana Brown

Bred for herding and guarding on Alpine farms, the Appenzell Cattle Dog has also taken well to urban life. The breed has a firm following in Switzerland but is not yet widely known elsewhere. Keen, alert, and full of energy, Appenzells are at their best when kept occupied and interested.

White blaze extends to sides of muzzle

Drop ears, raised forward when alert

Reddish brown markings on face

White chest

Tail carried in tight curl

Small, almond-shaped eyes

Dense, flat, shiny, tricolour coat

White feet

ENTLEBUCHER MOUNTAIN DOG

SMART IN APPEARANCE, THIS FAMILY DOG IS FULL OF HIGH SPIRITS

KC

Height range
42–50cm (17–20in)

Weight range
21–28kg (46–62lb)

Life span 11–15 years

Origin Switzerland

The smallest of several long-established Swiss mountain dogs, this cattle-droving breed from the Entlebuch Valley is gaining popularity as a house dog. Bouncing with high spirits, the Entlebucher Mountain Dog is confident and well-behaved within the family, but has strong protective instincts and is inclined to be wary around strangers.

High-set, drop ears

Back length longer than leg length

White chest

Reddish brown markings above eyes

Slightly curved, long tail

Short, harsh, glossy, tricolour coat

Reddish brown markings on legs

BERNESE MOUNTAIN DOG

A BEAUTIFULLY MARKED BREED WITH AN ATTRACTIVE PERSONALITY AND KIND NATURE

KC

Height range
58–70cm (23–28in)

Weight range
32–54kg (71–120lb)

Life span Under 10 years

Origin Switzerland

This lovely dog takes its name from the Swiss canton of Berne, where it traditionally worked as a haulage dog for basket-weavers. It is attractive not just in looks but also in temperament, and has become deservedly popular as a family dog. Although large and strong, the Bernese Mountain Dog is highly trainable and has gentle ways that are easy to live with. Generally, the breed is affectionate and reliable with children. The eye-catching tricolour coat needs plenty of grooming to maintain its silky texture and characteristic soft sheen.

Triangular, drop ears

White blaze on head

Broad head with well-defined stop

Long, bushy jet-black tail

Long, silky, slightly wavy, tricolour coat

Broad, deep chest with white markings

Reddish brown markings extend down to feet

GREAT SWISS MOUNTAIN DOG

THIS LARGE, POWERFUL, AND KIND DOG IS GOOD WITH CHILDREN AND OTHER PETS | KC

Height range
60–72cm (24–28in)

Weight range
36–59kg (79–130lb)

Life span 8–11 years

Origin Switzerland

Bred in the Swiss Alps, this huge, strong, striking dog was once used to haul wagons loaded with milk, cheese, and other produce. It was also used for cattle-herding and guard duties. A true working dog, the Great Swiss Mountain Dog has an agreeable temperament that makes it a sociable family companion for those with room to spare.

Tan spots over eyes

Triangular ears hang close to head

Broad, flattened skull

White chest

Tricolour coat has symmetrical pattern

Strong, muscular body

WHITE SWISS SHEPHERD DOG

THIS FAMILY-FRIENDLY DOG LIKES CHILDREN BUT CAN BE WARY OF STRANGERS | KC

Height range
53–66cm (21–26in)

Weight range
25–40kg (55–88lb)

Life span Over 10 years

Origin Switzerland

Pure white shepherd dogs were first brought into Switzerland from North America in the 1970s. Developed over the next two decades, it was recognized in Switzerland as a breed in 1991. Good-tempered and intelligent, it is suitable for both work and companionship. There are two coat types: medium-haired and long-haired.

High-set, erect ears

Arched neck with longer hair

Dark eyes

White coat

Bushy tail

Long-haired

TURKISH KANGAL DOG

A LOYAL AND INTELLIGENT DOG THAT CAN ADAPT WELL TO FAMILY LIFE

KC

Height range
71–81cm (28–32in)

Weight range
41–64kg (90–141lb)

Life span 12–15 years

Origin Turkey

Other colours

Cream   Steel Grey

All shades
of fawn

Considered a separate breed by some breed organizations, the Turkish Kangal is combined with the Anatolian Shepherd Dog by others. It is a large and gentle dog that was originally bred as a flock guardian. If kept as a pet, care must be taken to prevent it from becoming too territorial.

Tail carried over back when alert

Black mask and ears

Fawn coat

Slight dewlap on neck

Deep chest

ANATOLIAN SHEPHERD DOG

THIS PROTECTIVE AND LOYAL DOG NEEDS SUPERVISION WITH CHILDREN AND STRANGERS

KC

Height range
71–81cm (28–32in)

Weight range
41–64kg (90–141lb)

Life span 12–15 years

Origin Turkey

Other colours

Any colour

After a long history as a livestock-guardian, this hardy and powerful breed is still used in Turkey as a working dog. Bred for its courage and independence of spirit, the Anatolian Shepherd Dog respects the authority of a firm and loving owner. If kept as a companion dog, training and socializing should begin early.

Slight furrow down head

Mane of thicker hair around shoulders

Dark face mask

Long tail curls up at tip

Throat has dewlap

Fawn coat of various shades

AKBASH

Height range
69-79cm (27-31in)

Weight range
34-59kg (75-130lb)

Life span 10-11 years

Origin Turkey

A powerful Turkish breed developed for guarding flocks, Akbash-type dogs have probably been around for several thousands of years. Used on ranches in North America as a livestock and property guard, the Akbash is best suited to a working life and needs skilled handling to avoid behaviour problems. There are two coat types: long-haired and medium-haired.

Triangular, drop ears

Shorter hair on face

Weatherproof, coarse, white coat

Long-haired

Heavily feathered tail

Biscuit-coloured shading

Feathering on back of legs

CENTRAL ASIAN SHEPHERD DOG

FCI

Height range
65-78cm (26-31in)

Weight range
40-79kg (88-174lb)

Life span 12-14 years

Origin Central Asian Republics/ Russia

Other colours

Variety of colours

The nomadic herdsmen of Central Asia - the regions now known as Kazakhstan, Turkmenistan, Tajikistan, Uzbekistan, and Kyrgyzstan - have used dogs of this type to protect their flocks for hundreds of years. Once bred selectively in the former USSR, this rare breed needs early socialization. There are two coat types: short-haired and long-haired.

Moderate stop

Drop ears

Powerful shoulders

Large, rounded feet

Typical mastiff-type body

Dense, white coat with lemon markings

Short-haired

CAUCASIAN SHEPHERD DOG
THIS FIERCELY PROTECTIVE DOG DOES NOT MAKE AN IDEAL PET

FCI

Height range
67–75cm (26–30in)

Weight range
45–70kg (99–154lb)

Life span 10–11 years

Origin Russia

Other colours

Variety of colours

Developed from various large dogs, this shepherd dog was once used to guard flocks in the Caucasian regions. In the 1920s, selective breeding of this dog began in the former USSR and continued later in Germany. An excellent watchdog, it needs careful handling if it is to be a good companion.

Massive head

Triangular, drop ears with rounded tips

Heavily feathered tail

Deep chest

Dense, coarse, sable coat stands away from body

Darker muzzle

Puppy

Feet thickly insulated with white hair

LEONBERGER
THIS EXCELLENT FAMILY DOG IS GOOD-TEMPERED, CALM, AND FRIENDLY

KC

Height range
72–80cm (28–31in)

Weight range
45–77kg (99–170lb)

Life span Over 10 years

Origin Germany

Other colours

Sandy   Red

May have white markings.

Named after the Bavarian town of Leonberg, the Leonberger was developed in the mid-19th century as a result of cross-breeding between the St. Bernard (see p.72) and the Newfoundland (see p.74). After the two World Wars, Leonbergers had almost disappeared but the breed has recovered well and gained wide popularity for its splendid looks and friendly nature.

Feathered, high-set ears

Black tips to some hair

Mane on neck and chest

Black mask

Thick, fairly long, lion-gold coat

Broad chest

Slightly tucked-up belly

Feathered tail, lighter on underside

Feathered forelegs

ST. BERNARD

ALMOST UNRIVALLED FOR SIZE, THIS KINDLY GIANT HAS A DELIGHTFUL TEMPERAMENT

KC

Height range
70-75cm (28-30in)

Weight range
59-81kg (130-180lb)

Life span 8-10 years

Origin Switzerland

Other colours

Brindle

Originally crossbred from mastiff-type dogs by the monks of St. Bernard's Hospice in the Swiss Alps, this breed's sometimes exaggerated reputation as a mountain rescue dog extends worldwide. Affectionate and utterly trustworthy, the St. Bernard has many virtues. It is calm-natured, taking life at a moderate pace. The St. Bernard is comparatively rare as a house dog due to its colossal size, and the amount of space needed to accommodate its sheer bulk can hardly be over-estimated; food bills are another major consideration. There are two coat types: smooth and rough.

Massive head with wide skull

Slightly pendulous flews

Typical black shading

White markings on face

Characteristic white markings on legs

White collar

Broad, straight back

White patch

Flat, deep cheeks

Long, thick neck with pronounced dewlap

Bushy, white tail

Smooth, orange and white coat

Smooth-haired

TATRA SHEPHERD DOG

ALTHOUGH CALM WITH THE FAMILY, THIS DOG DOES NOT TAKE KINDLY TO STRANGERS

FCI

Height range
60–70cm (24–28in)

Weight range
36–59kg (79–130lb)

Life span 10–12 years

Origin Poland

Still used for protecting and herding flocks in the high Tatra mountains of Poland, this huge and handsome dog takes its duties just as seriously when guarding home and household. Usually gentle and well-mannered with those it knows, the Tatra Shepherd Dog is a force to be reckoned with if it perceives a threat. Firm and fair handling by an experienced owner, and a watchful eye for potential aggression, are essential if this breed is to be kept as a companion. The dog's extremely thick coat sheds heavily and requires frequent grooming.

Massively built body

Black nose with wide nostrils

Triangular drop ears with rounded tips

Long tail reaches hocks

Dense, slightly wavy, white coat

Lips and eyes have dark edges

Deep mane around neck

Hair shorter on lower legs and paws

NEWFOUNDLAND

A COLOSSAL BUT GENTLE AND FRIENDLY DOG WITH A LOVE OF SWIMMING

Height range
66-71cm (26-28in)

Weight range
50-69kg (110-152lb)

Life span 9-11 years

Origin Canada

Other colours

Dark brown

Although the Newfoundland is associated with the Canadian province of the same name, the dog's true origins are uncertain. Historically used by fishermen to retrieve nets, today it is sometimes used for sea rescues. The breed has a protective nature and is renowned for being gentle with children. Its large size rules this dog out as a pet for a small home.

Massive head

Bushy tail

Dense, coarse, slightly oily, black coat

Small, white markings on chest

Feathered forelegs

Large feet

LANDSEER

A BLACK AND WHITE NEWFOUNDLAND MADE FAMOUS BY AN ARTIST

Height range
66-71cm (26-28in)

Weight range
50-69kg (110-152lb)

Life span 9-11 years

Origin Canada

This colour variant of the Newfoundland (above) is regarded as a distinct breed in some countries. The Landseer is named after the mid-Victorian British painter Sir Edwin Landseer, who often painted these dogs. Apart from its bicoloured coat, this dog shares all the attributes of solid-coloured Newfoundlands, being placid, friendly, and dependable.

Black head with well-developed stop

Strong neck

Distinctive, black saddle

Black and white coat

Short hair in front of legs, feathered behind

PYRENEAN MOUNTAIN DOG

THIS GIANT-SIZED DOG IS SATISFIED WITH MODERATE EXERCISE AND LOVES FAMILY LIFE

KC

Height range
65-70cm (26-28in)

Weight range
40-50kg (88-110lb)

Life span 9-11 years

Origin France

Other colours

Pure white

One of the most imposing of all dogs, this breed comes from the French Pyrenees, where its traditional role was as a guarder of flocks. Thoroughly assimilated into modern family life, the Pyrenean Mountain Dog is calm-natured and unaggressive, reliable in the home, and good with children. Despite the dog's huge size and strength, it does not need an excessive amount of exercise and can be quite content with a gentle stroll. However, owners should be prepared to put their energies into grooming to keep the dog's thick coat looking its best.

Tan patches on head

Smallish, triangular ears

Heavy mane around neck and shoulders

Dark amber-coloured eyes with black rims

Dense, wavy, white coat

Plumed tail

Tan patch on rump

Double dewclaws on hind legs, hidden by hair

PYRENEAN MASTIFF

A GENERALLY GOOD-NATURED DOG WITH A NOBLE ATTITUDE, BUT SUSPICIOUS OF STRANGERS

KC

Height range
72–81cm (28–32in)

Weight range
54–70kg (120–154lb)

Life span 10 years

Origin Spain

A native of Spain, the Pyrenean Mastiff was originally kept for guarding mountain flocks. Large and courageous enough to take on a bear or a wolf, this breed is now often used as a house guard. Intelligent and calm, with the right training it can also be a good companion dog.

Dense, bristly textured, white coat

Small, almond-shaped eyes

Well-defined face mask

Double dewlap

Long, plumed tail

Irregular patch same colour as face mask

TIBETAN KYI APSO

A RARE MOUNTAIN DOG, POSSESSIVE OF HOME AND FAMILY

Height range
56–71cm (22–28in)

Weight range
31–38kg (68–84lb)

Life span 7–10 years

Origin Tibet

Other colours

Any colour

Only a handful of Kyi Apsos have appeared outside Tibet and the breed is elusive, even in its own country. Traditionally, this dog is a guard of flocks and homes. The Tibetan Kyi Apso has a characteristic springy gait, and is agile and capable of rapid bursts of speed.

Low-set, pendant ears

Tail carried high in a curl

Bearded face

Strong hind quarters

Dense, wiry, black coat

Neck broad relative to body

TIBETAN MASTIFF

ONE OF THE SMALLER MASTIFFS, THIS DOG MAY TAKE TIME TO TRAIN AND SOCIALIZE

KC

Height range
61–66cm (24–26in)

Weight range
36–100kg (80–220lb)

Life span Over 10 years

Origin Tibet

Other colours

Slate-grey   Gold

Black and slate-grey dogs may have tan markings.

With a history of guarding livestock in the Himalayas, the Tibetan Mastiff has strong protective instincts. In its native country, it should be approached with caution, but in the West, selective breeding has greatly reduced its aggressive traits. It is now an acceptable house dog and a good companion – although not overtly affectionate – but requires patience to train.

Short-haired, drop ears

Bushy tail carried curled over back

Coat forms mane around neck and shoulders

Dense, straight, black coat

Feathering between toes

Tan markings above eyes

TORNJAK

FRIENDLY AND OBEDIENT, BUT NEEDS TO BE WELL SOCIALIZED AS A PUPPY

FCI

Height range
58–72cm (23–28in)

Weight range
35–45kg (77–99lb)

Life span 10–12 years

Origin Bosnia and Herzegovina/ Croatia

Other colours

Usually bi-coloured with white dominating.

Also known as the Bosnian and Herzegovinian-Croatian Shepherd Dog, the Tornjak has only recently been seen outside its native countries. Shepherd dogs like these have defended flocks from predators in the Dinarides for centuries, but selective breeding did not start until 1978. A large, powerful dog, the Tornjak is intelligent and easy to train, but needs an experienced dog owner and plenty of space to exercise.

Dark, almond-shaped eyes

White coat with black patches

Tail well covered with long hair

Strong lower leg

SLOVAKIAN CHUVACH

THIS TOUGH AND FEARLESS DOG MAKES AN EXCELLENT HOUSE DOG GIVEN THE RIGHT TRAINING

FCI

Height range
59–70cm (23–28in)

Weight range
31–44kg (68–97lb)

Life span 11–13 years

Origin Slovakia

Originally a shepherd's guard dog from the Slovakian Alps, the Slovakian Chuvach has been developed successfully into a good house dog. This large, powerful breed retains the exceptional alertness and watchfulness that made it a superb defender of farms and livestock. Tactful training is needed to achieve the best results with this breed.

Short hair on face

Broad forehead with shallow furrow

High-set, drop ears

Profusely feathered, low-set tail

Slightly wavy, white coat

HUNGARIAN KUVASZ

CAN BE AFFECTIONATE, BUT THIS DOG MAY TURN AGGRESSIVE WHEN DEFENDING

KC

Height range
66–75cm (26–30in)

Weight range
32–52kg (71–115lb)

Life span 10–12 years

Origin Hungary

Probably the oldest and best known of Hungary's breeds, the Hungarian Kuvasz was once used as a shepherd's guard dog. The breed's naturally protective instincts may lead to aggressiveness, and this dog has the potential to become a liability in inexperienced hands. It takes firm training to make the Hungarian Kuvasz an acceptable house dog.

Broad head with minimal stop

Coarse, wavy, white coat

Muscular neck

Triangular, drop ears with rounded tips

Long, extremely muscular thighs

HOVAWART

THIS VERY HARDY, FAITHFUL COMPANION MAY TRY TO DOMINATE OTHER DOGS

KC

Height range
58-70cm (23-28in)

Weight range
28-45kg (62-99lb)

Life span 10-14 years

Origin Germany

Little known as a companion dog but growing in popularity, the Hovawart has a very long history – its forerunners are thought to have been used as farm dogs in the 13th century. The modern breed was developed in Germany in the first half of the 20th century. The Hovawart is very hardy, ready to go outdoors whatever the weather, and is a friendly and faithful house dog within a family. Although it has a strong-willed personality, the Hovawart is not difficult to train but may need careful handling in the presence of other dogs.

Black and gold coat

Triangular, drop ears

Medium-length, blonde coat

Bushy tail, may show a few white hairs

Skull and muzzle equal in length

Dense, black coat

Feathering on forelegs may be very long

Oval feet with arched toes

BEAUCERON

Height range
63–70cm (25–28in)

Weight range
29–39kg (65–85lb)

Life span 10–15 years

Origin France

Other colours

Grey, black, and tan

May have a few white chest hairs.

A herding and guard dog from the flatlands of the Beauce region in Central France, the Beauceron is an excellent worker and, in the right situation, a gentle family companion. This big, strong dog can be intolerant of other dogs; early training is needed to minimize potential problems.

Slightly sloping croup

Coarse-textured, short, black and tan coat

Broad head

Drop ears

Tan markings on muzzle

Double dewclaws on hind feet

Lower legs tan in colour

MAJORCA SHEPHERD DOG

Height range
62–73cm (24–29in)

Weight range
35–40kg (77–88lb)

Life span 11–13 years

Origin Spain

Comparatively rare worldwide, the Majorca Shepherd Dog is regarded with pride in Majorca, where it was once widely used as a shepherd dog, and is now popular as a show dog. Although usually willing to obey, this breed has strong herding instincts and can be defensive with strangers and other dogs.

Small, wide-set eyes

Tapering tail

Short, black coat

Small feet, with arched toes

ROTTWEILER
A BIG AND BURLY DOG SUITED TO FIRM AND RESPONSIBLE OWNERS

Height range
58-69cm (23-27in)

Weight range
38-59kg (84-130lb)

Life span 10-11 years

Origin Germany

Once used in southern Germany as a cattle dog, the Rottweiler has acquired an unfortunate image as a vicious guard dog and an intimidating status symbol. However, despite the breed's great strength, impressive swagger, and easily aroused protective responses, the Rottweiler is not naturally ill-tempered. With thoughtful training from a firm and experienced owner, who is alert to potential triggers of aggression, this dog makes a calm and obedient companion. Rottweilers are more agile than their size and sturdy build might suggest, and appreciate plenty of vigorous exercise.

Tan markings clearly defined on head

Small, drop ears

Broad, deep chest

Broad head with well-defined stop

Deep muzzle with firm flews

Short, smooth, shiny, black and tan coat

Tan chest markings

Tan markings on legs

SHAR PEI

A GENERALLY FRIENDLY TEMPERAMENT IS HIDDEN BEHIND THIS DOG'S SCOWLING FACE

KC

Height range
46–51cm (18–20in)

Weight range
18–25kg (40–55lb)

Life span Over 10 years

Origin China

Other colours

Variety of colours

The early uses of this native Chinese breed included herding and guarding livestock, hunting, and fighting. However, the Shar Pei's amiable nature and relatively compact size make it suitable as a pet for a town or country home. The dog's distinctive appearance has huge popular appeal and, at least for a while, owning a Shar Pei was a fashion statement. Some breeders sought to increase the Shar Pei's wrinkly looks by producing dogs with excessively loose and folded facial skin. However, this resulted in eye problems, and the practice is now largely discredited.

Square, sturdily built body

Broad muzzle with thick flews

Small, high-set, button ears

Puppy

Wrinkles on forehead give frowning expression

Loose skin on back and legs wrinkles when dog is seated

Tail carried high, and curved over

Back dips slightly behind withers

Wrinkled skin over shoulders and neck

Short, velvety, fawn coat

TAIWAN DOG
THIS BREED NEEDS WIDE OPEN SPACES AND IS INCLINED TO CHASE SMALL ANIMALS

FCI

Height range
43–53cm (17–21in)

Weight range
12–18kg (26–40lb)

Life span Over 10 years

Origin Taiwan

Other colours

Variety of colours

The Taiwan Dog, formerly known as the Formosan Mountain Dog, is something of a rarity, even in its native country. It is believed to have descended from the semi-wild dogs once used for hunting in the interior of Taiwan. The breed makes an intelligent family dog, but its hunting instincts need to be kept in check.

Sickle-shaped, high-set tail, profusely covered in hair

Erect ears

Short, hard, brindle coat

Black nose

Tucked-up belly

Strong, slender legs

MALLORCA MASTIFF
THIS SUPERB WATCHDOG COMBINES COURAGE WITH A CALM TEMPERAMENT

FCI

Height range
52–58cm (20–23in)

Weight range
30–38kg (66–84lb)

Life span 10–12 years

Origin Spain

Other colours

Black

The Mallorca Mastiff, also known as the Ca de Bou, has a background that includes fighting and bull-baiting. A powerful breed, it has the typical mastiff-type build and watchful nature. When handled firmly but quietly, this dog socializes well, but it is probably better suited to life as a guard dog rather than as a family pet.

Large, square head

Thick, tapering tail

Body length exceeds leg length

High-set, rose ears

Black mask

Brindle coat

Lower jaw slightly longer than upper (undershot)

Short, fawn coat

Strong neck with slight dewlap

White markings on feet

PRESA CANARIO

LARGE, POWERFUL, AND VERY STRONG-WILLED, THIS DOG IS NOT FOR NOVICE OWNERS

FCI

Height range
56-66cm (22-26in)

Weight range
40-65kg (88-143lb)

Life span 9-11 years

Origin Spain

Other colours

Brindle

May have white markings.

Bred in the Canary Islands in the early 19th century as a fighting dog, the Presa Canario is believed to include the Mastiff (see p.93) in its ancestry. Difficult to train and socialize, a Presa Canario is manageable if the owner understands and controls the dog's dominant nature. Early socialization is essential.

Square head with powerful jaw

Drop ears

Short, fawn coat

Darker muzzle

Pronounced dewlap

Tail extends to hock

Muscular body

Large, round, cat-like feet

DOGO ARGENTINO

BRED FOR HUNTING, THIS IS A GOOD-NATURED DOG IF SOCIALIZED WELL

FCI

Height range
60-68cm (24-27in)

Weight range
36-45kg (79-99lb)

Life span 10-12 years

Origin Argentina

Originating in the 1920s in Cordoba, Argentina, the Dogo Argentino was the creation of a local doctor who wanted a dog for hunting large game. Breeding from old fighting dogs such as mastiffs and the Bulldog (see p.94) produced this new dog. The Dogo Argentino has a kind temperament but can be overprotective.

Characteristic, slightly concave muzzle

Body length exceeds leg length

Long, thick tail

Short, white coat

Strong neck with skin folds at throat

Broad, deep chest

Powerful hind quarters

Round feet

FILA BRASILEIRO

THIS COURAGEOUS AND SELF-CONFIDENT DOG CAN BE WARY OF STRANGERS | FCI

Height range
60-75cm (24-30in)

Weight range
Over 40kg (Over 88lb)

Life span 9-11 years

Origin Brazil

Other colours

Any solid colour

Bred to guard large estates and livestock, the Fila Brasileiro does not fear intruders of any kind. Huge but beautifully proportioned, this dog exudes confidence and determination. Although the Fila Brasileiro is kind and quiet within a family, the average owner may find the breed's hunting and protective instincts difficult to manage.

Well-developed eyebrows

Large, drop ears

Broad chest with white markings

Forelegs more heavily boned than hind legs

White markings on feet

Massive, broad head

Short, smooth, brindle coat

Loose, thick skin forms dewlaps on throat

URUGUAYAN CIMARRON

THIS INTELLIGENT AND AGILE DOG NEEDS EARLY SOCIALIZING BUT MAKES A GOOD GUARD DOG | FCI

Height range
55-61cm (22-24in)

Weight range
33-45kg (73-99lb)

Life span 10-13 years

Origin Uruguay

Other colours

Fawn

Fawn coats may have black shading.

The ancestors of this breed were brought into Uruguay by Spanish and Portuguese colonists and crossed with local dogs. Bred by farmers in the remote area of Cerro Largo, the Uruguayan Cimarron was used for guarding and herding. Like many working breeds, it needs an experienced owner if kept as a companion.

Triangular ears with rounded tips

Dark muzzle

Muscular, well-defined hind quarters

Deep, broad chest

Strong, powerful jaws

Close-fitting, short-haired, brindle coat

Oval feet

White chest markings

Thick tail reaches hocks

Rounded, cat-like feet

ALAPAHA BLUE BLOOD BULLDOG

IF GIVEN REGULAR EXERCISE, THIS IS A GOOD DOG IN THE HOME BUT NEEDS CAREFUL TRAINING

Height range
46-61cm (18-24in)

Weight range
25-41kg (55-90lb)

Life span 12-15 years

Origin USA

Other colours

White

Dogs may have patches
of any colour.

Bulldog-type dogs were once commonly used as guards in the plantations of South Georgia. By the early 19th century such dogs were almost extinct, but dedicated breeding over the next 200 years regenerated the type and produced the Alapaha Blue Blood Bulldog. This dog is still rare and not widely known outside the United States. Muscular and intrepid, an Alapaha Blue Blood Bulldog has strong protective instincts, but it is easy to train to be a well-behaved and affectionate companion. Energetic outdoors, this dog is happiest when given plenty of exercise.

Short muzzle
with well-
defined stop

Broad,
flat head

Wide-set, triangular,
drop ears

Blue eyes

Black patch

Loose flews

Broad chest

Predominantly
white coat

Strong, muscular body

Cat-like feet

BOERBOEL

THIS DOG LOVES FAMILY BUT NOT STRANGERS AND REQUIRES RESPONSIBLE OWNERSHIP AKC

Height range
55–69cm (22–27in)

Weight range
68–91kg (150–200lb)

Life span 12–15 years

Origin South Africa

Other colours

Variety of colours

May have darker face mask.

The Boerboel was developed from the large, mastiff-type dogs brought by settlers to the Cape area of South Africa from the 17th century onwards. Affectionate with family and friends, the Boerboel is a formidable guard dog of huge size and strength. An experienced owner and early socialization are very important.

Characteristic massive, square head

Brow slightly wrinkled

Drop ears hang close to head

Darker tip to muzzle

Strong, muscular neck

Thick tail tapers slightly to tip

Powerful hind legs

Short, sleek, fawn coat

SPANISH MASTIFF

A HEAVYWEIGHT DEFENDER OF HOME AND FAMILY, THIS TERRITORIAL MASTIFF NEEDS EXPERT HANDLING FCI

Height range
72–80cm (28–31in)

Weight range
52–100kg (115–221lb)

Life span 10–11 years

Origin Spain

Other colours

Any colour

Once used for guarding livestock and homes in Spain, the Spanish Mastiff still carries out its traditional duties. The breed is also popular in its native country as a companion dog. Kind and loyal within the family, this breed can be aggressive with strangers and other dogs.

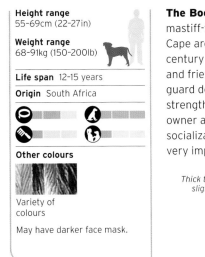

Almond-shaped eyes, small in proportion to head

Loose-fitting skin

Double dewlap

Fawn coat with some sabling

Drop ears

Long, bushy tail

Massively built but agile body

Upper lip overhangs lower lip

Large, cat-like feet

High-set tail,
held upright

Arched neck

Distinct stop

High-set
ears with
rounded tips

Expressive face with
dark brown eyes and
wrinkled forehead

Body square
in profile

Lower jaw
longer than
upper jaw
(undershot)

Short, broad
muzzle

Muscular
hind quarters

White chest

Tucked-up
belly

Smooth,
fawn coat

White feet and
lower legs

BOXER

THIS CLEVER, LOYAL, EXUBERANT, AND FUN-LOVING DOG IS IDEAL FOR AN ENERGETIC OWNER | KC

Height range
53-63cm (21-25in)

Weight range
25-32kg (55-71lb)

Life span 10-14 years

Origin Germany

Other colours

Black brindle

White markings should
not exceed a third of the
coat colour.

Once a Boxer-owner, always a Boxer-owner – this German breed is so big on personality that few who live with it ever look at another type of dog. The Boxer in its modern form was developed in the 19th century and its ancestry is thought to include mastiff-type dogs such as the Bulldog (see p.94) and the Great Dane (see p.95). Powerful and athletic, it was bred primarily for fighting and bull-baiting, but was also used for farm work, haulage, and for hunting and holding down large game such as wild boar. Because of its endurance and courage, the breed is used today as a police and military search-and-rescue dog and for guard work.

The Boxer's history, its proud, upstanding attitude, and forward-thrusting jaw give the impression of an intimidating dog, and it can certainly be protective of home and family, but it makes a wonderful companion. It is

loyal, affectionate, endearingly attention-seeking, and a boisterous but tolerant friend for children. This energetic breed suits fit, active owners as it retains its high spirits and playfulness into late maturity. Almost any sort of fun keeps a Boxer happy but, ideally, it requires a good two-hour walk every day with plenty of scope for romping around in the open. At home, given its stamina and curiosity, a Boxer enjoys a large garden where it has space to roam and interesting corners to explore.

This highly intelligent dog can be a handful to train but is obedient provided it receives calm and consistent commands and clear leadership. With early socializing, a Boxer is likely to get on well with any other pets in the family, although out on walks its hunting instincts may be aroused if there are birds or small animals to chase.

ST. MIGUEL CATTLE DOG

DEFENSIVE WITH STRANGERS, THIS GUARD DOG NEEDS AN OUTDOOR WORKING LIFE | FCI

Height range
48–60cm (19–24in)

Weight range
20–35kg (44–77lb)

Life span About 15 years

Origin Portugal

Other colours

Grey brindle

Also known as the Azores Cattle Dog, this robust cattle-herder and guard dog originally came from the Azorean island of São Miguel. The breed is quiet and obedient with a trusted owner but needs careful handling and early socialization where children or strangers are concerned.

Short, smooth, fawn-brindle coat

Thick, slightly curved, high-set tail

Triangular, drop ears

Wide mouth with powerful jaws

White marking on chest

Oval feet

ITALIAN CORSO DOG

THIS POWERFUL BUT GRACEFUL DOG NEEDS AN EXPERIENCED HANDLER | FCI

Height range
60–68cm (24–27in)

Weight range
40–50kg (88–110lb)

Life span 10–11 years

Origin Italy

Other colours

Grey   Stag-red

Brindle
May have white markings.

Descended from Roman fighting dogs, the Italian Corso is now used mainly for guarding and tracking. More graceful in build than many types of mastiff, this is nonetheless an extremely strong and robust breed. It can make a good house dog, but experienced and responsible ownership is essential.

Typical mastiff-shaped head

Short, glossy, black coat

Loose hanging flews

Powerful body

Fawn coat   **Puppy**

Dark muzzle

NEAPOLITAN MASTIFF

THIS CANINE HEAVYWEIGHT MAKES A LOYAL COMPANION FOR A RESPONSIBLE OWNER

KC

Height range
60–75cm (24–30in)

Weight range
50–70kg (110–154lb)

Life span Up to 10 years

Origin Italy

Other colours

Variety of colours

Said to have descended from the Molussus fighting dogs used in the Roman amphitheatre, the Neapolitan Mastiff has an intimidating appearance: huge, heavy-headed, and with a stern expression. The breed has mainly been used as a guard dog and by the police and armed forces. It needs a confident and capable owner.

Large head with loose-fitting skin

Moderate dewlap

Short, grey coat with hard texture

Tail thick at base, tapers to tip

Ears set well apart on broad skull

Deep muzzle with pendulous flews

White patch on tip of toe

DOGUE DE BORDEAUX

THIS NON-AGGRESSIVE GUARD DOG IS MORE AGILE THAN ITS SIZE SUGGESTS

KC

Height range
58–68cm (23–27in)

Weight range
45–50kg (99–110lb)

Life span 10–12 years

Origin France

This old French breed was once used for hunting and fighting. The Dogue de Bordeaux's instincts make it a natural guard dog but, lacking aggression, it is easier to train and socialize than some mastiff types. Experienced handling is still necessary, however, if this powerful and athletic dog is to fit comfortably into a family home.

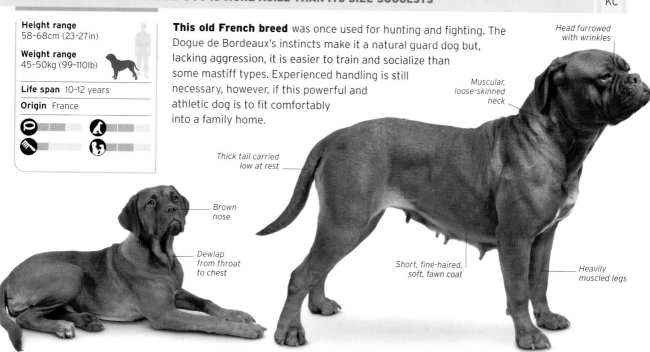

Head furrowed with wrinkles

Muscular, loose-skinned neck

Thick tail carried low at rest

Brown nose

Dewlap from throat to chest

Short, fine-haired, soft, fawn coat

Heavily muscled legs

BROHOLMER

FCI

Height range
70-75cm (28-30in)

Weight range
40-70kg (88-154lb)

Life span 6-11 years

Origin Denmark

Other colours

Black

Historically a hunting dog, and later a farm guard dog, the Broholmer is now almost exclusively kept at home. The breed had all but disappeared by the mid-20th century but was revived and "reconstructed" by enthusiasts, though it is rarely seen outside its native Denmark.

Large, heavy, broad head

Slightly pendulous flews

Short, flat, golden-red coat

White marking on chest

Low-set, broad tail

Darker muzzle

BULLMASTIFF

KC

Height range
61-69cm (24-27in)

Weight range
41-59kg (90-130lb)

Life span Under 10 years

Origin UK

Other colours

Red   Brindle

A cross between the Old English Mastiff and the Bulldog (see p.94), the Bullmastiff was developed to be a gamekeeper's guard dog. With a more reliable temperament than many other mastiff types, this breed makes an intelligent and faithful house dog. The Bullmastiff's square and solid frame houses a lively spirit and boundless energy.

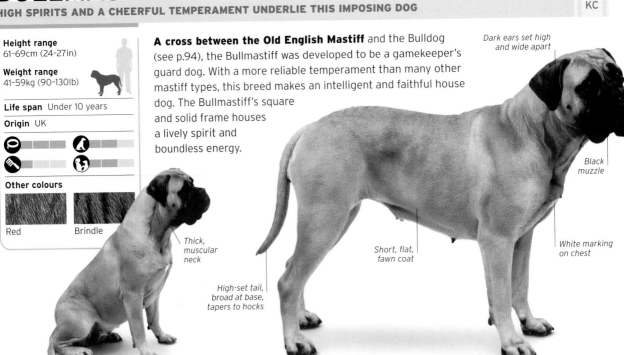

Dark ears set high and wide apart

Black muzzle

White marking on chest

Thick, muscular neck

High-set tail, broad at base, tapers to hocks

Short, flat, fawn coat

MASTIFF

THIS CALM, AFFECTIONATE DOG NEEDS PLENTY OF HUMAN COMPANY

KC

Height range
70–77cm (28–30in)

Weight range
79–86kg (175–190lb)

Life span Under 10 years

Origin UK

Other colours

Apricot   Black brindle

May have areas of white on body, chest, and feet.

With a history of guarding, fighting, and even bear-baiting, the Mastiff is surprisingly even-tempered and easy to get on with. Sheer size is probably the most serious drawback to housing, feeding, and exercising this enormous breed. A Mastiff likes company, preferably human, and is ready to offer loyalty and affection. It is intelligent and trainable but needs an owner with both the experience and physical strength to exert firm control and ensure that its guarding instinct does not get out of hand.

Wide-set, small eyes

Forehead wrinkles when alert

Pendulous flews

Small, flat, black ears, set high on head

Black muzzle

Short, fawn coat, thickest over neck and shoulders

Long, broad body

Straight, big-boned legs

BULLDOG

FULL OF CHARACTER, THIS DOG IS A SYMBOL OF COURAGE, DETERMINATION, AND TENACITY | KC

Height range
38-40cm (15-16in)

Weight range
23-25kg (51-55lb)

Life span Under 10 years

Origin UK

Other colours

Variety of colours

Once used for bull-baiting, and legendary for its refusal to let go of an adversary, the Bulldog has acquired a mellower reputation as a good-natured and lovable companion. The dog does have a stubborn streak as well as a protective instinct, and these traits need handling with tact, though they rarely develop into aggression. With a squat and massively muscled body, wrinkled head, and upturned nose, this breed has character rather than beauty. Despite its waddling gait, the Bulldog needs sufficient exercise to avoid it gaining too much weight.

Smooth, fawn coat

Broad, round, deep chest

Lower jaw longer than upper jaw (overshot)

Thick, short forelegs set wide apart

High-set, rose ears

Distinctive upturned nose

Thick, pendant lips

Sloping, muscular shoulders

Hind legs longer than forelegs

GREAT DANE

GENTLE AND EASY TO MAINTAIN, THIS DOG TAKES UP A LOT OF ROOM

KC

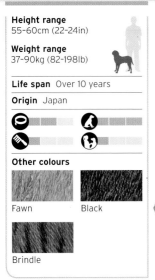

Height range
71–76cm (28–30in)

Weight range
46–54kg (101–119lb)

Life span Under 10 years

Origin Germany

Other colours

Blue

Black

Brindle

Elegance and dignity combined with gigantic size make the Great Dane one of the most impressive of all dogs. Once a hunting dog in Germany, the easy-going Great Dane is content to be a house dog, provided there is enough room for it to flop comfortably. As well as space, the breed needs plenty of exercise.

Long, arched neck
with no loose skin

Dark
shading
on head
and ears

Short,
harlequin coat

Deep, long,
fawn body

TOSA

FORMERLY BRED AS A FIGHTING DOG, THIS BREED NEEDS AN EXPERIENCED HANDLER

FCI

Height range
55–60cm (22–24in)

Weight range
37–90kg (82–198lb)

Life span Over 10 years

Origin Japan

Other colours

Fawn

Black

Brindle

The Tosa was developed from progressive crossbreeding between Japanese fighting dogs and Western breeds such as Mastiff (see p.93), the Bulldog (opposite), and Great Dane (above). Very large, strongly built, and possessing a latent fighting instinct, the Tosa is considered to be a dog that should only be owned by expert handlers.

Short,
red coat

Smallish,
high-set ears

Thick,
tapering tail

Small, white
marking

Dewlap
on neck

PULLING TOGETHER
A team of Siberian Huskies ploughs effortlessly through deep snow. With an experienced handler, these hardy and tireless dogs work superbly together.

SPITZ-TYPE DOGS

A team of huskies pulling a sled over icy wastelands epitomizes the type of dog known as a Spitz. In fact, this group has diverse uses, including herding, hunting, and guarding; many smaller types are kept solely as pets. Descent from wolves is apparent in many spitz dogs: the shape of the head, the typical wolf colouring, and an alert expression.

The smiling-faced Samoyed originated in Siberia

Many of the modern spitz breeds seen today originated in northern Arctic regions, though a number of them, including the Chow Chow and Akita, were developed in East Asia. The history of the spitz group remains unclear, but it is currently thought that they originated in Asia, some migrating alongside tribal movements into Africa and others across the Bering Strait to North America.

Breeds such as the Greenland Dog and Siberian Husky were used most famously for sled-hauling by the polar explorers of the 19th and early 20th centuries. These tough dogs worked in appalling weather conditions, often on a diet of poor food, and frequently ended up being eaten themselves when their owners ran out of rations. Such spitz-type sled dogs were also once widely used by North American hunters and fur-trappers. Today, the sled-hauling spitz breeds are popular for endurance racing and with tourists who want to try their hand at dog-driving. Other spitz dogs have been bred for hunting large game, such as wolf and bear, and for herding reindeer. The Akita, originally from Japan, was developed as a fighter and bear-hunter and now often works as a guard dog. Among the small, non-working spitz dogs are the Pomeranian, selectively bred down in size from a larger type of dog, and the newly created Alaskan Klee Kai, a miniature husky.

Spitz dogs, both large and small, have the characteristics of animals bred specifically for living in extremely cold climates. Typically, they have a very thick double coat, which varies in length and density according to the origin of a breed. Other features for preventing heat loss in low temperatures are pointed, densely-furred ears, and well-furred feet. An attractive addition to many breeds is the distinctive "spitz" tail that curls upwards over the back.

As house dogs, most spitz breeds are happy with family life, but they are not the easiest of dogs to train. Without sufficient exercise and amusement they can resort to disruptive behaviour such as digging holes and barking.

SMALLEST SPITZ
The tiny Pomeranian is the smallest of the spitz-type breeds. Although it was bred as a pet, this dog has a strong character and is full of indomitable spitz spirit.

EX-FIGHTER
The burly Akita was once a fighting dog in its native Japan.

CANADIAN ESKIMO DOG

THIS FRIENDLY DOG NEEDS A FIRM HAND BUT IS HAPPY BELONGING TO A HUMAN "PACK"

KC

Height range
50–70cm (20–28in)

Weight range
18–40kg (40–88lb)

Life span Over 10 years

Origin Canada

Other colours

Any colour

One of the oldest breeds of sled dog in the world, the Canadian Eskimo Dog, or Inuit Dog, is built for survival in the harshest conditions. This breed has a natural instinct for running with a pack and likes company, either canine or human. Training should be firm, ideally with plenty of fun.

Short hair lines ears

Short, straight, muscular neck

Thick, piebald coat has coarse outer hairs

Deep, broad chest

Powerful jaws

Tail carried up or curled over back

Large, round, arched feet

GREENLAND DOG

THIS DOG HAS GREAT STRENGTH AND ENDURANCE AND LOVES OUTDOOR ACTION

KC

Height range
51–68cm (20–27in)

Weight range
27–48kg (60–106lb)

Life span Over 10 years

Origin Greenland

Other colours

Any colour

The classic sled dog of polar expeditions, the Greenland Dog was used by Arctic peoples for hunting and transport long before European and American explorers discovered its worth. Powerful, strong-willed, and stubborn, though generally happy-natured, this dog needs patient training and does best in the hands of an expert.

Small, wide-set ears

Bushy tail curls loosely over back

Hair forms long "breeches" on hind quarters

Thick, weatherproof coat is dark above and light below

Muscular, compact body

Large feet with thick hair between toes

Sturdy, heavily boned legs

SIBERIAN HUSKY

KC

Height range
51–60cm (20–24in)

Weight range
16–27kg (35–60lb)

Life span Over 10 years

Origin Siberia

Other colours

Any colour

Long used as a sled dog by the indigenous peoples of eastern Siberia, the Siberian Husky has great endurance, an appetite for work, and resistance to extreme cold. The breed is still popular in the Arctic, particularly in sports such as dogsled racing. Siberian Huskies make peaceable and lovable companions but need vigorous exercise to burn off some of their energy. They have a strong pack instinct, and are unlikely to be happy living in isolation. A Siberian Husky tends to see small animals as natural prey, so caution is needed if other pets are kept.

Triangular, erect, high-set ears

Long, bushy tail

Fox-like head

Arched neck

Slightly sloping croup

Thick, medium-length, wolf-grey coat

Powerful, muscular thighs

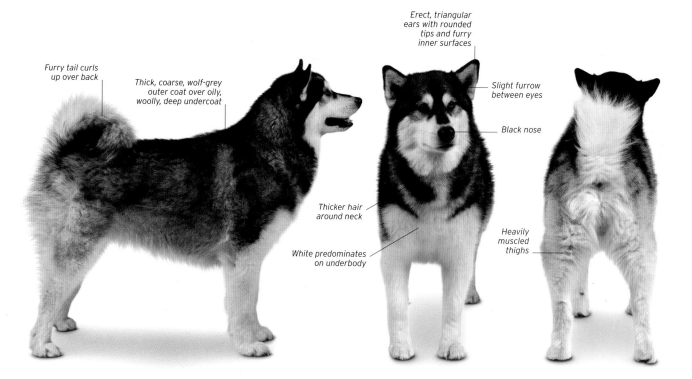

Furry tail curls up over back

Thick, coarse, wolf-grey outer coat over oily, woolly, deep undercoat

Erect, triangular ears with rounded tips and furry inner surfaces

Slight furrow between eyes

Black nose

Thicker hair around neck

White predominates on underbody

Heavily muscled thighs

ALASKAN MALAMUTE

A LARGE, SLED-PULLING DOG THAT CAN ADAPT WELL TO FAMILY LIFE

KC

Height range
58-71cm (23-28in)

Weight range
38-56kg (84-123lb)

Life span 12-15 years

Origin USA

Other colours

Variety of colours

All dogs have white underparts.

The wolf-like Alaskan Malamute is named after the Native American Mahlemut people, who bred these dogs to pull heavy loads and travel great distances across the snow when sleds were the only mode of transport. Today, it is still used to haul freight in remote North American locations, and successfully takes part in sled-racing competitions. Also used on polar expeditions, this breed has staggering amounts of stamina, strength, and tenacity combined with highly tuned senses of direction and smell.

For all its toughness, the Alaskan Malamute is a friendly dog, at least towards people, which means that it cannot be relied on as a guard dog. It likes children but is too big and boisterous to be left alone with a small child. The Alaskan Malamute, especially the male, tends to be intolerant of strange dogs, and without thorough socializing can quickly become aggressive. The breed also has a strong chasing instinct and can disappear far and fast in pursuit of small animals that it sees as prey. Owners should be cautious about where and when to exercise this dog off the lead. A quick learner, the Alaskan Malamute has a strong will, so needs firm handling and training in good habits right from the start.

The Alaskan Malamute settles well into domestic life as long as it has at least two hours of exercise each day and a garden to roam in. A bored dog, with energy to spare, can be destructive if left at home without supervision. Although its thick coat sheds in spring, there is a risk of overheating if the dog is over-exercised in hot weather, so it needs access to shade. The hardy Alaskan Malamute is happy to sleep outdoors, provided it has a companion.

ALASKAN KLEE KAI

THIS ENERGETIC MINI HUSKY IS CONFIDENT WITH OWNERS BUT WARY OF STRANGERS

Height range
Toy:
Up to 33cm (Up to 13in)
Miniature:
33-38cm (13-15in)
Standard:
38-44cm (15-17in)

Weight range
Toy:
Up to 4kg (Up to 9lb)
Miniature:
4-7kg (9-15lb)
Standard:
7-10kg (15-22lb)

Life span Over 10 years

Origin USA

Other colours

Any colour

This miniature version of the Alaskan Malamute (see p.100), was developed to be a house dog and is found in three sizes: toy, miniature, and standard. It fits well in a modestly sized home but, like its larger relative, has a great deal of energy and needs plenty of exercise to stay in good physical and mental health. Typical of husky-type breeds, the Alaskan Klee Kai appreciates company and likes to be treated as a pack member within a family. Reserved with strangers, this dog needs careful training and early socializing.

Eyes are different colours

Triangular, erect ears

Alert expression

Toy

Standard

Distinct stop

Tapering muzzle

Characteristic facial mask

Heavy-coated, brush-like tail

Dense, moderately long, wolf-grey coat

Miniature

CHINOOK

AKC

Height range
55-66cm (22-26in)

Weight range
23-41kg (51-90lb)

Life span 10-15 years

Origin USA

Developed as a sled dog at the beginning of the 20th century in the USA, the Chinook is the result of various crosses between mastiffs, the Greenland Dog (see p.98), and shepherd dogs. Active but gentle-natured, this is a fun-loving breed and makes an excellent all-round family dog.

Wide, slightly arched, head

V-shaped ears, slightly darker than body

Medium-length, sandy coat

Well-defined thigh muscles

Ruff of longer hair around neck

Deep, broad chest

Strong, well-muscled forelegs

Oval feet with webbed toes

KARELIAN BEAR DOG

FCI

Height range
52-57cm (20-22in)

Weight range
20-23kg (44-51lb)

Life span 10-12 years

Origin Finland

Developed in Finland, this fearless hunting dog was bred to challenge big game, particularly bear and elk. The Karelian Bear Dog has a strong fighting instinct, which does not turn into aggression against people but may cause trouble with other dogs. This breed is unlikely to settle well into domestic life.

Straight, harsh-textured, black and white outer coat

Straight nose bridge

High-set tail curled over back

Thicker hair on neck

Well-defined white markings are common

Strong-boned legs

Slightly tucked-up belly

WEST SIBERIAN LAIKA

AN INTELLIGENT AND ALERT DOG WITH A KEEN NOSE AND STRONG HUNTING INSTINCT

FCI

Height range
51-62cm (20-24in)

Weight range
18-22kg (40-49lb)

Life span 10-12 years

Origin Russia

Other colours

Variety of
colours

Bred for hunting in the forests of Siberia, this handsome
dog is very popular in its native country. The breed is strong
and confident, and eager to follow game, either large or small.
Although the West Siberian Laika
has a steady temperament, its
readiness to hunt makes it
unsuitable as a house dog
for most families.

High-set ears held erect

Sable coat on neck and shoulders forms longer collar

Tail carried in tight curl over back

Sandy coat

Oval, slightly deep-set eyes

Long, muscular upper forelegs

Feet with hair between toes

EAST SIBERIAN LAIKA

BORN TO HUNT, THIS DOG IS CALM AND EASY-GOING WITH PEOPLE

FCI

Height range
53-64cm (21-25in)

Weight range
18-23kg (40-51lb)

Life span 10-12 years

Origin Russia

Other colours

White

Karamis

Piebald

The popularity of this Russian hunting dog is widespread
in its own country and also reaches into Scandinavia.
Bred for work, the East Siberian Laika is tough, active,
and confident. Although it has a strong instinct for
following big game, it is controllable, steady-tempered,
and friendly with people.

V-shaped, erect ears, thickly lined with hair

Broad head

Straight, black coat with lighter woolly underlayer

White legs with darker speckles

RUSSIAN-EUROPEAN LAIKA

A STRONG AND WORKMAN-LIKE BREED, NOT SUITED TO FAMILY LIFE

FCI

Height range
48–58cm (19–23in)

Weight range
20–23kg (44–51lb)

Life span 10–12 years

Origin Russia

Other colours

White   Black

This Laika was only acknowledged as a distinct breed in the early 1940s. Strong but lean-limbed, the Russian-European Laika has been used mainly for hunting in Russia's northern forests. A steady worker, this dog is excellent when used for its traditional purpose but does not adapt well to a domestic lifestyle.

Narrow, triangular head

Black nose

Hair on hind legs forms "breeches"

Well-muscled, slender legs

Tail carried over back

Harsh-textured, black coat with white markings

FINNISH SPITZ

BRISK AND JAUNTY, THIS DOG ENJOYS FAMILY FUN AND IS USUALLY PATIENT WITH CHILDREN

KC

Height range
39–50cm (15–20in)

Weight range
14–16kg (31–35lb)

Life span 12–15 years

Origin Finland

Finland's national dog was bred for hunting small game and is still used for sport in Scandinavia. With its pert, fox-like appearance, luxuriant coat, and enthusiasm for play, the Finnish Spitz makes an appealing family pet. The breed has a tendency to bark a great deal; this should be discouraged at an early age.

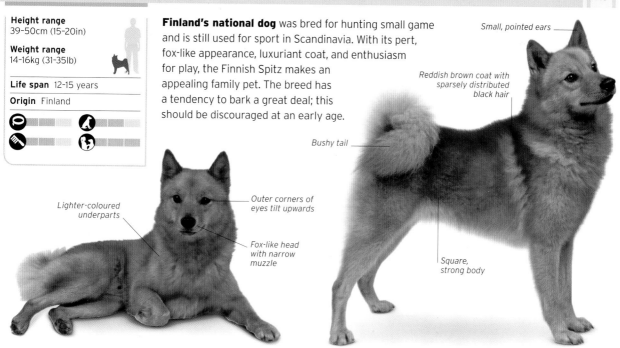

Small, pointed ears

Reddish brown coat with sparsely distributed black hair

Bushy tail

Lighter-coloured underparts

Outer corners of eyes tilt upwards

Fox-like head with narrow muzzle

Square, strong body

Long, bushy tail carried over back, falls to one side

Muscular, broad back

Dark eyes rimmed with black

Broad, wedge-shaped head

Erect, round-tipped ears, thickly lined with hair

Typical "smiling" expression

Ruff of longer, denser hair around neck

Thick, soft, white coat with silver-tipped outer hairs

Feathering on back of front legs

SAMOYED

THIS STRIKINGLY ATTRACTIVE DOG MAKES AN EXCELLENT FAMILY PET

KC

Height range
46–56cm (18–22in)

Weight range
16–30kg (35–66lb)

Life span Over 12 years

Origin Russia

Developed centuries ago by the nomadic Samoyed people of Siberia, this beautiful dog was used for herding and guarding reindeer and for sled-hauling. This tough, outdoor worker was also very much a family dog, taking its place in its owner's tent and enjoying human companionship. These dogs were brought to England in the 1800s and were first seen in the United States around a decade later. Numerous myths and unsubstantiated stories link the Samoyeds to the polar expeditions of the late 19th and early 20th centuries, but it appears likely that this breed was included among sled teams taken to the Antarctic during the heyday of polar exploration.

The modern Samoyed retains the sociable and easy-going temperament that made it so valued as part of a nomadic family. Behind the "smiling" expression characteristic of the breed is an affectionate nature and a desire to be friends with everyone. However, the Samoyed retains the watchdog instincts for which it was bred. Although never aggressive, it will bark at anything that arouses its suspicion. This dog craves company and likes to be kept occupied mentally and physically. Intelligent and spirited, a bored or lonely Samoyed will resort to mischief – whether it is digging holes or finding a way to escape through a fence. The breed responds well to thoughtful handling, but training requires patience and persistence on the part of its owner.

Daily grooming is essential to keep the Samoyed's magnificent, stand-out coat in order and maintain its distinctive silvery sheen. Seasonal shedding of the undercoat can be very heavy but, except in very warm conditions, normally occurs only once a year.

FINNISH LAPPHUND

THIS FRIENDLY AND LOYAL DOG, WITH SOME HERDING INSTINCTS, IS QUICK TO LEARN

KC

Height range
44-49cm (17-19in)

Weight range
15-24kg (33-53lb)

Life span 12-15 years

Origin Finland

Other colours

Any colour

Developed from the dogs used as reindeer-herders and guards by the Sami people of Lapland, the Finnish Lapphund is enjoying growing popularity, both in Finland and elsewhere. Affectionate and faithful, this adaptable breed is willing to work, but is equally happy as a family pet and watchdog.

Dark brown eyes

Long, dense, black coat

Erect ears

Profusely long-haired tail

Thick mane, especially in males

White markings on chest

Feathering on back of front legs

Tan markings on legs

Well-arched, oval feet

LAPPONIAN HERDER

BRED FOR HERDING, THIS DOG HAS A DOCILE TEMPERAMENT AND PLENTY OF ENERGY

FCI

Height range
46-51cm (18-20in)

Weight range
Up to 30kg (up to 66lb)

Life span 11-12 years

Origin Finland

Originally bred from Finnish Lapphunds (above), German Shepherd Dogs (see p.35), and working collies, this dog was recognized as a separate breed in the 1960s. The Lapponian Herder, or Lapinporokoira, is still kept for work by reindeer-hunters, and sometimes as a house dog. This breed has a calm and friendly nature.

Erect ears lined with dense hair

Tail extends below hock length

Dense, black coat

Tan markings on deep chest

Tan markings on face

Fairly wide-set, oval, dark eyes

Oval feet, covered with thick hair

Dark brown coat

SWEDISH LAPPHUND

FRIENDLY BUT NEEDING FIRM CONTROL, THIS DOG CAN BE NOISY AND RESTLESS IF LEFT ALONE

KC

Height range
40-51cm (16-20in)

Weight range
19-21kg (42-46lb)

Life span 9-15 years

Origin Sweden

Other colours

Brown

Black and brown

May have white mark on chest, feet, and tip of tail.

Similar to the Finnish Lapphund (opposite) in all but colour, the Swedish Lapphund was once used as a reindeer-herder by the nomadic Sami people. This breed is popular in Sweden as a house dog but remains uncommon elsewhere. It enjoys company and tends to bark if left alone for long periods of time.

Erect ears, set well apart

Moderate stop

Long-haired, bushy tail, curled over back

Wedge-shaped head

Dark brown eyes

Shorter hair on face

Dense, black coat stands out from body

Compact, oval feet

SWEDISH ELKHOUND

THIS POWERFUL AND AGILE DOG IS NOT SUITABLE FOR AN URBAN LIFESTYLE

FCI

Height range
52-65cm (20-26in)

Weight range
Up to 30kg (up to 66lb)

Life span 12-13 years

Origin Sweden

Developed in Sweden's northern forest regions, this large upstanding dog, also known as the Jämthund, was once kept for hunting elk, bear, and lynx. Popular with Sweden's military forces, this breed is the country's national dog. Although good with families, the Swedish Elkhound needs careful handling when around other dogs or pets.

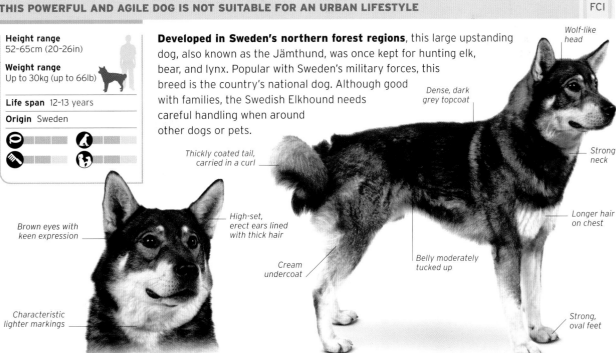

Wolf-like head

Dense, dark grey topcoat

Strong neck

Longer hair on chest

Thickly coated tail, carried in a curl

Brown eyes with keen expression

High-set, erect ears lined with thick hair

Cream undercoat

Belly moderately tucked up

Characteristic lighter markings

Strong, oval feet

NORWEGIAN ELKHOUND

THIS CALM DOG IS GOOD WITH CHILDREN, BUT MAY BARK AT STRANGERS

KC

Height range
49-52cm (19-20in)

Weight range
20-23kg (44-51lb)

Life span 12-15 years

Origin Norway

Believed to have existed in Scandinavia for many hundreds of years, the Norwegian Elkhound was once used for tracking game, and is sturdy enough for sled hauling. Impervious to cold and wet weather, this dog likes to be outdoors. The breed has a strong hunting instinct and needs patient training.

Black muzzle

Tightly curled tail carried high

Clearly defined stop on head

Thick ruff around neck

Short, compact body

Black-tipped hairs on outer, grey coat

BLACK NORWEGIAN ELKHOUND

THIS DOG FORMS STRONG FAMILY BONDS, BUT MAY BE A LITTLE STUBBORN TO TRAIN

FCI

Height range
43-49cm (17-19in)

Weight range
18-27kg (40-60lb)

Life span 12-15 years

Origin Norway

This breed is a smaller, rarer version of the grey-coated Norwegian Elkhound (above). Originally bred for tracking game, it is versatile enough to be a sled dog, herder, watchdog, or family companion. It tends to bark readily but can be taught to stop on command.

Pointed ears with wide base

Short, thick tail curls over back

Broad top of head

Muzzle tapering but not pointed

Solid black, weatherproof coat

Small, white marking on feet

HOKKAIDO DOG

FEARLESS YET GENTLE AT HOME, THIS DOG NEEDS SUPERVISION WITH OTHER ANIMALS | FCI

Height range
46-52cm (18-20in)

Weight range
20-30kg (44-66lb)

Life span 11-13 years

Origin Japan

Other colours

Variety of
colours

Dogs of this type were brought to the Japanese island of Hokkaido by the migrating Ainu people (Ainu Dog is the breed's alternative name). Although medium-sized, the Hokkaido Dog was bold and tough enough to hunt bears. Careful training and socializing can make this dog a good companion and home guardian.

Strong, straight back

Thick tail curled over back

Muscular neck

Smallish, dark, triangular eyes

Harsh, straight, sesame-coloured coat

SHIKOKU

THIS BREED RESPONDS READILY TO AFFECTION, BUT SHOULD NOT BE TRUSTED WITH SMALL PETS | FCI

Height range
46-52cm (18-20in)

Weight range
16-26kg (35-57lb)

Life span 10-12 years

Origin Japan

Other colours

Sesame and
black sesame

Once used as a boar-hunter in remote mountain regions of Japan, the Shikoku remained largely inaccessible for crossbreeding. As a result, this breed is very true to its origins. Resilient, agile, and keen to chase other animals, the Shikoku is challenging to train but forms a close bond with people it loves and trusts.

Firmly erect ears

Typical "spitz" tail

Dark eyes have keen expression

Moderately long, wedge-shaped muzzle

Muscular, thick neck

Deep chest

Red-sesame coat

Powerful hind quarters

AKITA

Height range
61-71cm (24-28in)

Weight range
32-59kg (71-130lb)

Life span 10-12 years

Origin Japan

Other colours

Any colour

Merle not permitted.

This breed was first developed in 19th-century Japan as a fighting dog, before breeders in the USA took an interest. Also known as the American Akita, this handsome dog has a quiet dignity but tends to be domineering with other dogs. Without an experienced owner to set the rules at a young age, it may become wayward or aggressive.

Triangular, erect ears

Black overlay

Black face mask

Thick, bushy tail curls over back

Well-developed, muscular hind quarters

Deep, wide chest

Harsh, fawn outer coat stands away from body

White chest markings extend down to legs

AKITA INU

Height range
58-70cm (23-28in)

Weight range
35-55kg (77-120lb)

Life span 10-12 years

Origin Japan

Other colours

White

Brindle

Sesame

Smaller than the Akita, it is thought that the Japanese Akita Inu originated from northern Japanese hunting dogs. Once considered a type of Akita, it was recognized as a distinct breed in the 1990s. The Japanese Akita Inu can be territorial and protective so needs to be well trained and socialized from puppyhood.

Distinctive red-fawn coat

Relatively small, dark brown eyes

Triangular ears with rounded tips

Thick, muscular neck

White (urajiro) markings

Round feet with thick pads

CHOW CHOW

THIS DOG IS LOYAL TO ITS OWNER BUT STANDOFFISH WITH STRANGERS

KC

Height range
46-56cm (18-22in)

Weight range
21-32kg (46-71lb)

Life span 8-12 years

Origin China

Other colours

Cream

Gold

Black

Blue

Dogs like the Chow Chow have been known in China for around 2,000 years. It was used for guarding and hunting, and may have been a source of meat and fur. No other dog looks quite like it, with its stocky build, scowling face, and unique blue-black tongue. It is very independent and may have a stubborn streak, so needs firm training and early socializing. There are two varieties: rough-coated and smooth-coated.

Small, thick, rounded ears

Distinctive stop

Tail carried over back

Profuse, red coat stands out from body

Lighter hair on back of legs

Small, round feet

Rough-coated

THAI BANGKAEW DOG

A DOG THAT IS EAGER TO PLEASE ITS FAMILY BUT CAN BE ALOOF WITH STRANGERS

Height range
41-55cm (16-22in)

Weight range
16-22kg (35-50lb)

Life span 12-14 years

Origin Thailand

Other colours

Variety of colours

White with well-defined coloured patches.

This breed is named after the village in Thailand where it is said to have originated. However, the pure bred dogs seen today are all descendants of selective breeding that started in 1957. The Thai Bangkaew Dog can be a devoted companion and watchdog but new dog owners may find its stubbornness too challenging.

White coat with red patches

Moderately long, well-feathered tail

High-set ears relatively small compared to size of head

Deep chest extends to the elbows

Strong, straight forearms

KOREAN JINDO

THIS INDEPENDENT DOG HAS A STRONG HUNTING INSTINCT AND NEEDS EARLY SOCIALIZING

Height range
46–53cm (18–21in)

Weight range
9–23kg (20–51lb)

Life span 12–15 years

Origin Korea

Other colours

White

Red

Black and tan

Named after the Korean island of Jindo where it originated, the breed is popular in Korea but something of a rarity elsewhere. Used to hunt game, both large and small, the Korean Jindo's keen instinct for chasing other animals may be difficult to curb.

Stiff, fawn hairs stand away from body

Erect, pointed ears, lined with dense hairs

Longer coat on backs of thighs

Thicker hair on neck

Tucked-up belly

Rounded, cat-like feet

JAPANESE SHIBA INU

THIS KEEN, PERKY, FAST-MOVING DOG HAS A STRONG URGE TO HUNT

Height range
37–40cm (15–16in)

Weight range
7–11kg (15–24lb)

Life span 12–15 years

Origin Japan

Other colours

White

Black and tan

Red dogs may have a black overlay (red sesame).

Japan's smallest hunting dog, the Japanese Shiba Inu is a "national treasure" and has been known in its native country for hundreds of years. Bold and lively, the Japanese Shiba Inu makes a happy family dog. However, it can be unreliable with other pets, if not socialized early on, and needs to have its hunting instinct controlled outdoors.

Small, triangular ears incline slightly forward

Dark brown eyes are keen and alert

Longer-haired tail carried in high curl

Coarse-haired, red coat

Rounded, cat-like feet

Whitish under-markings

KAI

THIS ONE-MAN DOG IS GOOD AT GUARDING BUT IS BEST KEPT ON A LEAD OUTDOORS

FCI

Height range
48–53cm (19–21in)

Weight range
11–25kg (24–55lb)

Life span 12–15 years

Origin Japan

Other colours

Range of red brindles

One of the oldest and purest of Japan's native dog breeds, the Kai was given the status of "national treasure" in 1934. An active and athletic hunter, used to running in packs, this dog may settle reasonably well into being a home companion but is not recommended for a novice owner.

High-set tail carried curved over back

Strong, thick neck

Erect ears incline slightly forward

Head broad with well-defined stop and tapering muzzle

Black coat changes from solid colour to brindle as dog matures

KISHU

THIS NATURAL HUNTER IS GOOD WITH OTHER DOGS BUT CAN BE SELF-WILLED

FCI

Height range
46–52cm (18–20in)

Weight range
13–27kg (29–60lb)

Life span 11–13 years

Origin Japan

Now rare but much prized, the Kishu was possibly bred hundreds of years ago for hunting large game in Japan's mountainous Kyushu region. A "national treasure", this dog is quiet and faithful but can be a handful as a companion because of its strong instinct to chase.

Erect ears incline forward

Some longer, black hairs

Short, straight, well-muscled back

Thick, fringed tail carried in curl over back

Dark brown eyes

Short, straight, coarse, red coat

Dense, white coat

White markings on feet and lower legs

JAPANESE SPITZ

SUITABLE FOR SMALL HOMES, THIS SOCIABLE AND CONFIDENT SPITZ LOVES EXERCISE | KC

Height range
30-37cm (12-15in)

Weight range
5-10kg (11-22lb)

Life span Over 12 years

Origin Japan

Although the Japanese Spitz looks like a miniature version of the Samoyed (see p.106), there is no evidence that the two have a common descent. The breed was developed in Japan, and the popularity of this bright and energetic little dog has spread worldwide. Persistent barking is characteristic but can be controlled with training.

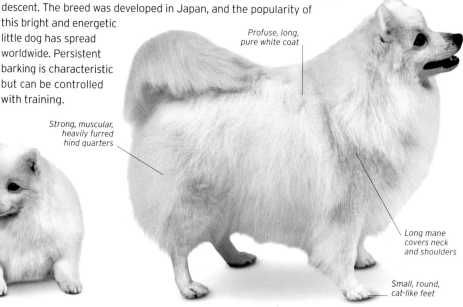

Small ears carried erect

Profuse, long, pure white coat

Strong, muscular, heavily furred hind quarters

Small, round, black nose

Long mane covers neck and shoulders

Small, round, cat-like feet

EURASIER

THIS FAMILY-LOVING DOG IS A LITTLE RESERVED WITH STRANGERS BUT NOT EASILY PROVOKED | KC

Height range
48-60cm (19-24in)

Weight range
18-32kg (40-71lb)

Life span Over 12 years

Origin Germany

Other colours

Any colour

Coat should not be all white, liver, or with white patches.

A modern and still rare breed, the Eurasier was created in Germany in the 1960s from crossing the Russian Samoyed (see p.106), Chow Chow (see p.113), and German Wolfspitz (see p.118). A good companion dog, it is even-tempered and calm but watchful. It readily forms close family bonds.

Harsh-textured, topcoat

Straight, strong back

Triangular, erect ears

Collar of longer hair

Fawn coat with black hairs

Dark face mask

ITALIAN VOLPINO

SMALL BUT INTREPID, THIS ALERT DOG HAS A BRIGHT AND PLAYFUL PERSONALITY

FCI

Height range
25–30cm (10–12in)

Weight range
4–5kg (9–11lb)

Life span Up to 16 years

Origin Italy

Other colours

Red

A favourite in Italy for over a century, this appealing little dog was kept by nobility as a pampered pet, and by farmers as a watchdog. Quick to bark at strangers, the Italian Volpino alerted bigger guard dogs to potential trouble. Lively and fun-loving, the breed is suitable for almost any type of home.

Short muzzle

Long-haired tail carried in curl

Thick collar of hair around neck

Well-feathered hind quarters

Long, dense, white coat

Round eyes

SCHIPPERKE

THIS SHARP, INQUISITIVE DOG IS PROTECTIVE DESPITE ITS SMALL SIZE

KC

Height range
25–33cm (10–13in)

Weight range
6–8kg (13–18lb)

Life span Over 12 years

Origin Belgium

Other Colours

Variety of colours

Sometimes called the Belgian Barge Dog, this breed was once used by Flemish river-boatmen to guard their barges and keep down rat populations. In the house, the Schipperke has lost none of its watchful instincts and is wary of strangers. A dog with a lively and likeable personality, it is an entertaining companion.

Small, triangular ears

Wedge-shaped, fox-like head

Dense, black coat

Tail naturally very short

Long "culottes" on back of thighs

Thickset body

Distinctive mane and cape around neck and shoulders

KEESHOND

THIS NON-AGGRESSIVE WATCHDOG IS EASY TO TRAIN, AFFECTIONATE, AND SOCIABLE

KC

Height range
43–46cm (17–18in)

Weight range
15–20kg (33–44lb)

Life span 12–15 years

Origin The Netherlands

The Keeshond was used in the 18th century by the river-boatmen and farmers of Holland as a watchdog. Not aggressive, this intelligent and outgoing breed has an amiable nature that makes it a much-loved companion dog. The Keeshond is willing to learn, and mixes well with people and other pets.

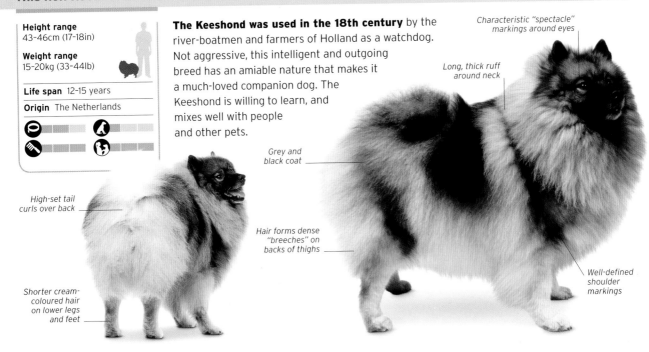

Characteristic "spectacle" markings around eyes

Long, thick ruff around neck

Grey and black coat

High-set tail curls over back

Hair forms dense "breeches" on backs of thighs

Well-defined shoulder markings

Shorter cream-coloured hair on lower legs and feet

GERMAN WOLFSPITZ

INTELLIGENT AND QUICK TO LEARN, THIS GOOD WATCHDOG IS EXCELLENT WITH FAMILIES

Height range
43–55cm (17–22in)

Weight range
27–32kg (60–71lb)

Life span 12–15 years

Origin Germany

The German Wolfspitz is one of the oldest-known European dogs. It has given rise to the Keeshond (above) and in some countries the two are not regarded as separate types. Highly trainable, it is eager to be a part of family life. Suspicious of strangers, this dog barks readily but is not aggressive.

Bushy tail

Short, straight back

Small, triangular, erect ears

Long, grey and black topcoat

Fox-like head with bright expression

Thick mane over neck and shoulders

Small, cat-like feet

GERMAN SPITZ

A BUSTLING AND HAPPY DOG, WITH GOOD WATCH INSTINCTS, AND SUITABLE FOR ANY HOME

KC

Height range
Klein:
23-29cm (9-11in)
Mittel:
30-38cm (12-15in)
Gross:
42-50cm (17-20in)

Weight range
Klein:
8-10kg (18-22lb)
Mittel:
11-12kg (24-26lb)
Gross:
17-18kg (37-40lb)

Life span 14-15 years

Origin Germany

Other colours

Variety of
colours

There are three sizes of the German Spitz - Klein (small) and Mittel (standard) are both recognized by KC, and Gross (giant) is recognized by FCI. They all are descendants of the herding dogs once used by nomadic tribes of the Arctic. German Spitzes need patient training because they have an independent spirit that can turn into wilfulness without firm leadership. Once their place in the family has been established, these cheerful and affectionate dogs are excellent companions for owners of all ages. Thorough and regular grooming sessions are needed to prevent the immensely thick coat from becoming matted.

Black coat

Gross

White coat

Klein

Wolf-sable coat

Short hair on face

Compact, square body

Moderately broad head

Tail curls over back

Thick frill around neck and shoulders

Long feathering on backs of legs

Profuse double coat with long, orange-sable outer hair

Mittel

ICELANDIC SHEEPDOG

A SMART, CHEERFUL, VOCAL, AND COMPANIONABLE DOG

FCI

Height range
42–46cm (17–18in)

Weight range
9–14kg (20–31lb)

Life span 12–15 years

Origin Iceland

Other colours

Grey

Chocolate brown

Black

Tan and grey dogs may have black masks.

Also called the Friaar Dog, this hardy, muscular breed was brought to Iceland by early settlers. Its agility over rugged terrain and shallow water plus its keen barking make it perfect for herding livestock. As a pet, it requires plenty of exercise. There are two coat types: long-haired and short-haired.

Erect ears slightly rounded at tip

Smallish, rectangular, powerful body

Black pigmented lips

Typical spitz tail curls over back

White markings on face

Thick, waterproof tan coat with white markings

Long-haired

NORWEGIAN LUNDEHUND

THIS ACROBATIC, PROTECTIVE HUNTER HAS AN INDEPENDENT STREAK

FCI

Height range
32–38cm (13–15in)

Weight range
6–7kg (13–15lb)

Life span 12 years

Origin Norway

Other colours

White

Grey

Black

Black and grey coats have white markings; white coat has dark markings.

Also called the Norwegian Puffin Dog, this amazingly agile dog can tilt its head back over its shoulder and splay its forelegs out sideways. Once used as a puffin-hunter, these traits, as well as an extra toe on each foot, enabled the dog to reach precarious nests. As a pet, it needs plenty of training and exercise.

Triangular, erect ears

Very pronounced stop

Black tips to some of the hairs

Dense, reddish brown coat sheds quite heavily

Wedge-shaped head

Six toes on each foot

NORDIC SPITZ

THIS LIVELY, LOVING, LONG-LIVED DOG HAS NO DOG ODOUR

FCI

Height range
42–45cm (17–18in)

Weight range
8–15kg (18–33lb)

Life span 15–20 years

Origin Sweden

This small, light spitz is Sweden's national dog, though it is little known outside its native country. Its local name, Norbottenspets, means "spitz from the county of Bothnia". It was once used to hunt squirrels and, more recently, game birds. A bright-eyed, bushy-tailed dog, the Nordic Spitz is not difficult to train as a house pet, but requires regular, energetic exercise.

Fox-like head with typical tan markings

Compact body

Well-defined tan patch on hind quarters

Short, straight, white coat

Erect, black ears

NORWEGIAN BUHUND

THIS WORKING FARM DOG NEEDS AN ENERGETIC, OUTDOOR-LOVING OWNER

KC

Height range
41–46cm (16–18in)

Weight range
12–18kg (26–40lb)

Life span 12–15 years

Origin Norway

Other colours

Red

Coat may be wolf-sable. Red, wheaten, and wolf-sable coats may have a black mask, ears, and tip to tail.

This medium-sized, agile farm dog was once used to guard against bears and wolves. Today, the breed thrives when it has plenty of exercise and constant training. A keen barker that moults heavily twice a year, this may not be the ideal dog for a house-proud owner.

Pronounced stop

Long, thick, harsh, wheaten topcoat with soft, woolly undercoat

Tightly curled tail carried over back

Triangular, erect ears

Longer hair on top of hind leg

Black coat

White hairs on chest

PAPILLON

THIS DAINTY AND DELIGHTFUL DOG IS A LIVELY AND INTELLIGENT COMPANION

KC

Height range
20–28cm (8–11in)

Weight range
2–5kg (5–11lb)

Life span 14 years

Origin France/Belgium

Other colours

Black and white

White

White coats may have any colour patches except liver.

Also known as the Continental Toy Spaniel, this little dog makes a charming companion. Often portrayed in European court paintings (the breed was a particular favourite of Marie Antoinette), the Papillon has eye-catching "butterfly-wing" ears and distinctive facial markings. A drop-eared variety is known as the Phalène (French for "moth"). These dogs love human companionship and enjoy plenty of play and exercise. They require early socializing with other dogs and strangers. The long, fine, silky coat needs daily grooming to prevent mats forming.

Long-fringed, "butterfly-wing" ears

Drop ears

Phalène

Long, plumed tail falls over back

Full, soft, tricolour coat

Fine, pointed muzzle on rounded head

Elongated hare-like feet

POMERANIAN

KC

Height range
22–28cm (9–11in)

Weight range
2–3kg (5–7lb)

Life span 12–15 years

Origin Germany

Other colours

Any solid colour

Should be free from black or white shading.

Smallest of the German spitz-type dogs (see p.119), the Pomeranian was selectively bred down to "toy" size during the 19th century. Intelligent and attention-seeking, the Pomeranian readily returns affection and will become devoted to its owner. Amazingly fast for their size, these dogs should be supervised if running loose. The thick coat is not difficult to groom.

Heavily plumed tail carried over back

Smooth-haired, fox-like face

Longer hair on hind quarters

Soft, fluffy, orange coat

Abundant frill around neck, shoulders, and chest

AMERICAN ESKIMO DOG

AKC

Height range
Toy:
23–30cm (9–12in)
Miniature:
30–38cm (12–15in)
Standard:
Over 38–48cm (Over 15–19in)

Weight range
Toy:
3–5kg (6–10lb)
Miniature:
5–9kg (10–20lb)
Standard:
11–16kg (24–35lb)

Life span 12–13 years

Origin USA

Despite its name, this is not a true Eskimo breed, but was developed in Germany and probably brought to the USA by German settlers in the 19th century. Once seen performing tricks in travelling circuses, the American Eskimo Dog is a fast learner and eager to please. The breed comes in three sizes: toy, miniature, and standard.

Triangular, erect, slightly blunt-tipped ears

Long, white guard hairs form topcoat

Round eyes, set well apart with black rims

Jet-black lips

Profuse ruff at neck and chest

Toy

Toy

HIGH SPEED
On the racetrack, Greyhounds have been recorded as reaching top speeds of around 45 mph (72 kph). They are one of the fastest living animals.

SIGHT HOUNDS

Canine speed merchants, the sight hounds – or gazehounds as they are sometimes called – are hunting dogs that locate and follow their prey primarily by using their keen eyesight. Streamlined, lightly framed, but powerful, a sight hound in pursuit of quarry moves fast and turns with great flexibility. Many dogs in this group were bred to hunt specific prey.

Dogs like these Irish Wolfhounds were used for hunting in Roman times

As shown by archaeological evidence, lean, leggy dogs have been hunting alongside humans for thousands of years, but the early development of modern sight hounds is not entirely clear. It is likely that many crosses involving a diversity of other breeds, including terriers, went into the creation of classic sight hounds such as the Greyhound and the Whippet.

Most sight hounds are easily recognizable as a type. Selective breeding has developed characteristics designed to promote speed: strong, supple backs and an athletic build enable the body to stretch out at full gallop; long-striding, elastic limbs, and powerful hind quarters to provide impulsion. Another characteristic is a long, narrow head that either lacks a pronounced stop or, as in the case of the Borzoi, has no stop at all. Typically in a sight hound bred to hunt and snap up small prey, the head is carried low when the dog runs at full stretch. Another common feature of sight hounds is a deep chest accommodating a larger than usual heart and allowing for good lung capacity. Short or fine silky coats tend to be the norm among this group of dogs; only the Afghan Hound is very long-haired.

Graceful and aristocratic, sight hounds during their history have been the favoured hunting dogs of the wealthy and well born. Greyhounds, or at least coursing dogs very similar to the modern breed, were kept by the pharaohs of ancient Egypt. Salukis were, and occasionally still are, used by sheikhs for hunting gazelle in the desert. In pre-Soviet Russia the spectacular Borzoi was the dog of choice for the nobility and even royalty, specifically bred for running down and killing wolves.

Today, sight hounds are used for racing and coursing and are very often kept as pets. Usually non-aggressive, although sometimes a little aloof, sight hounds make attractive family dogs but need handling with caution when out of doors and may be best exercised on a lead. Their instinct to chase small animals can be strong enough to override all obedience training. A sight hound chasing after what it perceives to be prey is almost impossible to stop.

HOME LIFE
Many former racing Greyhounds settle down well as family companions. Their desire to chase can be channelled into play.

ARISTOCRAT
The long-nosed Borzoi looks purely decorative, but this dog was once used in Russia for hunting and could bring down a fully grown wolf.

GREYHOUND

THE SWIFTEST OF ALL DOGS, BUT DOCILE AND GENTLE AT HOME

KC

Height range
69–76cm (27–30in)

Weight range
27–30kg (60–66lb)

Life span 11–12 years

Origin UK

Other colours

Any colour

Capable of reaching 45mph (72km/h) in short bursts, the sleek and powerful Greyhound is purpose-built for running. Although the modern Greyhound was developed in the UK, the breed's earliest ancestors may have been the similar-looking dogs depicted in Egyptian tombs dating back some 4,000 years BCE. Originally bred to hunt hare, today these dogs are raced for sport. As a pet, the Greyhound needs only moderate daily exercise, and is happy lounging around at home the rest of the time.

Small rose ears, fine in texture

Straight, long forelegs

Muscular, long, slightly arched neck

Long and narrow head

Short, smooth, brindle coat

Deep chest housing powerful lungs and heart

Long, low-set, tapering tail

ITALIAN GREYHOUND

THIS MINIATURE, SATIN-SKINNED GREYHOUND ENJOYS CREATURE COMFORTS

KC

Height range
32–38cm (13–15in)

Weight range
4–5kg (9–11lb)

Life span 14 years

Origin Italy

Other colours

Variety of colours

Black and blue with tan markings, and brindle not permitted.

This mini-greyhound was a much favoured pet in the courts of the Renaissance, and still loves to be pampered. Despite its small size, the Italian Greyhound is fast and can reach 40mph (60km/h) in a sudden chase. The breed's short coat makes it susceptible to the cold but it does need regular outdoor exercise.

Large eyes

Long, flat, narrow head

Very fine muzzle

Long, slender, gracefully arched neck

Short, satin-soft, red-fawn coat

Fine, supple skin

Rose ears placed well back

Very fine-boned legs

Long, fine tail set very low

Adult and Puppies

HUNGARIAN GREYHOUND

THIS VIGILANT HOUSE DOG IS PACKED WITH SPEED AND STAMINA

FCI

Height range
62–70cm (24–28in)

Weight range
25–40kg (55–88lb)

Life span 12–14 years

Origin Hungary

Other colours

Any colour

This dog, once used for hunting hare and fox, may have entered Hungary with the Magyars over 1,000 years ago. Not as fast as a Greyhound (opposite) but tougher and tireless, the Hungarian Greyhound (or Magyar Agár) needs a regular run. It makes a faithful and protective companion.

Large rose ears, raised when alert

Broad, straight, and firm back

Length of body slightly greater than height

Short, dense, smooth, white coat

Powerfully muscled hind quarters

Deep, rounded chest

Elongated muzzle and wedge-shaped head

Long tail reaches hock

Rose ears

Muscular, elegant outline

Fine-haired, short, silver-fawn coat

Darker muzzle

Fawn coat with white markings

Well-muscled hind quarters

Tucked-up belly

Deep chest

Long, tapering tail reaches as far as hock

Neat, oval feet with well-arched toes

WHIPPET

THE ULTIMATE SPRINTER, THIS DOG IS CALM, SWEET-NATURED, AND ADORING AT HOME

KC

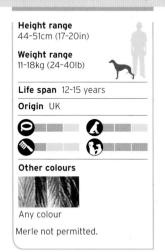

Height range
44–51cm (17–20in)

Weight range
11–18kg (24–40lb)

Life span 12–15 years

Origin UK

Other colours

Any colour

Merle not permitted.

The fastest domesticated animal for its weight, the Whippet is capable of speeds of up to 35mph (56kph). It has impressive powers of acceleration, and can twist and turn at speed with dexterity. This elegant little dog was developed in the north of England in the late 19th century by crossing the Greyhound (see p.126) with various terriers. Originally bred for hunting hare, rabbit, and other small game, the Whippet soon became popular as an affordable sporting dog. Whippet racing, held wherever there was enough space for dogs to sprint a couple of hundred metres, became a regular fixture for working men of mill and mining towns. Today, it is still used for racing, as well as lure coursing and agility trials, but is mostly kept as a pet.

Quiet, docile, and affectionate, the Whippet behaves well in the house and is gentle with children. A sensitive breed, it needs tactful

handling and is easily distressed by rough play or harsh commands. With its delicate skin and short, fine hair, the Whippet needs to wear a coat in cold weather. Its own coat is almost odour-free, without a "doggy" smell even when wet. Puppies with long coats are occasionally born but are not officially recognized.

The Whippet has abundant energy and should be given regular exercise and, in safe areas, plenty of opportunity to run free. It is generally good with other dogs but has a strong hunting instinct and chases cats and small animals if given the chance. A Whippet will tolerate, or at least ignore, a household cat if the two are raised together, but it should not be left unsupervised with other family pets such as rabbits or guinea pigs. This breed is wary with strangers, so it makes a reasonable watchdog. Towards its owners, the Whippet shows unswerving loyalty.

BORZOI

THIS NOBLE RUSSIAN HOUND COMBINES SPEED, ELEGANCE, AND A CERTAIN NONCHALANCE

KC

Height range
68–74cm (27–29in)

Weight range
27–48kg (60–106lb)

Life span 11–13 years

Origin Russia

Other colours

Variety of
colours

This large, frilly-haired, almost feline dog is arguably the most aristocratic of sight hounds. Once known as the Russian Wolfhound, it was bred to hunt wolves for tsars and nobles; often over 100 of these dogs would chase wolves through the snowbound tundra. Outside Russia the Borzoi has been bred for many years for companionship. Today, the dog is happy in a regular home environment but needs plenty of long walks and runs. It also requires a routine of brushing and bathing to keep its long, wavy coat lustrous.

Distinctive
roman nose

Silky, long, white
coat, with red marks

Short, smooth
coat on head

Narrow, refined
head with
imperceptible
stop

Profuse frill
on neck

Slightly arched back

Short hair on
front of legs

Long-haired,
low-set tail

Hare-shaped feet
with well-padded toes

SALUKI

THIS SLIM-FRAMED, SLEEK, GAZELLE-HUNTER IS LOYAL AND COURAGEOUS

KC

Height range
58-71cm (23-28in)

Weight range
16-29kg (35-65lb)

Life span 12 years

Origin Persia

Other colours

Variety of colours

Reputed to be one of the few breeds that were mummified with the pharaohs of the Sumerian Empire, the Saluki (named after an ancient city) is esteemed in the Middle East for its swiftness over sand and is used for hunting with falcons. It is not an especially demonstrative or tactile pet and may seem somewhat aloof. There are two coat types: smooth and feathered.

Long, slender, supple neck

Smooth, soft, silky coat

Long, narrow head

Deep, narrow chest

Slight feathering on back of legs

Black coat with tan markings

Pendant ears with long, silky, golden hair

Feathered coat

Feathered coat

POLISH GREYHOUND

THIS POWERFUL CHASER IS A FAST BUT FAMILY-FRIENDLY HOUND

FCI

Height range
68-80cm (27-31in)

Weight range
65-85kg (143-187lb)

Life span 12-15 years

Origin Poland

Other colours

All colours

Possibly a mix of the Greyhound (see p.126) and the Borzoi (opposite) in origin, the Polish Greyhound is stronger and sturdier than other sight hounds. It is bred to hunt bustard (a large, crane-like bird) and wolves, and is a popular track racer. The Polish Greyhound requires firm training, plenty of exercise, and regular brushing.

Long, powerful, muscular neck

Long tail, strong at base

White mark on chest

Black and tan coat

White blaze on head

Short, sable coat

White tail tip

IRISH WOLFHOUND

A LOYAL, DIGNIFIED, AND DOCILE HOUND, THIS GENTLE GIANT IS THE WORLD'S TALLEST BREED

KC

Height range
71–86cm (28–34in)

Weight range
48–68kg (105–150lb)

Life span 8–10 years

Origin Ireland

Other colours

Variety of colours

This seriously large and heavy dog can reach well over 1.8m (6ft) tall when standing on its hind legs. Once used to hunt wolves by Irish chieftains and kings, it later served as an army dog and is the Regimental Mascot of the Irish Guards. It makes a gentle companion and guard dog.

Dark, oval, full eyes

Small rose ears

Strong, muscular, and well-arched neck

Rough, harsh, steel-grey hair

Long head with tapering muzzle

Hair especially wiry and long over eyes and under jaw

Deep chest

Very strong, curved nails

DEERHOUND

THIS FAST, FEARLESS, FRIENDLY DOG HAS A ROMANTIC SCOTTISH PAST

KC

Height range
71–76cm (28–30in)

Weight range
37–46kg (82–101lb)

Life span 10–11 years

Origin UK

Other colours

Red-fawn or sandy-red

Black brindle

Once the preserve of Scottish stag-hunting nobility, this shaggier version of the Irish Wolfhound (above) is now as much at home in a cosy sitting room as by a baronial log fire. It is lazy and companionable indoors so long as it has a strenuous walk every day and garden space to roam in.

Small, rose ears

Pointed muzzle

Long, strong neck

Coat softer on head and chest

Silky haired, lighter-coloured moustache and beard

Harsh, thick, wiry, dark blue-grey coat

Long tail, thick at base, carried low

White toes

AFGHAN HOUND

GLAMOROUS, ALOOF, AND HIGH-MAINTENANCE, THIS BREED IS THE SUPERMODEL OF DOGS KC

Height range
63–74cm (25–29in)

Weight range
23–29kg (51–64lb)

Life span 12–14 years

Origin Afghanistan

Other colours

Any colour

The glossiest and most elegant of dogs, the exact origin of the breed is unknown but it is thought to have been brought along trade routes to Afghanistan, where tribal chieftains used it to track deer, wild goats, and snow leopards. The Afghan Hound's long, luxurious coat protected it from the extreme climate of its original mountain home. In the 1930s Marx Brother "Zeppo" brought the breed to the USA; and it has since been popular with celebrities. However, this independent and lively companion is also at home in sports and obedience events.

Dark eyes, almost triangular-looking, slanting slightly upwards

Abundant top knot

Pendant ears covered with long, silky hair

Long muzzle and skull

Tail is relatively bare, carried in a ring and raised when moving

Long, silky, gold coat has fine texture except along short, close saddle

Feet strong and covered with thick, long hair

RAMPUR GREYHOUND

A SPEEDY, POWERFUL HUNTING DOG THAT IS NOT SUITABLE FOR URBAN LIFE

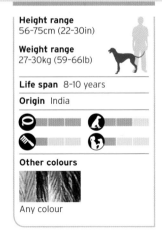

Height range
56–75cm (22–30in)

Weight range
27–30kg (59–66lb)

Life span 8–10 years

Origin India

Other colours

Any colour

Now rare, the Rampur Greyhound was once the favourite sporting companion of Indian princes. Used mainly to hunt jackal and deer, this powerful dog was also capable of bringing down wild boar. The breed's origins are uncertain, but may include crosses between the English Greyhound and native Indian breeds chosen for their strength and tenacity.

Long, narrow, pointed nose on flat skull

Short, black coat

Deep, narrow chest

Arched feet and strong claws for good grip at speed

Tucked-up belly

Tan markings on lower leg

Powerful hind quarters and long legs

Long, thin, tapering tail

SLOUGHI

THIS ELEGANT AND RACY DOG BONDS WITH FAMILY MEMBERS BUT IS ALOOF WITH STRANGERS   KC

Height range
61–72cm (24–28in)

Weight range
20–27kg (44–60lb)

Life span 12 years

Origin North Africa

Long established in North Africa, where it is much prized as a hunting dog, the Sloughi has only recently become known in Europe and the USA. This quiet-natured breed is a pleasant companion and likes home life. A Sloughi needs early socializing with other household pets as its urge to chase small animals is strong.

Lean, muscular body with curved topline

Elongated, wedge-shaped muzzle

Prominent breastbone

Darker face and ears

Tough, fine, close-fitting, sandy coat

Neck arched and elegant

Long, thin, oval feet

SPANISH GREYHOUND

BRED TO HUNT, THIS GENTLE BUT UNDEMONSTRATIVE DOG CAN ADAPT TO HOME LIFE

FCI

Height range
58-72cm (23-28in)

Weight range
20-30kg (44-66lb)

Life span 12 years

Origin Spain

Other colours

Any colour

Thought to be a descendant of dogs that came into the Iberian Peninsula with the Celts, around 500BCE, the Spanish Greyhound is a fast-footed hunter. Once kept only by royalty, the breed became widely popular for coursing and racing. Spanish Greyhounds are not hard to train as house dogs but have high exercise requirements. There are two coat varieties: smooth-haired and wire-haired.

Very shallow stop

Long, straight back

Sandy coloured coat

Lean, long head

Almond-shaped eyes

Compact, well-muscled body

Long tail ending in a fine point

Wire-coated variety may have moustache and beard

Wire-haired

AZAWAKH

CAPABLE OF ASTONISHING SPEED, THIS SMALL-GAME HUNTER CAN BE KEPT AS A PET

KC

Height range
60-74cm (24-29in)

Weight range
15-25kg (33-55lb)

Life span 12-13 years

Origin Mali

This long-legged hound comes from the desert areas of the southern Sahara. The Azawakh is used by nomadic tribes for hunting, guarding, and as a companion dog. It has an exceptionally fine skin, beneath which the muscular, rangy frame is clearly apparent. With kind, firm handling and a daily run, the Azawakh settles well as a house pet.

Head is narrow and chiselled

Neck long, fine, muscular, and slightly arched

Short, fawn coat

Wide-set, pendant ears

Muscles and bones visible beneath fine skin

Long, tapering tail has a white brush tip

Characteristic white stockings

Typical white bib

PACK HUNTING
Fox-hunting with pack hounds was once a familiar rural sight. The modern alternative is drag-hunting – where hounds follow an artificial scent.

SCENT HOUNDS

A keen sense of smell is an essential part of being a dog. The sharpest noses belong to the scent hounds, which track prey more by following scent than by using their eyes as the sight hounds do (see pp.124–25). These dogs, some of which hunt in packs, have a natural ability to pick up a trail, even if it is days old, and will follow it single-mindedly.

The Otterhound is one of the rarest scent hound breeds

It is not known exactly when certain dogs were first recognized for their exceptional ability to hunt by scent. The origins of the modern scent hound possibly date back to the mastiff-type dogs of the ancient world, brought into Europe by traders from the region that is now Syria. By the Middle Ages hunting with packs of scent hounds was a widespread and popular sport, the quarry including fox, hare, deer, and wild boar. Pack-hunting arrived in North America in the 17th century with English settlers who brought their own foxhounds with them.

Scent hounds come in all sizes, but typically have substantial muzzles packed with odour-detecting sensors, loose, moist lips that also aid scent detection, and long, pendant ears. Bred for staying power rather than speed, they are strong-bodied, especially in the forequarters. The breeds of scent hound known today were selectively developed not only according to the size of prey that they followed but to the countryside that the hunts covered. The English Foxhound, for example, is comparatively fleet and lightly built for leading a mounted hunt over mostly open terrain. Similar in general appearance but much smaller, the Beagle hunted hare, sometimes in thick undergrowth, with followers on foot. Some short-legged dogs were bred to follow or dig out quarry below ground. The best known of these small scent hounds is the Dachshund, an agile little dog, adept at getting in and out of tight spots. The Otterhound, which hunted its quarry in rivers and streams, sometimes swimming for much of the time, has a water-repellent coat and more extensive webbing between its toes than most dogs.

Hunting with a pack of hounds is currently banned in England, Wales, and Scotland, and so the future of some pack hounds, such as the

EVER POPULAR
Long-eared and low-slung, the Basset Hound was once much admired for its hunting ability and is now loved for its appearance alone.

English Foxhound or Harrier is uncertain. Although usually gregarious and good with other dogs, pack hounds rarely make satisfactory house pets. They need space, are often vocal, and their eagerness to follow any scent trail can make them difficult to train.

AMERICAN COONHOUND
This Bluetick Coonhound is a typical example of the large, handsome coonhounds popular in the United States for hunting and trials.

BRUNO JURA HOUND

THIS MOUNTAIN HUNTING DOG IS SWEET-TEMPERED BUT NOT OFTEN SEEN AS A COMPANION

Height range
45–57cm (18–22in)

Weight range
16–20kg (35–44lb)

Life span 10–11 years

Origin Switzerland

One of two similar breeds of hound developed in the Swiss Jura mountain region, this is one of four laufhunds (see p.176) that probably descended from older, heavier French breeds. Used mainly for hare-hunting, it has a powerful nose and great strength and agility when working on steep terrain. Restless and ever on the go, this breed does not enjoy indoor confinement.

Eyes dark in colour

Strong muzzle

Domed head smaller than in St. Hubert Jura Hound (below)

Long, large ears set well back and low

Thick, short coat

Tapering tail, curves slightly upwards

Black blanket on tan coat

Rounded feet with strong nails and tough pads

ST. HUBERT JURA HOUND

ROBUST, AGILE, AND SKILLED AT TRACKING, THIS DOG IS BEST KEPT FOR OUTDOOR WORK

Height range
45–58cm (18–23in)

Weight range
15–20kg (33–44lb)

Life span 10–11 years

Origin Switzerland

Sharing a common history with the Bruno Jura Hound (above) and closely resembling it, the St. Hubert Jura Hound is distinguished by its larger size and smoother coat. A keen tracker, the St. Hubert Jura Hound bays loudly when following a scent. It has great stamina for hunting hare, foxes, or deer.

Massive, domed head

Loose upper lip covers lower lip

Back straight, broad, and muscular

Dark hazel to brown eyes

Large, pendant ears

Smooth, short, tan coat with black blanket

Forelegs straight and strong

BLOODHOUND

KC

Height range
58–69cm (23–27in)

Weight range
36–50kg (79–110lb)

Life span 10–12 years

Origin Belgium

Other colours

Black and tan | Liver and tan

Originally developed in Belgium by the monks of the Abbaye de Saint-Hubert, the Bloodhound (known in Belgium as the St. Hubert Hound) may have been among the dogs brought to England with William the Conqueror in 1066. Massive, wrinkly, and droopy-eared, this is the classic sleuthhound of detective stories. The Bloodhound is renowned for its superlative tracking abilities over varied terrain and can pick up a scent that is several days old. Good-natured and mild-mannered, this dog is also an excellent family companion for those with room to spare.

Very long, pendant ears

Long, thick, tapering tail

Deep-set eyes give solemn expression

Smooth, short, weatherproof, shaded red coat

Heavy, loose upper lip

Pronounced dewlap

Lower ears curl inwards

Long, pendant ears fold in on leading edge

Head well-covered with hair

Rough, waterproof, black and tan coat

Hair slightly longer on underside of tail

Deep chest

Large, round feet with well-developed webbing between toes

High-set tail reaches hock

OTTERHOUND

EASY-GOING AND AFFECTIONATE, THIS DOG HAS RETAINED A STRONG HUNTING INSTINCT

KC

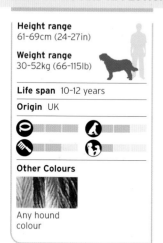

Height range
61–69cm (24–27in)

Weight range
30–52kg (66–115lb)

Life span 10–12 years

Origin UK

Other Colours

Any hound colour

As its name suggests, this shaggy-coated hound was once used for hunting otters. Though its exact origins are uncertain, dogs of a similar type, working in packs, were known in England from about the 18th century, and there are records of otter-hunting with pack hounds as far back as the 12th century. When otters became a protected species, and otter-hunting was banned in the UK in 1978, the number of Otterhounds declined sharply. The breed is now considered rare, with fewer than 60 puppies being registered by the Kennel Club each year. Small numbers of Otterhounds are found in other countries, including the USA, Canada, and New Zealand.

The Otterhound is a strong, energetic dog that, given sufficient exercise, readily adapts to life in the home. It is intelligent and good-natured but, as is the case with many former pack hounds, can be difficult to train. Being large and boisterous, the breed is not recommended for small homes or families with elderly members or young children, as there is a risk of them being knocked over. The Otterhound is best suited to owners who enjoy outdoor activities and have a large garden or access to open spaces where the dog can run safely. Bred for hunting in water, this hound loves swimming and will splash around happily in streams for hours, if given the opportunity.

The Otterhound's dense, coarse coat is slightly oily, and therefore water-repellent. Regular grooming is usually enough to keep the long topcoat free from tangles; in wet weather mud tends to collect but can be brushed out easily when dry. The dog's longer facial hair may need washing occasionally.

GRIFFON NIVERNAIS

TOUGH AND INDEPENDENT, THIS DOG CAN BE NOISY AND NEEDS A FIRM OWNER

FCI

Height range
53-62cm (21-24in)

Weight range
23-25kg (51-55lb)

Life span 12-15 years

Origin France

One of the oldest French sporting dogs, this breed has bloodlines that include the Otterhound (see p.140) and the English Foxhound (see p.158). Used for tracking wild boar, the Griffon Nivernais has great endurance. It may work individually but usually hunts in a pack. The rough, tousled coat provides protection against thick vegetation.

High-set tail

Eyes dark with lively, penetrating gaze

Large, black nose

Dense, rough, shaggy, sandy coat overlaid with black

GRAND GRIFFON VENDEEN

THIS WELL-PROPORTIONED, PASSIONATE HUNTER IS INTELLIGENT AND FAMILY-FRIENDLY

FCI

Height range
60-68cm (24-27in)

Weight range
30-35kg (66-77lb)

Life span 12-13 years

Origin France

Other colours

Fawn

Black and tan

Black and white

Tricolour

Fawn dogs can have black overlay.

There are four varieties of Griffon Vendéen and this one, as its name implies, is the largest; it is also the longest established. The Grand Griffon Vendéen is used for hunting deer and wild boar, and usually works as a pack hound. This attractive dog has a beautiful musical voice and an appealing personality.

Narrow ears, covered in fine hair, and inward turning

Eyebrows pronounced, but not covering eyes

Long, feathered tail

Front of muzzle has square appearance

Coarse, bushy, white and orange coat

GRAND BASSET GRIFFON VENDEEN
THIS SHORT-LEGGED BREED IS A DEDICATED WORKING HUNTER

KC

Height range
39–44cm (15–17in)

Weight range
18–20kg (40–44lb)

Life span 12 years

Origin France

This basset-type Griffon Vendéen hound was originally developed for hunting hare. Today, it is used for tracking all types of game from rabbits to wild boar. Brave and tenacious when on the trail, the short-legged Grand Basset Griffon Vendéen is adept at working in difficult countryside such as dense scrub.

Long, pendant ears

White coat with orange markings

Long, broad, drop ears

Flat, hard hair with thick undercoat

White coat with black and orange markings

PETIT BASSET GRIFFON VENDEEN
ENERGETIC AND OUTGOING, THIS FAMILY DOG IS CHEERFUL, CONFIDENT, AND CURIOUS

KC

Height range
33–38cm (13–15in)

Weight range
11–19kg (24–42lb)

Life span 12–14 years

Origin France

Smallest of the Griffon Vendéen breeds, the Petit Basset Griffon Vendéen is an alert, active, and vigorous hound, capable of a long day's hunting. Short legs, a body twice the dog's height, and a thick, rough coat make this breed ideal for work in dense, brambly undergrowth. Full of restless energy, like all hounds, the Petit Basset Griffon Vendéen is a family dog for people who enjoy spending time outdoors.

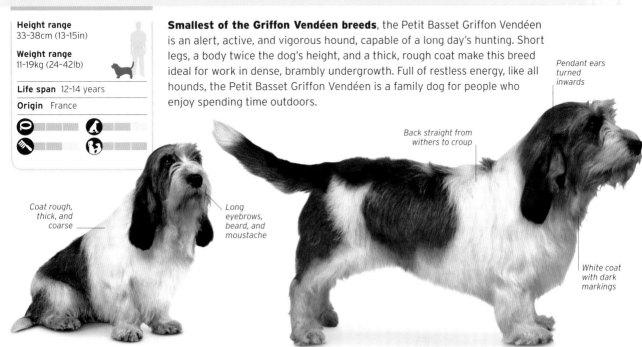

Pendant ears turned inwards

Back straight from withers to croup

Coat rough, thick, and coarse

Long eyebrows, beard, and moustache

White coat with dark markings

BRIQUET GRIFFON VENDEEN
SHAGGY AND COARSE-HAIRED, THIS IS A HAPPY-GO-LUCKY SCENT HOUND

FCI

Height range
48-55cm (19-22in)

Weight range
16-24kg (35-53lb)

Life span 12 years

Origin France

Other colours

Fawn with black overlay

Black and tan

White and black

Black, tan, and white

Briquet means "medium sized" – an apt description for this well-proportioned hound. A handsome and determined chaser of wild boar and roe deer, it is a scaled-down version of the Grand Griffon Vendéen (see p.142), from which it was bred. This hound hunts in a pack but can adapt to urban life if introduced to it early on.

Long, pendant ears set below eye level

Bushy eyebrows noticeable but not covering the eye

Brown nose

Long, white and orange hair

BASSET HOUND
THIS LOW-SLUNG, FLOPPY-EARED DOG IS GENTLE-NATURED AND A SUPERB TRACKER

KC

Height range
33-38cm (13-15in)

Weight range
18-27kg (40-60lb)

Life span 10-13 years

Origin France

Other colours

Variety of colours

Any recognized hound colour.

Equally happy by the fireside or on the moors, the Basset Hound was bred by French monks to hunt in heavy cover. Unlike its depiction as a buffoon in some cartoons, this consummate sniffer dog is very intelligent and extremely tenacious. As a family pet, the Basset Hound is placid and affectionate.

Eyes soft, sad-looking, and slightly sunken

Broad and level back

Long, deep body – heaviest-boned of all dogs for its height

Dark nose with large, wide-open nostrils

Short, tricolour coat

Body low but allows free movement over all types of terrain

BASSET ARTESIEN NORMAND

THIS SHORT-LEGGED, DETERMINED HUNTING DOG IS A LIVELY, DEVOTED FAMILY PET

FCI

Height range
30-36cm (12-14in)

Weight range
15-20kg (33-44lb)

Life span 13-15 years

Origin France

Other colours

Tan and white

This low-slung, long-bodied dog from the Artois and Normandy regions of France, is renowned for searching, tracking, flushing out, and pursuing hare, rabbit, and deer - either individually or in small packs. This elegant hound has a very deep bark, perhaps surprising for its size. Like many hounds, it requires experienced training.

Muzzle same length as skull

Long, low-set ears

Close, short, smooth, tricolour coat

High-set, tapering tail

Large, black nose

BASSET FAUVE DE BRETAGNE

AN AGILE, COMPACT FAMILY DOG WITH AN EASY-GOING, CHEERFUL DISPOSITION

KC

Height range
32-38cm (13-15in)

Weight range
16-18kg (35-40lb)

Life span 12-14 years

Origin France

This versatile and nimble hound has the same qualities as the breed from which it is derived: the Griffon Fauve de Bretagne (see p.146). It is courageous and has a well-developed sense of smell, which makes it ideal for tracking, and search and rescue. Although wiry, a weekly brush and comb is all that its coat requires.

Slightly tapering muzzle with brown nose

Tail medium length and set high

Ears covered in shorter, darker hair than on body

White spot on broad chest

Gold-wheaten coat

GRIFFON FAUVE DE BRETAGNE

THIS HARDY, WIRY RABBIT-CHASER IS AN EASY-GOING FAMILY DOG WHEN OFF DUTY

KC

Height range
48-56cm (19-22in)

Weight range
18-22kg (40-49lb)

Life span 12-13 years

Origin France

One of the oldest French hounds, with ancestors dating back to the 1500s, the Griffon Fauve de Bretagne was bred in Brittany to guard against wolves. Today, it is a versatile hunter and lively housedog. Its short-legged cousin is the Basset Fauve de Bretagne (see p.145).

Dark brown eyes

Low-set ears curl in on front edge

Wiry, very rough, red-wheaten coat

Compact feet

Tail carried in a sickle shape

Black nose

Broad chest

ISTRIAN WIRE-HAIRED HOUND

THIS TOUGH BUT GENTLE HOUND IS SUITED TO HUNTING FOX AND HARE IN MOUNTAINOUS TERRAIN

FCI

Height range
46-58cm (18-23in)

Weight range
16-24kg (35-53lb)

Life span 12 years

Origin Croatia

With its boundless tenacity and passion for hunting, the Istrian Wire-haired Hound is similar to the smooth-coated variety (opposite). Due to its stubborn nature it can be difficult to train, so is not an ideal pet. It is known as the Istarski Oštrodlaki Gonic in its homeland on the Istrian peninsula of Croatia.

Oval-shaped, dark eyes

Orange speckling on ears

Black nose

Tail has orange hairs at base

Broad, deep chest extends to elbows

Harsh, snow-white topcoat is dull and bristly

Cat-like, narrow feet

ISTRIAN SMOOTH-COATED HOUND

RESEMBLING A LONG-LEGGED FOXHOUND, THIS IS THE OLDEST OF THE BALKAN HOUNDS

FCI

Height range
44-56cm (17-22in)

Weight range
14-20kg (31-44lb)

Life span 12 years

Origin Croatia

Originally bred for hunting hare and fox in the vast open terrain of Istria, the handsome and well-built Istarski Kratkodlaki Gonic, as it is known in its native land, displays a stunning snow-white coat. It is kept across the Istrian peninsula as a working dog but also makes a contented housedog in a rural household.

Long, narrow, pear-shaped head

Orange markings on broad, level back

Large, dark eyes

Broad, thin, drop ears

Orange markings on face extend to include ear

Short, smooth, snow-white coat

Black nose

STYRIAN COARSE-HAIRED MOUNTAIN HOUND

THIS RARE WORKING DOG IS IDEAL FOR HIGH ALTITUDE AND HUNTING ON ROUGH TERRAIN

FCI

Height range
45-53cm (18-21in)

Weight range
15-18kg (33-40lb)

Life span 12 years

Origin Austria

Other colours

Red

May have white marking on chest.

This medium-sized dog has the agility to twist and turn on difficult, steep terrain, having developed its hunting skills in the mountains of Austria and Slovenia. It can make a calm and good-natured pet. It is also known as the Peintingen Hound after its 18th-century developer, who crossed a Hanoverian Scent Hound (see p.178) with an Istrian Wire-haired Hound (opposite).

Moderate stop

Broad back

Darker-coloured drop ears covered with fine hair

Expressive, brown eyes

Black nose

Rough, coarse, fawn coat

AUSTRIAN BLACK AND TAN HOUND

SUPPLE AND TIRELESS, THIS DOG IS SUITED TO TRACKING PREY ACROSS MOUNTAINOUS TERRAIN

FCI

Height range
48–56cm (19–22in)

Weight range
15–23kg (33–51lb)

Life span 12–14 years

Origin Austria

Sometimes known as the Brandlbracke, the Austrian Black and Tan Hound has descended from the Celtic Hound. Popular locally, it was bred to seek out hare and track down wounded animals with its highly tuned senses of smell and direction. It works eagerly and has a calm temperament.

Tan markings above eyes

Body length longer than leg length

Drop ears

Smooth, short, thick, black and tan, close-fitting coat with silky sheen

Tucked-up belly

Long, tapering tail hangs down at rest

Tan markings on lower legs

SPANISH HOUND

A STRONG-WILLED HUNTING DOG OF NOBLE ANCESTRY

FCI

Height range
48–57cm (19–22in)

Weight range
20–25kg (44–55lb)

Life span 11–13 years

Origin Spain

The ancestors of the Spanish Hound date back to the Middle Ages. Also known as Sabueso Español, this dog is a specialized, lone hare-hunter that will track its prey all day, following the commands of an experienced owner. There is considerable variation in the height of this breed: males being much larger than females.

Long, straight muzzle

Compact, sturdy, rectangular body, longer than leg length

Long, pendant ears

Fine, smooth hair over loose skin

Curved tail, held sabre-like

Broad chest

Short, white and orange coat

SEGUGIO ITALIANO

THIS INTELLIGENT AND SWEET-NATURED HOUND MAKES A GOOD ACTIVE COMPANION

KC

Height range
48–59cm (19–23in)

Weight range
18–28kg (40–62lb)

Life span 10–14 years

Origin Italy

Other colours

Wheaten

Black and tan

Originally bred as a boar-hunter, this Italian hound is today more often used to track hare and rabbits. It is a fast sprinter and has the stamina for running long distances. Usually calm and quiet, when at work the Segugio Italiano emits an excited and distinctive, high-pitched bark. It is good with children and other dogs provided it is well trained, has access to open spaces, and is exercised regularly. Generally cautious, even a well-trained dog is likely to take off if it spots a rabbit. There are two coat varieties: wire-haired and short-haired.

Large, dark, oval eyes

Black nose

Back arches towards croup

Elongated head with small stop

Smooth, red coat

White tip to tail

Low-set, pendant ears

Oval feet

Short-haired

SEGUGIO MAREMMANO

A WORKING DOG MORE SUITED TO HUNTING THAN BEING A PET

Height range
46–53cm (18–21in)

Weight range
13–23kg (29–51lb)

Life span Over 10 years

Origin Italy

Other colours

Brindle

White markings permitted.

A scent hound specialized for hunting wild boar either alone or in packs, the Segugio Maremmano is not well known outside Italy. Primarily a working dog, it can be either smooth- or rough-haired and where permitted the tail is docked to just under one half of its length.

Dark, slightly oval eyes

Tail with sabre-shaped carriage

Muzzle slightly shorter than skull

Body line rises gently from chest to abdomen

Black and tan coat

Triangular ears lie flat against head

Dark tan coat with white markings

HARRIER

THIS SUPREMELY ACTIVE AND EAGER HOUND IS AN ENTHUSIASTIC EXPLORER AND TRACKER

FCI

Height range
48–55cm (19–22in)

Weight range
19–27kg (42–60lb)

Life span 10–12 years

Origin UK

Once popular for pack hunting, this handsome, classically proportioned hound was probably developed as a smaller version of the English Foxhound (see p.158). Originally used to hunt hare with foot followers, Harriers later hunted foxes with mounted followers. Today, the dog makes a great outdoor companion and agility competitor.

Long muzzle more pointed than square

Short, dense, hard, white coat with black and tan markings

Long tail set high, carried upright, and slightly curved

V-shaped, pendant ears

Prominent black nose

Feet have thick pads for working on rough terrain

BEAGLE HARRIER

A GOOD COMPANION DOG WITH A VERY CALM TEMPERAMENT, BUT KEEN TO FOLLOW SCENT

FCI

Height range
46–50cm (18–20in)

Weight range
19–21kg (42–46lb)

Life span 12–13 years

Origin France

Larger than a Beagle (see p.152) but smaller than a Harrier (above), this attractive little hound is thought to have both these breeds in its ancestry, although it may not be the result of a direct cross. Beagle Harriers are not often seen outside France, where they have been used for hunting small game since the late 1800s. This dog has a pleasant temperament and makes a good family pet.

Square, compact body

Eyes have eager and intelligent expression

Narrow muzzle on broad head

Tricolour coat

Deep, broad chest

Rounded, cat-like feet

ANGLO-FRANCAIS DE PETITE VENERIE
THIS WORKING PACKHOUND IS NOT SUITED TO AN URBAN LIFESTYLE

FCI

Height range
48–56cm (19–22in)

Weight range
16–20kg (35–44lb)

Life span 12–13 years

Origin France

Other colours

Tan and white

Also known as the Petit Anglo-Français, this hound was developed in France and is the result of cross-breeding between English and French scent hounds, a few hundred years ago. The breed is now rare and mostly seen in Continental Europe, where it is still used for small game hunting (to which its name, Petite Vénerie, alludes).

Large, brown eyes

High-set, thin tail

Low-set, pendant ears

Short, dense, glossy, tricolour coat

PORCELAINE
THIS INSTINCTIVE HUNTER IS TRAINABLE AS A HOUSE DOG BUT NEEDS AN ACTIVE LIFE

FCI

Height range
53–58cm (21–23in)

Weight range
25–28kg (55–62lb)

Life span 12–13 years

Origin France

Possibly the oldest of the French pack hounds, with origins in the Franche-Comté on the French–Swiss border, this breed is named for the distinctive glaze-like sheen of its beautiful white coat. It is used primarily for hunting deer and wild boar. If kept as a pet, this hound needs plenty of exercise and tactful training.

Long, lean, finely chiselled head

Well-developed black nose

Highly characteristic orange ticking on ears

Black, pigmented spots on skin

Low-set, thin, pendant ears

Very short, fine, white coat

Long, sloping, muscular shoulders

White tip to
tail (stern)

Typical tan
markings on face

Well-defined
stop

White blaze
on head

Black nose

Pendant
ears with
rounded tips

Straight,
level topline

Short, dense,
tricolour coat

BEAGLE

ONE OF THE MOST POPULAR SCENT HOUNDS, THIS DOG IS ACTIVE, HAPPY-GO-LUCKY, AND AMIABLE   KC

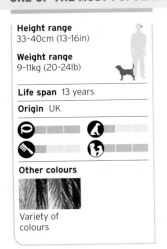

Height range
33-40cm (13-16in)

Weight range
9-11kg (20-24lb)

Life span 13 years

Origin UK

Other colours

Variety of
colours

A sturdy, compact dog with a merry disposition, the Beagle looks rather like an English Foxhound (see p.158) in miniature. The Beagle's origins are unclear, but it appears to have a long history, possibly being developed from other English scent hounds such as the Harrier (see p.150). In England, from the 16th century onwards, packs of small beagle-type hounds were kept to hunt hare and rabbit, but it was not until the 1870s that a standard for the modern Beagle was recognized. Since then the breed has remained remarkably popular, at first for hunting and now as a companion dog. This versatile hound has also been used by law enforcement agencies to sniff out drugs, explosives, and other illegal items.

The Beagle's friendly and tolerant nature makes it an excellent pet, provided it has plenty of company and exercise – it does not easily tolerate long periods of solitude,

which may lead to behavioural problems. A typical scent hound, this dog is highly active and has a strong instinct for following a trail. Left alone in an inadequately fenced garden, or allowed to run off the lead, a Beagle can disappear swiftly and stay away for hours. The breed has a loud bark and can be noisy, which may irritate neighbours if the barking becomes excessive. Fortunately, Beagles are relatively easy to train, and do best with an owner who combines fondness with firmness and clear leadership. This breed is good with children old enough to understand how to handle a dog, but cannot be considered safe with small family pets.

In the United States two sizes are recognized, based on the height of the dog at the withers: those under 33cm (13in) and those between 33cm (13in) and 38cm (15in).

SCHILLERSTOVARE
THIS RARE, TIRELESS TRACKER HUNTS SOLO AND IS THE SWIFTEST SWEDISH HOUND

FCI

Height range
49-61cm (19-24in)

Weight range
15-25kg (33-55lb)

Life span 10-14 years

Origin Sweden

A rare breed, the Schillerstovare is much prized for its hunting speed and stamina, especially over snow. This dog's thick coat insulates it well from its native climate. It tracks alone, rather than in a pack, and emits a deep-throated bay to pinpoint the position of its prey – hare or fox. The breed is named after its breeder, farmer Per Schiller.

Medium-sized muzzle well proportioned to head

Strong, long neck

Short, glossy, tan coat with thick undercoat

Well-cut black blanket "saddles" back, neck, sides of trunk, and top of tail

High-set, drop ears narrow towards the tip

Black nose

HAMILTONSTOVARE
SWEDEN'S MOST POPULAR FOXHOUND IS VERY LOYAL AND A GOOD COMPANION AND PROTECTOR

KC

Height range
46-60cm (18-24in)

Weight range
23-27kg (51-60lb)

Life span 10-13 years

Origin Sweden

Developed by Count Adolf Patrick Hamilton, a founder of the Swedish Kennel Club, this handsome, easy-going hound loves to roam fields and flush out small game. The Hamiltonstovare is a mix of English Foxhound (see p.158) stock (it has also been called the Swedish Foxhound) and Holstein Hound, Hanovarian Haidbrake, and Courlander Hound.

White blaze on face

Dense, strong, close-lying coat

Short, dense, soft undercoat

Tricolour coat with no one colour dominating

White "socks" on lower legs and feet

SMALANDSSTOVARE

THIS ROBUST ALL-WEATHER HUNTER AND WORKER FORMS A STRONG BOND WITH ITS OWNER

FCI

Height range
42–53cm (17–21in)

Weight range
15–20kg (33–44lb)

Life span 12 years

Origin Sweden

This Swedish Hound, also known as the Småland Hound, is thought to date back to the 16th century and takes it name from the dense forest of Småland in southern Sweden where it was used to hunt fox and hare. It has a distinctive black coat with tan markings similar to that of a Rottweiler (see p.81).

High-set, medium-length ears with rounded tips

Head shorter and more wedge-shaped than most hounds

Typical tan marking above eyes

Thick, shiny, black and tan coat

Small, white markings on toes

Square, well-muscled body

Naturally short tail

HALDEN HOUND

THIS NORWEGIAN FOXHOUND IS A RELATIVELY RARE HUNTING AND FAMILY DOG

FCI

Height range
50–65cm (20–26in)

Weight range
23–29kg (51–64lb)

Life span 10–12 years

Origin Norway

The largest of the four stovare breeds, this hound loves a speedy chase over snowy open spaces. Like other Norwegian dogs bred as hunting companions, the Halden Hound is not widely known outside its native land. It was developed in Halden in the southeast, by crossing an English Foxhound (see p.158) with a local "beagle".

Tan shading on head

Thick tail carried low

Eyes dark brown

Drop ears lie close to head

White coat with black patches

Broad, deep chest

NORWEGIAN HOUND

A BEAUTIFULLY COATED HARE-HUNTER AND FIRST-CLASS FAMILY HOUND

FCI

Height range
47-55cm (19-22in)

Weight range
16-23kg (35-51lb)

Life span 11-14 years

Origin Norway

Other colours

Tricolour

Trusting, friendly, and easy to handle when not hunting, the Norwegian Hound, or Dunker, is designed to track hare in snow in temperatures as low as -15°C (-59°F). Originally named after Captain Wilhelm Dunker, this hound was bred from other Norwegian and Russian hare-hounds in the early 1800s.

Gently sloping stop

Drop ears with rounded tips

Large, dark, expressive eyes

Black nose

White chest and shoulders

Blue marbled back

Tapering tail reaches below hock

Straight, hard, dense, blue marbled coat with pale fawn and white markings

White socks

FINNISH HOUND

A CALM AND FRIENDLY DOG AT HOME AND AN ENERGETIC AND TIRELESS TRACKER ON THE MOVE

FCI

Height range
52-61cm (20-24in)

Weight range
21-25kg (46-55lb)

Life span 12 years

Origin Finland

By far Finland's most popular hunting dog, this hound is bred to drive hare and fox in the country's snowy forests. It hunts with unfailing eagerness, but at home it is an easy-going and manageable pet. Although generally placid, the Finnish Hound can sometimes be shy of strangers.

White blaze on head

Back edge of ear turns outwards

Dark brown eyes

Well-developed, black nose

Close-lying, straight, dense, tricolour coat

HYGEN HOUND

A BRIGHT HUNTING DOG, LIVELY COMPANION, AND RELIABLE HOUSE WATCHDOG

FCI

Height range
47–58cm (19–23in)

Weight range
20–25kg (44–55lb)

Life span 12 years

Origin Norway

Other colours

Yellow-red

Black and tan

Yellow-red coats have black shading.

A more lightweight dog than the Norwegian Hound (opposite), this breed from Ringerike and Romerike in eastern Norway is purpose built for the snowy Arctic expanses and has the stamina to bound through them tirelessly. Quite compact like the Smålandsstövare (see p.155), this is a quick-thinking hunter that loves long walks.

Head and snout shorter and wider than Norwegian Hound (opposite)

Black nose

Thin, soft, drop ears with rounded tips

White blaze on head

Tail with black shading and white tip

Dense, shiny, harsh, red-brown coat with white markings

AMERICAN FOXHOUND

BRED FOR SPEED AND DISTANCE, THIS DOG NEEDS AN ENERGETIC OWNER

FCI

Height range
53–64cm (21–25in)

Weight range
18–30kg (40–66lb)

Life span 12–13 years

Origin USA

Other colours

Any colour

These dogs have the most august of patrons – the first president of the United States, George Washington. He bred them from French and English hounds to produce a taller and more athletic, stand-alone breed. American Foxhounds love running in packs, hunting singly, or competing in field trials.

Hazel eyes

Moderate stop

Close, hard, white coat with tan patches

Straight, square-cut muzzle

Long, broad, drop ears

Chest narrower than English Foxhound (see p.158)

Fox-like feet with well-arched toes

ENGLISH FOXHOUND

A GOOD-NATURED, ACTIVE DOG WITH A SUNNY APPROACH TO LIFE

KC

Height range
58-64cm (23-25in)

Weight range
25-34kg (55-75lb)

Life span 10-11 years

Origin UK

Other colours

Variety of colours

Any recognized hound colour.

The ancestry of the English Foxhound goes back centuries. By the 1800s more than 200 packs of foxhounds were kept in England for hunting foxes over a variety of terrain. An active, bold, and passionate hunter, this hound is highly responsive to training but can also be stubborn and self-willed, especially when on the scent. Historically kennelled in packs rather than kept as house dogs, the English Foxhound nevertheless makes a good companion, is very friendly towards people, and is excellent with children. Would-be owners should be aware that these hounds can retain their playfulness, liveliness, and stamina into old age.

Large eyes with friendly expression

Back broad and level with a slight rise over strong loins

Black nose

Flat-lying, pendant ears

High-set tail

Short, dense, weatherproof, tricolour coat

Very straight front legs

Round, cat-like feet

CATAHOULA LEOPARD DOG

THIS SKILFUL, STRONG-WILLED HUNTER IS SUITED TO AN EXPERIENCED OWNER

Height range
51–66cm (20–26in)

Weight range
23–41kg (51–90lb)

Life span 10–14 years

Origin USA

Other colours

Variety of colours

This striking-looking Louisiana herding dog and hunter of wild boar and raccoon is a mix of Spanish colonial greyhound, mastiff, and native Red Wolf. It can work well in swamps, forests, and more open terrain. Named after a parish in its home state, the Catahoula Leopard Dog is an alert watchdog, wary of strangers, but calm and dedicated to its household.

Eyes may be different colours

White marking on chest

Short, tight, blue-merle coat

Spotted pattern gives rise to "leopard" name

PLOTT HOUND

RUTHLESS AND DETERMINED WHEN HUNTING, THIS HOUND IS RESPONSIVE AND ALERT AT HOME

AKC

Height range
51–64cm (20–25in)

Weight range
18–27kg (40–60lb)

Life span 10–12 years

Origin USA

This powerful, brindled hound is used for hunting raccoon, though it also hunts big cats, bear, coyote, and wild boar. It is one of only a few breeds with acknowledged American origin. The original Plott Hound was bred in the 1750s in the Smokey Mountains by the Plott family, using boar-hunting Hanoverian Hounds brought over from Germany.

Neck and topline long, lean, and muscular

Brindle coat

Prominent brown or hazel eyes

Broad, soft ears set moderately high

Powerfully built body for speed and stamina

Compact feet with white toes

BLACK AND TAN COONHOUND

MAINLY USED FOR HUNTING, THIS DOG IS CALM AND FRIENDLY IN THE HOME

KC

Height range
58–69cm (23–27in)

Weight range
23–34kg (51–75lb)

Life span 10–12 years

Origin USA

This big hunting dog probably descends from the Bloodhound (see p.139) and a now-extinct old English breed called the Talbot Hound. Tough and powerful, the Black and Tan Coonhound is a superb tracker of raccoon, opossum, and even cougar, baying loudly when it has chased its quarry up a tree.

Ear low and set
well back

Tail set slightly
below level
of back

Well-
developed
flews

Rich tan
on muzzle

Coal-black coat

REDBONE COONHOUND

THIS DOG NEEDS A LOT OF EXERCISE AND MAY FIND CHASING IRRESISTIBLE

AKC

Height range
53–69cm (21–27in)

Weight range
21–32kg (46–71lb)

Life span 11–12 years

Origin USA

Bred in the southern states of the USA, the handsome, glossy-coated Redbone Coonhound has been a popular hunting dog for over a century. Fast and agile over almost any type of terrain, this hound is well known for its prowess in tracking raccoon, bear, and cougar. Trainable as a companion dog, this coonhound is sociable and affectionate.

Slightly higher at
withers than at hip

Round eyes
set well apart

Powerful,
agile body

Short, smooth,
solid red coat

Compact,
well-padded,
cat-like feet

BLUETICK COONHOUND

THIS ENERGETIC WORKING BREED NEEDS SUPERVISION OUTDOORS   AKC

Height range
53–69cm (21–27in)

Weight range
20–36kg (44–79lb)

Life span 11–12 years

Origin USA

A breakaway breed, originally regarded as the English Coonhound, the Bluetick Coonhound has had its devoted followers since the 1940s. Although mainly used to track raccoon and opossum, this hound also hunts deer and bear. Happiest when working, the Bluetick Coonhound has proved to be highly successful at obedience and agility trials.

Large nose

Clear, keen eyes

Long, deep, broad muzzle

Ticking on coat produces characteristic colour

Thickly mottled, dark blue coat

TREEING WALKER COONHOUND

THIS POPULAR COONHOUND MAKES AN EXCELLENT COMPANION WHEN SOCIALIZED   AKC

Height range
51–68cm (20–27in)

Weight range
23–32kg (51–71lb)

Life span 12–13 years

Origin USA

Other colours

White

White coats have tan or black spots.

This fast and efficient racoon-hunter has been recognized as a distinct breed since the 1940s. In the USA this breed is much admired for its outstanding abilities in coonhound competitions. It is a dog that appreciates a friendly home environment and loves people.

Black saddle

Long, narrow muzzle

Large, bright, brown eyes

Muscular shoulders and neck

Smooth, tricolour coat

AMERICAN ENGLISH COONHOUND
THIS AMERICAN-BRED HUNTER IS FULL OF ATHLETIC POISE AND PACE

AKC

Height range
58-66cm (23-26in)

Weight range
21-41kg (46-90lb)

Life span 10-11 years

Origin USA

Other colours

Red and white   White and black

May also have a blue and white ticked coat.

This energetic and intelligent dog evolved from English Foxhounds (see p.158) that were brought to the New World. It was bred to adapt to rougher terrain, hunting fox by day and raccoon by night. It shows an effortless trot and never appears to get tired. Quite similar to the Treeing Walker Coonhound (see p.161), it can adopt both the "cold nose" trail (straddling an old track for hours to locate the animal that left it) or follow a scent fast in pursuit of a fresh, active trail. As a pet, it needs firm handling but in return will be a devoted companion and good guard dog.

Muscular, reasonably long neck

Tricolour coat with ticking

Kind, hound-like expression

Pendant ears

Flews cover lower jaw

Red and white ticked coat

ARTOIS HOUND

THIS FRIENDLY, LIKEABLE FRENCH HOUND MAKES A WELL-BEHAVED HUNTING COMPANION | FCI

Height range
53–58cm (21–23in)

Weight range
28–30kg (62–66lb)

Life span 12–14 years

Origin France

The sometimes precocious Artois Hound is an excellent hunting companion that needs lots of exercise. It can be distinguished from other French scent hounds by its flat, open, pendant ears. The Artois Hound has a strong directional sense, a very keen nose, precise pointing, speed on the move, and drive. Its ancestry goes back to the Great Artois Hound (and back to the Saint Hubert), while some English blood also modified the breed. In the early 1990s this robust and courageous hunter of hare, deer, and boar was brought back from near extinction, although it is still rare.

Black saddle

Pronounced stop

Broad head with moderately long muzzle

Large, round, dark-coloured eyes

Slightly elongated feet

Strong, broad back

Ears practically flat, distinguishing it from other French scent hounds

Tricolour coat

Wide chest

ARIEGEOIS

AN ELEGANT DOG, THIS IS THE SMALLEST OF THE HOUNDS FROM THE SOUTH OF FRANCE

FCI

Height range
50-58cm (20-23in)

Weight range
25-27kg (55-60lb)

Life span 10-14 years

Origin France

A relative newcomer - France officially recognized it in 1912 - this dog is also called the Ariege Hound, after the dry, rocky region it comes from on France's border with Spain. Its forebears include the Grand Gascon-Saintongeois (opposite), the Grand Bleu de Gascogne (opposite), and local medium-sized hounds. The Ariégeois excels as a hare-hunter but is also known for its friendly nature.

Pale tan spot over eye

Black mottling

Smaller and more finely boned than Grand Bleu de Gascogne (opposite)

Low-set, soft, pendant ears

Brown eyes with gentle expression

Pale tan on cheeks

Tail extends to hocks

Strong neck

Clearly defined, jet-black marking

Short, white coat

Elongated, hare-like feet

GASCON-SAINTONGEOIS

THIS ROE-DEER PACKHOUND HAS AN AMIABLE TEMPERAMENT

FCI

Height range
Petit:
53-62cm (21-24in)
Grand:
62-72cm (24-28in)

Weight range
Petit:
24-25kg (53-55lb)
Grand:
30-32kg (66-71lb)

Life span 12-14 years

Origin France

This rare breed, from the Gascony area of France, is also known as the Virelade Hound after the Baron de Virelade who crossed the Saintongeois with the Grand Bleu de Gascogne (below), and the Ariégeois (opposite). It is a high-stamina hunter, with a fine-tuned sense of smell. There are two sizes: Petit and Grand.

Occiput (back part of head) very pronounced

Traces of tan on cheek

Long, thin, pendant ears

White coat with sparse, black speckling

Oval eyes with black rims

Black patches cover ears and surround eyes

Well-developed flews

Grand

GRAND BLEU DE GASCOGNE

A LARGE WORKING HOUND WITH GREAT STAMINA AND TENACITY

KC

Height range
60-70cm (24-28in)

Weight range
36-55kg (80-120lb)

Life span 12-14 years

Origin France

This large trail hound has a powerful voice, is solidly built, and is recognizable by the dark mottling on its white skin, which creates a shimmering blue colour. Unsuitable for city living, it needs plenty of exercise. Originally used to hunt wolves, its quarry today is hare. Its scenting skills are highly developed and it is single-minded when on a trail.

Well-developed stop

Black marks cover ears and surround eyes

Low-set, pendant ears curl inwards

Tan markings on face

Well-developed flews

Black patch

Strong, smooth, weather-resistant, slate-blue coat

Long, oval-shaped foot

PETIT BLEU DE GASCOGNE
THIS KEEN-NOSED HOUND IS READY TO FOLLOW SCENT BUT IS EASILY BORED   FCI

Height range 50-58cm (20-23in)
Weight range 40-48kg (88-106lb)
Life span 12 years
Origin France

Bred down in size from the Grand Bleu de Gascogne (see p.165), the Petit Bleu de Gascogne was developed for hunting hare but is also used to pursue larger game. With a fine nose and a musical voice, this hound works well either as an individual or in a pack. If kept as a companion, it needs a firm hand and a lot of exercise.

Dark chestnut eyes · Black patch · Short, slate-blue coat · Tan markings on feet and legs

Pendant, low-set ears · Long, refined muzzle · Well-developed dewlap

BLUE GASCONY GRIFFON
THIS ALL-WEATHER HUNTER IS TIRELESS AND FULL OF SPIRIT   FCI

Height range 48-57cm (19-22in)
Weight range 17-18kg (37-40lb)
Life span 12-13 years
Origin France

A cross between the Petit Bleu de Gascogne (above) and wire-coated hounds, this dog has a coarse, shaggy coat that allows it to work in harsh conditions. A comparatively rare breed, it was specifically developed to hunt deer, fox, and rabbit. It has stamina rather than great speed and a remarkably efficient nose.

Tan markings on muzzle · Long, wiry eyebrows · Long, pendant ears · Coat denser and longer on shoulders

Harsh, shaggy, slate-blue coat · Long tail tapers to thin point

BASSET BLEU DE GASCOGNE
THIS ELEGANT BASSET HOUND HAS A DELIGHTFUL TEMPERAMENT BUT CAN BE STRONG-WILLED

KC

Height range
30–38cm (12–15in)

Weight range
16–20kg (35–44lb)

Life span 10–12 years

Origin France

In 12th-century France blue hounds of this type were used to hunt wolves, deer, and boar. The modern breed of Basset Bleu de Gascogne was established in the 20th century and is not as widely known as some other Gascony hounds. A low-slung dog, it is not fast moving but makes up for lack of speed with great determination, tracking quarry for hours once on the scent. This hound is an enthusiastic outdoor companion as well as a fine household pet but, like many hounds, takes patience to train and socialize.

Long muzzle with black nose and wide nostrils

Long, pendant ears

Short, dense coat with clearly defined, black saddle

Tan spot above each oval eye

Long tail extends below hock

Moderately developed flews

A mix of black and white hairs give coat slate-blue appearance

Strong, oval feet with black nails

POITEVIN

A REAL BOUNDER THROUGH THE THICKETS, THIS HOUND IS BRAVE AND BIG-HEARTED

FCI

Height range
62–72cm (24–28in)

Weight range
60–66kg (132–146lb)

Life span 11–12 years

Origin France

Other colours

White and orange

Wolf-coloured hair also often occurs.

This big, courageous hound is adept at fast and furious pack hunting over rough ground, and once hunted the wolves that used to roam the province of Poitou below Vendée and Brittany in western France. Today, after several infusions of "new blood", this powerfully muscled breed shows great prowess and stamina in pursuing wild boar and deer in packs, and can hunt all day. It is a very hard worker that will follow its quarry through water and bays a lot. It is the longest-serving of the French pack hounds.

Muzzle narrows towards nose

Saddle of black hair over back

Large, brown eyes

Long, narrow head

Arched back

Thin, cone-shaped ears

Sleek, shiny, tricolour coat

Well-muscled body with deep, narrow chest

Rounded feet

BILLY

A SUPERB HUNTING DOG AND EASY-GOING FAMILY PET

FCI

Height range
58-70 cm (23-28in)

Weight range
25-33kg (55-73lb)

Life span 12-13 years

Origin France

A sleek, attractive breed built for speed, the Billy has remained relatively obscure even in its native France. Its forebears are the now extinct Montemboeuf, Ceris, and Larye breeds. Its quirky name comes from Château de Billy in Poitou where Gaston Hublot du Rivault bred this instinctive deer hunter in the late 1800s.

Clearly defined stop

Strong, slightly arched back

Long, strong tail

Mottling resembles café au lait

Short, harsh, white coat

Slightly arched forehead

FRENCH TRICOLOUR HOUND

THE YOUNGEST OF THE FRENCH HOUNDS, AND SIMILAR TO THE POITEVIN IN LOOKS AND ABILITY

FCI

Height range
60-72cm (24-28in)

Weight range
34-35kg (75-77lb)

Life span 11-12 years

Origin France

Perhaps the most popular hound in France, the French Tricolour Hound was blended from the Poitevin (opposite) and Billy (above) to try to create a home-grown pack hound without English Foxhound (see p.158) blood (though there is a hint of Great Anglo-French Tricolour Hound, see p.170). Today, these strong, well-muscled pack dogs hunt game such as deer and wild boar.

Large, brown eyes

Deep chest

Short, fine, tricolour coat

Lips squarer and more substantial than in the Poitevin (opposite)

GREAT ANGLO-FRENCH TRICOLOUR HOUND

THIS HOUND IS HAPPIEST WHEN HUNTING IN A PACK

FCI

Height range
60-70cm (24-28in)

Weight range
30-35kg (66-77lb)

Life span 10-12 years

Origin France

Like several French scent hounds, the name says what it is: a tricoloured dog with cross-Channel connections – the "Great" refers to the game it hunts, such as red deer, not the dog's size. Its coat and character come from the tricolored Poitevin (see p.168), and the powerful muscles and stamina from the English Foxhound (see p.158).

Broad, pendant ears

Short, quite coarse, tricolour coat

Black blanket

Fairly broad chest

Rounded feet

GREAT ANGLO-FRENCH WHITE AND BLACK HOUND

A BIG, ENERGETIC DOG USED FOR LARGE GAME HUNTING

FCI

Height range
62-72cm (24-28in)

Weight range
30-35kg (66-77lb)

Life span 10-12 years

Origin France

This Anglo-French scent hound is one of three colour-based varieties recognized as separate breeds. It originated in the 1800s from a mix of Bleu de Gascogne and Gascon Saintongeois hounds crossed with English Foxhound (see p.158). Most live in kennels in France, and are used to hunt deer in packs. Very few of these powerful, sturdy hunters are kept as domestic pets.

Deep-set, brown eyes

Pale tan on cheek

Pale tan marking above eyes

Long tail ends in sharp point

Black mantle

Short, white coat

FRENCH WHITE AND BLACK HOUND

A SWIFT-FOOTED, STAMINA-PACKED HUNTER THAT GIVES ENDLESS CHASE

FCI

Height range
62–72cm (24–28in)

Weight range
26–30kg (57–66lb)

Life span 10–12 years

Origin France

There is a growing population of these big, powerful dogs in France, and it is perhaps not surprising given that this handsome breed is highly regarded for hunting roe deer in packs. It is a friendly dog but more likely to form a close relationship with its master in kennels than an owner in a modern house. It may have links with the famous Hound of Saintonge, whose own origins are uncertain but which was bred to hunt wolves. The modern French White and Black Hound is a mix of Bleu de Gascogne and Gascon Saintongeois hounds.

Black mantle

Long, thin tail

Tan marking above eyes

Pendant ears

Slightly arched back with dipping croup

Short, dense, white and black hair

Bluish speckling on legs

GREAT ANGLO-FRENCH WHITE AND ORANGE HOUND

BRED TO LIVE AND WORK IN A PACK, THIS HOUND IS NOT A GOOD CHOICE FOR APARTMENT LIFE | FCI

Height range
60–70cm (24–28in)

Weight range
34–35kg (75–77lb)

Life span 10 years

Origin France

One of three breeds of the Great Anglo-French pack-hunting dogs produced in the early 19th century, this hound is the result of crossing the English Foxhound (see p.158) with a large, French scent hound – the Billy (see p.169). Although trainable and kind-natured, this dog lives to hunt and is too energetic to be happy in complete domesticity.

Drop ears with rounded tips

Well-defined stop

Orange patch

Large, dark brown eyes

Deep chest

Sleek, short, relatively thin, white coat

FRENCH WHITE AND ORANGE HOUND

THIS BREED REQUIRES STRENUOUS EXERCISE BUT MAY SETTLE IN A SPACIOUS HOME | FCI

Height range
62–70cm (24–28in)

Weight range
27–32kg (60–71lb)

Life span 12–13 years

Origin France

Rarely seen, the French White and Orange Hound is a relatively new hunting dog – only gaining recognition in the 1970s. Easier to manage than most packhounds, this dog is usually reliable with children and other dogs but must be supervised around small pets. It loves action and should not be kept in a confined space.

Large head in proportion to body

Drop ears twist slightly at tip

Muscular thighs

Short, fine-textured, white and orange coat

WESTPHALIAN DACHSBRACKE

THIS ENERGETIC DOG HAS AN EVEN TEMPERAMENT BUT NEEDS FIRM TRAINING

FCI

Height range
30–38cm (12–15in)

Weight range
15–18kg (33–40lb)

Life span 10–12 years

Origin Germany

A short-legged version of the German Hound (see p.175), this sturdy little dog was bred to hunt small game in areas too thickly overgrown for larger dogs to penetrate. Playful and cheerily good-natured, the Westphalian Dachsbracke makes a delightful companion and is well suited to family life.

Bridge of nose slightly arched

Black mantle

Body length greater than leg length

White tip to tail

Puppy

White blaze extends down muzzle

White collar and chest

Smooth, red coat

ALPINE DACHSBRACKE

THIS FRIENDLY DOG IS HAPPY TO BE OUT ALL DAY IN ALL WEATHERS

FCI

Height range
34–42cm (13–17in)

Weight range
12–22kg (26–49lb)

Life span 12 years

Origin Austria

Other colours

Vieräugl (black and tan)

Hunting dogs very similar in appearance to the Alpine Dachsbracke existed hundreds of years ago and may have been the predecessors of this small hound. In the 1930s the modern breed was recognized as one of Austria's top scent hounds. Sturdy and tireless, and bred to hunt, the Alpine Dachsbracke is not an ideal house dog.

Well-defined stop

Dense, dark deer-red coat, interspersed with black hairs

Slightly arched head with definite furrow

Drop ears with well-rounded tips

White markings on chest

Longer hairs on underside of tail

Well-muscled, long body

Prominent chest bone

Short, sturdy legs

Strong, round feet

DACHSHUND

Height range
Miniature:
13–15cm (5–6in)
Standard:
20–23cm (8–9in)

Weight range
Miniature:
4–5kg (9–11lb)
Standard:
9–12kg (20–26lb)

Life span 12–15 years

Origin Germany

Other colours

Variety of
colours

Despite their small size, Dachshunds need plenty of exercise and mental stimulation to maintain their cheerful and loving temperament. Strong-willed, they tend to ignore commands when on the scent of prey. Dachshunds will bark protectively at unexpected visitors but are good with older children. There are three coat types: smooth-haired, long-haired, and wire-haired. The long-haired varieties need daily grooming. Two sizes are recognized by the KC, miniature and standard; but three sizes, based on chest circumference, are recognized by the FCI.

Black and tan
coat, coarse
to touch

Forefeet bigger and
broader than hind feet

Wire-haired

Shiny, black
and tan coat

Smooth, red coat   **Smooth-haired**

Hair shorter
on head

Very
shallow stop

Pendant,
feathered ears

Body much longer
than leg length

Long, silky,
shaded red coat

Long-haired

GERMAN HOUND

USUALLY GOOD WITH CHILDREN AND OTHER DOGS, THIS HOUND PREFERS OUTDOOR LIFE

FCI

Height range
40-53cm (16-21in)

Weight range
16-18kg (35-40lb)

Life span 10-12 years

Origin Germany

For centuries numerous hunting dogs of the type known as brackes existed in Germany. Today the German Hound, or Deutsche Bracke, is one of the few to survive. This hound, bred by combining several bracke varieties, is still used mainly for hunting. Although good-natured, the German Hound does not adapt well to life indoors.

White blaze on head

Slightly arched back with black blanket

Broad, pendant ears

Short, smooth, tan coat

White chest markings

Distinctive flesh-pink nose, edged with black

White markings on feet

DREVER

THIS SPORTING DOG IS RARELY KEPT SOLELY FOR COMPANIONSHIP

FCI

Height range
30-38cm (12-15in)

Weight range
14-16kg (31-35lb)

Life span 12-14 years

Origin Sweden

Other colours

Variety of colours

In the early 20th century a small, short-legged hound from Germany, the Westphalian Dachsbracke, was imported to Sweden. The breed proved popular as a game tracker, and by the 1940s the Swedes had developed their own version, the Drever. Because of its strong hunting instinct, this breed is best kept as a sporting dog.

Drop ears with rounded tips

Large head in proportion to body

White neck hair extends down to chest

Body length greater than leg length

Smooth, tricolour coat

Long, thick tail with white tip

White feet

SCHWEIZER LAUFHUND

A NOBLE-HEADED, KEEN AND LEAN HOUND WITH ROMAN ROOTS

FCI

Height range	
47–59cm (19–23in)	
Weight range	
15–20kg (33–44lb)	
Life span 12 years	
Origin Switzerland	

This breed, also known as the Swiss Hound, is a keen-nosed tracker that moves easily across Alpine terrain. It is bred to sniff out the track of hare, fox, and roe deer with its long muzzle. There are four distinct varieties – Bernese, Lucerne, Schwyz Laufhunds, and the Bruno Jura (p.138) – each named after a Swiss canton and identified by its coat colours. (A further variety, the Thurgovia, has died out.) The fine sculpted head and well-proportioned body lends the Schweizer Laufhund an air of nobility. At home they are relaxed and quite docile.

Forehead lacks any furrow or wrinkle

White coat with orange patches

Schwyz

Blue coat, a result of a combination of white and black hairs

Light to dark tan markings on cheeks

Lucerne

Elegant tail carried hanging down

Firm, straight back

Pendant ears set below eye level

Slim, elegant, domed head

Finely chiselled, narrow muzzle

White coat with black patches

Bernese

SCHWEIZER NEIDERLAUFHUND

A SMALLER, SHORTER-LEGGED, HIGHLY VOCAL SWISS HOUND

FCI

Height range
33–43cm (13–17in)

Weight range
8–15kg (18–33lb)

Life span 12–13 years

Origin Switzerland

This reduced version of the Schweizer Laufhund (opposite) was bred specifically to make the most of the Swiss cantons' high-mountain game reserves. Being slower than the Schweizer Laufhund, it can track big game more efficiently than its larger cousin (which is too fleet of foot in an enclosed area). This short-barrelled, stocky version has a great nose for game such as wild boar, badger, and bear. The Bernese Neiderlaufhund comes in a smooth-haired and a rarer rough-coated version with a small beard. The other Neiderlaufhunds are the Schwyz, Jura, and Luzerne Niederlaufhund.

Harsh, dense, white coat with black and tan markings

Soft undercoat

Bernese rough-coated

White coat with orange patches

Friendly, alert facial expression

Schwyz

Tan marking over eyes

Lucerne

Long tail carried down when active

Long, pendant ears

White coat with black and tan patches

Bernese

BAVARIAN MOUNTAIN HOUND

AMENABLE TO TRAINING, THIS HOUND NEEDS PLENTY OF PHYSICAL AND MENTAL ACTIVITY

KC

Height range
44–52cm (17–20in)

Weight range
25–35kg (55–77lb)

Life span 10 years

Origin Germany

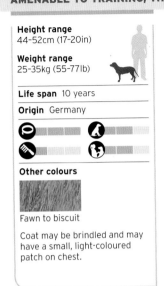

Other colours

Fawn to biscuit

Coat may be brindled and may have a small, light-coloured patch on chest.

This handsome hound, with a relatively light build, was first bred in the 1870s specifically to work in mountainous regions. A peerless tracker, the Bavarian Mountain Hound is used to follow large game, such as wild boar and deer. Steady-natured, though needing a lot of exercise, it makes a good family dog.

Dark, alert eyes

Broad, flat head

Dark mask

Back rises slightly towards hind quarters

Broad, pendant ears

Short, harsh, close-fitting, red coat

HANOVERIAN SCENT HOUND

BRED FOR STRENUOUS WORK, THIS SUPERB TRACKING DOG IS NOT A GOOD HOUSE DOG

FCI

Height range
48–55cm (19–22in)

Weight range
25–40kg (55–88lb)

Life span 12 years

Origin Germany

A classic big game tracker, dogs of this type have been well established since the Middle Ages, when they were taken hunting on leads. The modern breed, little changed in appearance, is still used for tracking wounded game. Intensely loyal to a trusted handler, this dog is cautious with strangers.

Strongly defined stop

Strong, long back

Pendulous flews

Long tail with slight curve

Slight wrinkling on forehead

High-set, broad, pendant ears

Short, thick, harsh-textured, dark brindled, deer-red coat

DOBERMANN

THIS LOYAL AND OBEDIENT FAMILY DOG COMBINES STRENGTH WITH GRACE

KC

Height range
65–69cm (26–27in)

Weight range
30–40kg (66–88lb)

Life span 13 years

Origin Germany

Other colours

Isabella

Blue

Brown

Reportedly created around 1860 by a German tax official called Louis Dobermann, this dog is the result of a number of crossings thought to include the German Shepherd Dog (see p.35), the Rottweiler (see p.81), the Greyhound (see p.126), and the Weimaraner (see p.246). From these, the Dobermann inherited a collection of admirable traits, including guarding and tracking abilities, intelligence, endurance, speed, and good looks. Widely used for police and security work, this breed is also popular as a town or country house dog. Dobermanns love being part of family life – the more active the better.

Typical rust-red markings

Almond-shaped eyes

Flat-topped, long head

Back slopes gently down towards croup

Smooth, short, black and tan coat

Compact, cat-like feet

BLACK FOREST HOUND

A MOUNTAIN HUNTING DOG WITH AN EXCEPTIONAL SENSE OF SMELL AND DIRECTION

FCI

Height range
40–50cm (16–20in)

Weight range
15–20kg (33–44lb)

Life span 11–12 years

Origin Slovakia

The Black Forest Hound, or Slovenský Kopov, originated in the foothills and snowy mountain forests of central Eastern Europe. It is used to hunt boar, deer, and other game in small packs or alone. Local hunters like the breed because it can follow a scent for hours through dense thickets, protected by its coarse coat.

Eyelids always black

Slightly tapered, black nose

Black coat with tan markings

Oval-shaped feet with well-arched toes

Tan spots above eyes

Drop ears with rounded tips

Tan-coloured muzzle

POLISH HOUND

THIS LITHE AND PERSISTENT DOG HAS A FRIENDLY CHARACTER

FCI

Height range
55–65cm (22–26in)

Weight range
20–32kg (44–71lb)

Life span 11–12 years

Origin Poland

Evolving from a heavier bracke and lighter scent hound, this rare breed emerged as a large game hunter in Poland's thick mountainous forests. The ancestors of this hound hunted in packs for Polish nobility during the Middle Ages. The Polish Hound displays superb tracking abilities regardless of how fast it is running.

Tip of ears twist

Short, fawn coat

Moderately pronounced dewlap

Black saddle

TRANSYLVANIAN HOUND

MEDIUM-SIZED AND SHORT-HAIRED, THIS IS A RARE HUNGARIAN HUNTING DOG

FCI

Height range
55-65cm (22-26in)

Weight range
25-35kg (55-77lb)

Life span 10-13 years

Origin Hungary

Also known as the Hungarian Hound, or Erdélyi Kopó, this hardy hunting dog was once the preserve of Hungarian kings and princes. Then, as now, its keen sense of direction, and hardiness in heavy, snowbound Carpathian forests and climate extremes made it the large game hunter of choice. However, it remains an extremely rare breed.

Tan spots above dark brown eyes

Black lips

Drop ears widen and then taper to a rounded tip

Clearly defined tan markings

Coarse, short, black coat

POSAVAZ HOUND

THIS VERY HARDY SCENT HOUND HAS BEEN BRED TO HUNT HARE AND FOX

FCI

Height range
46-58cm (18-23in)

Weight range
16-24kg (35-53lb)

Life span 10-12 years

Origin Former Yugoslavia

The Croatian name for the Posavaz Hound, Posavski Gonic, can be translated as "scent hound from the Sava Valley", and its robust build makes it ideally suited to the dense underbrush of the Sava River basin. Passionate in the hunt, this hound is quite docile in the home.

Straight, dense, reddish wheaten coat

Large, dark eyes

Flat, thin, drop ears with rounded tips

Long, narrow head

White muzzle

White collar and chest

BOSNIAN ROUGH-COATED HOUND
AN IMPLACABLE HUNTER ON THE TRAIL BUT QUIET AND GENTLE AT HOME

FCI

Height range
45–56cm (18–22in)

Weight range
16–25kg (35–55lb)

Life span 12 years

Origin Bosnia and Herzegovina

Other colours

Tricolour

Formerly known as the Illyrian Hound, this breed has been a huntsman's companion since the 19th century. A hardy, solidly built dog, it has a thick, coarse-haired coat that enables it to work in bitterly cold weather and through thick undergrowth.

Large, oval, chestnut-brown eyes

Dark red, drop ears

Blackish area on back extends from neck to tail

Long, wiry, bicolour coat has thick undercoat

Reddish yellow hair on chest and legs

Cat-like front feet

MONTENEGRIN MOUNTAIN HOUND
THIS CLASSIC BALKAN SCENT HOUND MAKES A GOOD COMPANION DOG

FCI

Height range
44–53cm (17–21in)

Weight range
20–25kg (44–55lb)

Life span 12 years

Origin Serbia

Also known as the Serbian Mountain Hound, this rare dog from the Planina region of Serbia has a calm, gentle nature that is appreciated by non-hunting owners. Nevertheless, it remains a superb hound for hunting fox and hare, or even larger animals such as deer and wild boar.

Tan markings on face

Long, pendant ears

Tail carried sabre fashion

Moderately developed flews

Tan markings on chest

Glossy, black and tan coat – rough to the touch

SERBIAN TRICOLOURED HOUND

A LOYAL, DEPENDABLE WORKER AND LOVING COMPANION

FCI

Height range
44-55cm (17-22in)

Weight range
20-25kg (44-55lb)

Life span 12 years

Origin Serbia

Once regarded as a variety of the Montenegrin Mountain Hound (opposite), this rare breed has striking white markings that distinguish it from its relative. Used to hunt fox and hare, or occasionally larger game, it also makes a gentle and devoted family dog.

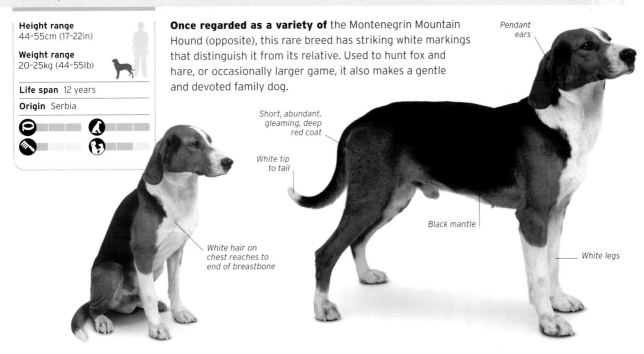

Pendant ears

Short, abundant, gleaming, deep red coat

White tip to tail

Black mantle

White hair on chest reaches to end of breastbone

White legs

SERBIAN HOUND

HAPPIEST IN COMPANY, THIS HOUND NEEDS PLENTY OF OUTDOOR ACTION

FCI

Height range
44-56cm (17-22in)

Weight range
20-25kg (44-55lb)

Life span 12-14 years

Origin Serbia

This pack-hunting dog with a booming voice tracks game of all sizes from rabbit to elk and boar. Away from the hunt, it is sweet-natured and makes a good companion for an active family, especially if there are other dogs around. The Serbian Hound is also a fine watchdog.

Black markings on either side of temples

Slanting, oval eyes

Pendant ears

Prominent chest bone

Black mantle

Smooth, tan coat

HELLENIC HOUND

THIS FAST AND POWERFUL HOUND HAS A STRONG CHARACTER AND A GREAT NOSE FOR SCENT

FCI

Height range
45–55cm (18–22in)

Weight range
17–20kg (37–44lb)

Life span 11 years

Origin Greece

Descended from the traditional scent hounds of ancient Greece, the Hellenic Hound has a musical hunting voice that carries over long distances. Once used to hunt boar and hare, if trained with care, the breed can be a pleasant companion, but without plenty of space to run in can develop bad behaviour.

Shallow stop

Back long in proportion to height

Graceful, powerful neck

Short, smooth, black and tan coat

Typical hound-shaped head

Tan markings on face

Drop ears with rounded tips

Tail tapers to pointed tip

MOUNTAIN CUR

THIS TOUGH AND COURAGEOUS DOG IS A NATURAL HUNTER BUT RESPONDS WELL TO TRAINING

Height range
41–66cm (16–26in)

Weight range
18–27kg (40–60lb)

Life span 12–16 years

Origin USA

Other colours

Variety of colours

Originating in North America when early settlers from Europe crossed their hunting dogs with native dogs, the Mountain Cur was first recognized in the 1950s. It is still used for hunting racoon and larger game such as bears. Mountain Curs are not indoor dogs, but with the right training they make good companions.

Short, dense, red coat

Muscular back

Strong, muscular neck

White markings on chest

Broad head

Drop ears

Large, dark eyes

White tips on toes

RHODESIAN RIDGEBACK

BOISTEROUS AND HIGHLY STRUNG, THIS DOG NEEDS AN ENERGETIC OWNER

KC

Height range
61-69cm (24-27in)

Weight range
29-41kg (64-90lb)

Life span 10-12 years

Origin Zimbabwe

The distinctive ridge of hair along this dog's back, growing in the opposite direction to the rest of the coat, instantly identifies it. Native to Zimbabwe (formerly Rhodesia), the breed may have descended from dogs brought to southern Africa by European settlers. Because the Rhodesian Ridgeback was once used in packs to hunt lions, it is sometimes known as the African Lion Hound. Despite the breed's fierce image, it is kind-natured and affectionate, and is a good family companion for experienced owners. This dog needs to be kept occupied, as it may develop behavioural problems if bored or under-exercised.

Black nose

Long tail tapers from base

Characteristic ridge of hair

Drop ears, slightly darker than rest of coat

Dark muzzle

Small, white markings on chest

Sleek, short, red-wheaten coat

White markings on toes

Compact feet

DIGGING INSTINCT
Intent on his task, this Airedale Terrier is doing what comes naturally – excavating a hole. Most terriers are inveterate diggers and tunnellers.

TERRIERS

Tough, fearless, self-confident, energetic – a terrier can claim all of these descriptions, and more. The terrier group takes its name from the Latin word *terra* (earth), referring to the original use of various types of small dog as hunters of underground-dwelling vermin, such as rats. However, some modern terriers are large dogs, bred for different purposes.

Once a fighting dog, the Bull Terrier is now a family favourite

Many breeds of terrier originated in the UK, where they were traditionally regarded as hunting dogs for the working man. Some are named after the regions they first came from: Norwich Terrier, Yorkshire Terrier, and Lakeland Terrier. Others are known by the types of animal they used to hunt: for example, Fox Terrier and Rat Terrier.

Terriers are by nature quick to react and show great persistence when on the track of quarry. They possess independent, some would say wilful, characters and are ready to stand their ground against larger dogs. The dogs developed for hunting below ground, including the much-loved Jack Russell and Cairn Terriers, are small, sturdy, and short-legged. Terriers with longer legs, such as the Irish Terrier and the beautiful Soft-coated Wheaten Terrier, were once used for hunting above

ground and also as guard dogs for protecting flocks. The largest terriers of all include the Airedale Terrier, originally bred for hunting otter, and the impressively built Russian Black Terrier, which was specifically developed for military use and guard duties.

In the 19th century, a different type of terrier became popular. Crosses between terriers and bulldogs produced such dogs as the Bull Terrier, the Staffordshire Bull Terrier, and the American Pit Bull Terrier, breeds intended for the vicious and now illegal sports of pit-fighting and bull-baiting. With their broad heads and powerful jaws, these dogs suggest a close affinity with mastiffs and are, in fact, likely to be related to that group.

Most types of terrier are today kept as pets. Intelligent and usually friendly and affectionate, they make excellent companions and watchdogs. Because of their inherent traits, terriers need to be trained and socialized early to prevent problems

with other dogs and pets. Hunting-type terriers also love to dig and can wreak havoc in a garden if unsupervised. The modern breeds of those dogs historically used for fighting are now largely free from aggression and, when properly trained by an experienced owner, are usually trustworthy with families.

MIXED HISTORY
Terriers have highly variable origins. This Miniature Pinscher has Whippets in its ancestry.

LIVELY COMPANION
The sparky Jack Russell is among the best known of various small working terrier breeds now enjoying popularity as pets.

WEST HIGHLAND WHITE TERRIER

A CHEEKY AND CHEERFUL CHARACTER, THIS TERRIER CAN BE BOSSY WITH OTHER DOGS

KC

Height range
25–28cm (10–11in)

Weight range
7–10kg (15–22lb)

Life span 9–15 years

Origin UK

One of the best loved of all small terriers, the "Westie" was developed in Scotland in the 19th century from Cairn Terriers (opposite). This hardy little dog's original role was to hunt fox, badger, and vermin such as rats. Today, West Highland White Terriers are suitable town or country pets for all types of home. They have boundless energy and are always ready for walks or to play with children. Early social training is recommended for this breed, as they have large egos for their size and can be overbearing with other dogs.

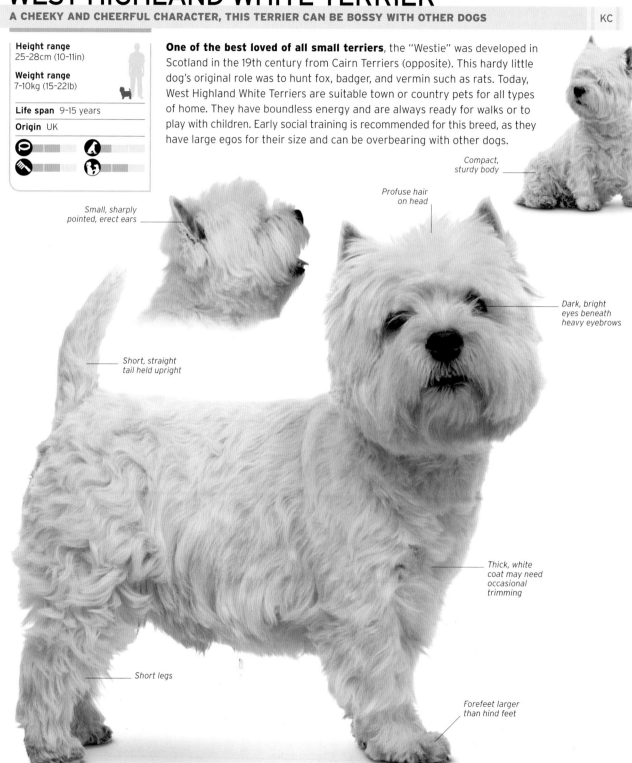

Compact, sturdy body

Profuse hair on head

Small, sharply pointed, erect ears

Dark, bright eyes beneath heavy eyebrows

Short, straight tail held upright

Thick, white coat may need occasional trimming

Short legs

Forefeet larger than hind feet

CAIRN TERRIER

THIS LIVELY DOG IS IDEAL WITH CHILDREN BUT MAY CHASE OTHER PETS

KC

Height range
28–31cm (11–12in)

Weight range
6–8kg (13–18lb)

Life span 9–15 years

Origin UK

Other colours

Near black

Red

Coat may be brindled.

Originating in the Western Isles of Scotland, the Cairn Terrier was bred for hunting vermin. Amusing and full of character, this sturdy terrier is small enough for apartment life and energetic enough for romping round a large country home; it fits in anywhere. The Cairn Terrier's urge to chase anything that moves should be discouraged early on.

Dark ears with shorter hair

Harsh, coarse, wheaten coat

Shaggy eyebrows overhang dark, hazel eyes

Cream coat

Grey coat

Forefeet larger than hind feet

SCOTTISH TERRIER

THIS SMALL DOG HAS GREAT DIGNITY AND IS ALERT AND READY TO BE PROTECTIVE

KC

Height range
25–28cm (10–11in)

Weight range
9–11kg (20–24lb)

Life span 9–15 years

Origin UK

Other colours

Wheaten

Coat may be brindled.

This breed was first named in the late 19th century, but dogs of this type existed in the Scottish Highlands much earlier. Powerful and agile, despite their short stature, "Scotties" were bred as vermin-hunters like the West Highland White Terrier (opposite) and Cairn Terrier (above). Affectionate and watchful, the Scottish Terrier is a good home companion.

Bushy eyebrows

Harsh, wiry, black coat, needs regular grooming and clipping

Long head

Pointed, erect ears

Long, dense beard

Body thickset, but not heavy

CESKY TERRIER

TOUGH, FEARLESS, AND SOMETIMES WILFUL, THIS DOG NEEDS PATIENT TRAINING

KC

Height range
25-32cm (10-13in)

Weight range
6-10kg (13-22lb)

Life span 12-14 years

Origin Czech Republic

Other colours

Liver

Can have yellow, grey, or white markings on the beard and cheeks, neck, chest, belly, and limbs, sometimes with white collar or a white tip to the tail.

A 20th-century breed developed for burrowing work, this dog is also known as the Czech or Bohemian Terrier. It is still used as a working dog, and its natural wariness of strangers makes it a useful watchdog. For a terrier, this dog has a relatively relaxed, playful character and it is sometimes simply kept as a companion. However, the breed retains some terrier stubbornness and an inclination to snap, so needs consistent training from an early age. The typical clip of the coat is short on the body, leaving long curtains of hair on the face, legs, and belly.

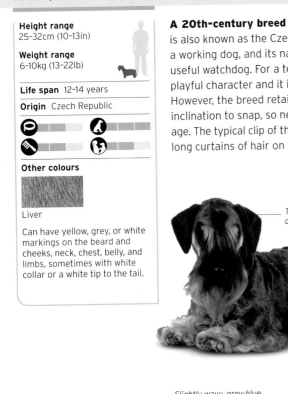

Triangular, drop ears

Yellow-white colour of lower leg and feet matches beard

Hair left long on front of head

Slightly wavy, grey-blue coat has silky sheen

Tail carried low at rest

Long hair forms beard

Forefeet are larger than hind feet

SEALYHAM TERRIER

THIS POWERFUL, INTELLIGENT, AND SPIRITED DOG IS AN ATTRACTIVE BUT CHALLENGING BREED

KC

Height range
25-30cm (10-12in)

Weight range
8-9kg (18-20lb)

Life span 14 years

Origin UK

Originally bred in Wales to tackle badgers and otters, this breed has no working role today but is kept as a pet. Their territorial nature makes Sealyham Terriers good watchdogs but they can be aggressive towards other dogs, and an innate stubbornness means that persistence in training is required. The show clip is distinctive, but requires regular maintenance.

Medium-sized, dark, round eyes

Tapering tail carried erect but not curled

White coat

Clipped hair gives jaw square appearance

Small, drop ears

Chest is broad and deep between short legs

NORFOLK TERRIER

THIS STURDY, CHEERFUL DOG IS HAPPY IN A TOWN OR COUNTRY HOME

KC

Height range
22-25cm (9-10in)

Weight range
5-6kg (11-13lb)

Life span 14-15 years

Origin UK

Other colours

Red

Black and tan

Coat may be grizzled.

This small terrier was bred from various rat-catching dogs, and is an energetic hunter. Because ratters work in packs, this breed is more sociable with other dogs than most terriers, but cannot be trusted with other pets. It makes a good guard dog or companion for families with older children.

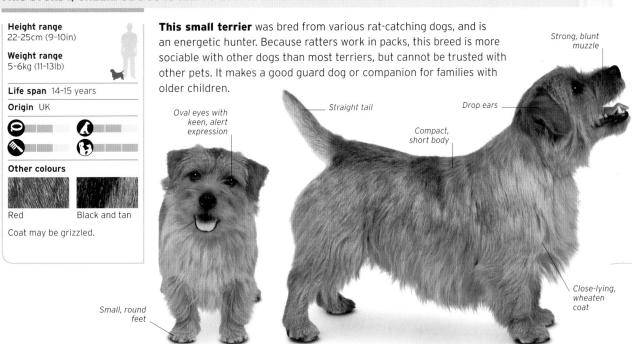

Strong, blunt muzzle

Straight tail

Drop ears

Oval eyes with keen, alert expression

Compact, short body

Close-lying, wheaten coat

Small, round feet

*Tail darker than
rest of body*

*Small, erect,
V-shaped ears*

*Long facial hair (topknot)
tied back with ribbon*

*Dark eyes have
intelligent, alert
expression*

*Fine, silky, dark
steel-blue coat*

*Black
nose*

Level back

*Long coat parted
in centre from
nose to end of tail
for show purposes*

*Rich, bright
tan facial
and chest hair*

YORKSHIRE TERRIER

THIS DOG'S CUTE LOOKS AND DIMINUTIVE SIZE BELIE A FEISTY TEMPERAMENT

KC

Height range
20–23cm (8–9in)

Weight range
Up to 3kg (Up to 7lb)

Life span 12–15 years

Origin UK

Oblivious to its tiny toy stature, the Yorkshire Terrier has the bravery, energy, and confidence that might be expected of a dog several times its size. An intelligent dog, it responds well to obedience training. However, it is inclined to take advantage of owners who let it get away with behaviour that would be unacceptable in a larger dog and can become yappy, snappy, and demanding. With proper handling, this terrier displays its natural character: sweet, affectionate, loyal, and spirited.

The Yorkshire Terrier was developed to catch the rats and mice that infested the woollen mills and mine shafts in the north of England. It was gradually miniaturized through breeding from the smallest individuals, and over time became a fashion accessory that was carried around by its lady owner. However, such pampering is at odds with the Yorkshire Terrier's dynamic nature and it is much happier when allowed to walk for at least half an hour each day. The long,

glossy show coat is wrapped around folded papers and secured with elastic bands to protect it outside the show ring. It is very time-consuming to maintain but the dogs generally love the extra attention.

CLIPPED COAT

Owners who do not intend to show their dogs usually clip the coat short every few months.

Puppy

BIEWER TERRIER

A FRIENDLY DOG WITH A LARGER THAN LIFE PERSONALITY

Height range
18-28cm (7-11in)

Weight range
2-4kg (4-8lb)

Life span 16 years

Origin Germany

Despite its small size, the Biewer Terrier enjoys long walks and is a loyal and entertaining companion. It is a colour variant of the Yorkshire Terrier that first appeared in Germany in 1984 when a blue, white, and gold puppy appeared in a litter produced from a cross between two normally coloured Yorkshire Terriers. Imported to the US in 2003, the dog's popularity increased, and it has become popular in other countries too.

Black lips, nose, and eye rims

Long, silky blue, white and gold coat

Tail has long plume

AUSTRALIAN SILKY TERRIER

THIS AFFECTIONATE AND SOCIABLE BREED NEEDS FIRM LEADERSHIP

KC

Height range
Up to 23cm (Up to 9in)

Weight range
Up to 4kg (Up to 9lb)

Life span 12-15 years

Origin Australia

This attractive dog was produced from crosses between the Yorkshire Terrier (see p.192) and the Australian Terrier (see opposite) in the late 19th century. A typical terrier, the Australian Silky Terrier has a fondness for digging holes, and its instinct to chase may put other small pets at risk. Regular grooming is needed to keep this dog's long coat tangle-free.

Lighter-coloured topknot falls over eyes

Long, silky, grey-blue and tan coat

V-shaped, erect ears

Upturned, high-set tail

Hair parts down centre of back

Small, cat-like feet hidden by long, tan hair

AUSTRALIAN TERRIER
THIS JOYFUL DOG IS GOOD WITH FAMILIES BUT BARKS AT STRANGERS

KC

Height range
Up to 26cm (Up to 10in)

Weight range
Up to 7kg (Up to 15lb)

Life span 15 years

Origin Australia

Other colours

Blue with tan

This terrier is likely to have been the result of crosses between various terriers, including the Cairn Terrier (see p.189), the Yorkshire Terrier (see p.192), and the Dandie Dinmont Terrier (see p.217), which were brought to Australia by British settlers in the 19th century. Diminutive yet spirited, the "Aussie" is an excellent house dog but is best exercised on a lead because of a strong instinct to chase.

Hair forms soft topknot on top of head

Distinct stop

Shorter hair on muzzle

Straight back

Erect ears

Harsh, straight, dense, red coat

Shorter hair on lower legs

Slight feathering on forelegs

PARSON RUSSELL TERRIER
THIS ENERGETIC DOG, WITH A STRONG HUNTING INSTINCT, NEEDS FIRM HANDLING

KC

Height range
33-36cm (13-14in)

Weight range
6-8kg (13-18lb)

Life span 15 years

Origin UK

Other colours

White

May have black markings.

Created in England in the 19th century by the Reverend John Russell, this long-legged strain of the Jack Russell Terrier (see also p.196) is intelligent, high-spirited, and restless, and needs a loving home where fun is a priority. Behavioural problems, such as excessive barking or snappiness, may occur if it is under-exercised or left alone for long periods. There are smooth-haired and rough-haired varieties; both have a harsh texture.

Eyebrows of longer hairs

High-set, white tail with tan base

V-shaped, button ears

Tan markings mostly occur on head

Short, rough, white coat

Fairly deep-set, dark eyes

Longer legs than Jack Russell Terrier

Rough-haired

JACK RUSSELL TERRIER
THIS ACTIVE DOG IS A FEISTY BUNDLE OF ENERGY

KC

Height range
25–30cm (10–12in)

Weight range
5–6kg (11–13lb)

Life span 13–14 years

Origin UK

Other colours

White with
black

Bouncy and bold, this working terrier is named after the Reverend John Russell, who bred them in the 1800s to flush out foxes. Today, this breed makes an excellent rat-catcher and an affectionate and exuberant companion. It has shorter legs than its more squarely built cousin, the Parson Russell Terrier (see p.195). There are two coat types: smooth-haired and wire-haired.

Flat top to head

Tail upright
when active

Body length exceeds
leg length

Black nose

Small, dark,
expressive eyes

Smooth-haired

Black lips

White coat
with black
and tan
markings

Predominantly
white coat with
tan markings

Wire-haired

Round feet

GLEN OF IMAAL TERRIER
A RUTHLESS AND BRAVE HUNTER, THIS TERRIER IS GENTLE AND LOYAL WITH THE FAMILY

KC

Height range
36cm (14in)

Weight range
16–17kg (35–37lb)

Life span 13–14 years

Origin Ireland

Other colours

Blue   Brindle

This sturdy little dog is more active than its size suggests. It comes from County Wicklow and was used in badger trials until these events were banned in the late 1960s. Now the Glen of Imaal Terrier makes a sensitive, devoted pet as long as it has a calm and firm owner.

Broad, slightly
domed head with
well-developed stop

Harsh, medium-length,
wheaten coat has
soft undercoat

Shorter-haired,
small, semi-
erect ears

Round,
brown eyes

Short legs

Strong,
compact feet

NORWICH TERRIER

A PLUCKY AND FRIENDLY FAMILY PET WITH AN ENDEARING PERSONALITY

KC

Height range
25–26cm (10in)

Weight range
5–6kg (10–12lb)

Life span 12–15 years

Origin UK

Other colours

Wheaten   Red

Red coats may be interspersed with black hairs (grizzled).

One of the smallest working terriers, the Norwich Terrier, like its cousin the Norfolk Terrier (see p.191), strikes a happy balance between courage and gentleness. With its easy-going nature, it is good with children but will bark at strangers. Like all ratting terriers, it is playful and loves to chase.

Erect ears differentiate the Norwich Terrier from the Norfolk Terrier (see p.191)

Dark, bright, oval-shaped eyes

Short, compact back with black shading

Long, coarse hair on neck creates ruff around face

Tan coat

Short, straight, strong forelegs

Rounded, cat-like feet

BOSTON TERRIER

A HIGHLY INTELLIGENT, DETERMINED, FRIENDLY, AND ALERT COMPANION DOG

KC

Height range
38–43cm (15–17in)

Weight range
5–11kg (11–24lb)

Life span 13 years

Origin USA

Other colours

Brindle

Brindle coats have white markings.

Dubbed "the American Gentleman" for its quirky yet dapper looks and docile nature, the Boston Terrier makes a good house pet for town or country. This mix of bulldog and several terrier types has lost its ratting instincts and enjoys human company. It has a boisterous streak and needs regular exercise.

Square head with flat top

Erect, pointed ears

Short muzzle with black nose

Low-set, naturally short tail

Wide-set, round, dark eyes

Black coat with white markings

Small, round, compact feet

BULL TERRIER

A FORMIDABLE-LOOKING DOG, BUT KIND AND WELL BEHAVED WITH THE RIGHT OWNER

KC

Height range
53-56cm (21-22in)

Weight range
23-32kg (51-71lb)

Life span 10-12 years

Origin UK

Other colours

Variety of colours

Largely the result of cross-breeding between the Bulldog (see p.94) and terriers of various types, the Bull Terrier was developed for pit-fighting in 19th-century England. A failure at vicious sports, this dog achieved greater success as a pet. The modern breed is normally good-natured and does well with a firm owner.

Thin, close-set, erect ears

Narrow, dark eyes

White tip to tail

Distinctive, long, oval head

Convex profile

Hind legs short from hock to foot

Wide chest

Brindle coat with white markings

MINIATURE BULL TERRIER

THIS SMALL AND STRONG DOG LOVES FUN AND BOISTEROUS GAMES

KC

Height range
Up to 36cm (Up to 14in)

Weight range
11-15kg (24-33lb)

Life span 10-12 years

Origin UK

Other colours

Variety of colours

This scaled-down version of the Bull Terrier (above) had almost disappeared by the 1920s. The breed was revived in the following decades, though it is still uncommon. Like its larger relative, the Miniature Bull Terrier needs early training and socializing to ensure it is a good family pet.

Typical oval head

Incomplete white collar

Short, harsh, glossy, black coat

White blaze on forehead

Round feet

AIREDALE TERRIER

KC

Height range
56–61cm (22–24in)

Weight range
18–29kg (40–64lb)

Life span 10–12 years

Origin UK

Justly known as the "King of Terriers", the Airedale Terrier is big, square, and strong. Originating in the valley of the Aire River in Yorkshire, this breed was first developed in the mid-19th century by local hunters who wanted a robust terrier for catching vermin and larger game such as otters. The breed's subsequent uses have included guarding and military work, but it is also a popular companion. Friendly, intelligent, and full of character, this dog, like many terriers, loves the thrill of the chase and can get up to mischief when bored.

Long, flat head

Wiry, wavy, rich tan coat

Tail carried high when alert

Drop ears

Bearded muzzle

Level back

Dark grizzle saddle

RUSSIAN BLACK TERRIER

THIS BIG, TOUGH, AND VERY PROTECTIVE DOG IS USUALLY FRIENDLY AND MANAGEABLE

KC

Height range
66-77cm (26-30in)

Weight range
38-65kg (83-143lb)

Life span 10-14 years

Origin Russia

First developed in the 1940s, this massively built and hardy terrier was the special creation of the Soviet Army in the former USSR. The breeders' aim was to produce a large dog suitable for military work and able to withstand the severe cold of Russian winters. Among many breeds used in its development were the Giant Schnauzer (see p.41), the Rottweiler (see p.81), and the Airedale Terrier (see p.199). Still relatively uncommon, the Russian Black Terrier is becoming more widely recognized outside its native land. Formidable in size and appearance, the breed is not naturally aggressive and with responsible handling is a friendly and well-adjusted house dog.

Dense beard and whiskers on muzzle

High-set tail, may curve over back

Large, compact feet covered with hair

Drop ears with shorter hair

Wavy, black coat

Long thighs

Square, muscular body

IRISH TERRIER

THIS TERRIER IS WELL-MANNERED IN THE HOUSE BUT NEEDS FIRM CONTROL AROUND OTHER DOGS

KC

Height range
46–48cm (18–19in)

Weight range
11–12kg (24–26lb)

Life span 12–15 years

Origin Ireland

Other colours

Wheaten

This handsome breed emerged in County Cork in Ireland and is believed to have a long history, though its earliest ancestry is unknown. The Irish Terrier has a delightful temperament and can be trusted with children, but outside the home it is inclined to be belligerent towards other dogs.

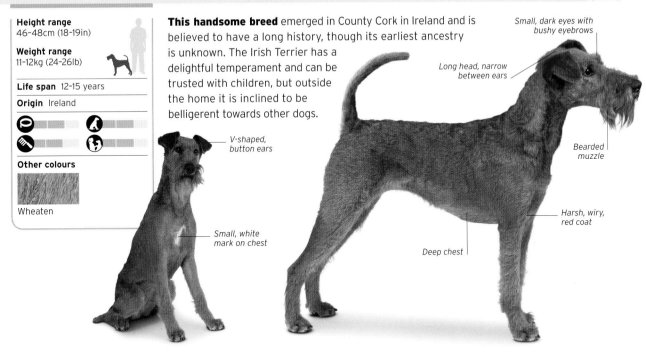

Small, dark eyes with bushy eyebrows

Long head, narrow between ears

V-shaped, button ears

Bearded muzzle

Small, white mark on chest

Harsh, wiry, red coat

Deep chest

WELSH TERRIER

THIS SMART, NEAT DOG IS HIGH-SPIRITED BUT EASY TO TRAIN

KC

Height range
Up to 39cm (up to 15in)

Weight range
9–10kg (20–22lb)

Life span 9–15 years

Origin UK

Other colours

Black grizzle and tan

Once used in packs for hunting foxes, badgers, and otters, the Welsh Terrier was recognized as a breed in the 1880s, and this medium-sized terrier has gained attention as a show dog. Although lively and energetic, the Welsh Terrier is easier to manage than many other terriers and is a good house dog.

Small, dark eyes

High-set, small, button ears

Tail held upright

Wiry, black and tan coat

Head flat between ears

Square, compact body

Small, round, cat-like feet

Long thighs

GERMAN HUNTING TERRIER
THIS TIRELESS, FEARLESS, INDEPENDENT DOG ENJOYS A WORKING LIFE

FCI

Height range
33–40cm (13–16in)

Weight range
8–10kg (18–22lb)

Life span 13–15 years

Origin Germany

This classic hunter is the result of Welsh and English terriers being crossed by four Bavarian dog breeders. The German Hunting Terrier is happy to sleep outdoors by night and hunt all day, above or below ground and across all types of terrain, and even water. It needs plenty of exercise and clear leadership. There are two coat types – rough-coated and smooth-coated.

Small, oval, dark eyes

Straight, long back

Strong neck

Tan markings on chest

Rough, wiry, black and tan coat

Rough-coated

Forefeet often broader than hind feet

Triangular, button ears

Smooth-coated

KERRY BLUE TERRIER
A LIVELY, PLAYFUL, AND BOISTEROUS DOG WITH A BIG HEART

KC

Height range
46–48cm (18–19in)

Weight range
15–17kg (33–37lb)

Life span 14 years

Origin Ireland

The national dog of Ireland is born black, but its coat colour gradually changes to blue before the age of two. A versatile farm and guard dog, the Kerry Blue Terrier is intelligent and makes an affectionate and biddable pet as long as it is well trained and handled firmly.

Long, lean head

Dark eyes with keen expression

Beard covers strong jaw and black nose

Blue coat

Neck runs into sloping shoulders

Soft, wavy, luxuriant coat

Deep chest

SOFT-COATED WHEATEN TERRIER

THIS HAPPY-GO-LUCKY, AFFECTIONATE DOG MAKES A FAITHFUL FAMILY FRIEND

KC

Height range
46–49cm (18–19in)

Weight range
16–21kg (35–46lb)

Life span 13–14 years

Origin Ireland

Similar to the other Irish terrier breeds, the Soft-coated Wheaten Terrier is probably one of the oldest Irish breeds. It has been used as a ratter and a guard dog, and for herding livestock. The breed has a puppy-like temperament even into adulthood, so although good with children, it can be too boisterous with toddlers. A highly intelligent dog, the Soft-coated Wheaten Terrier responds well to training.

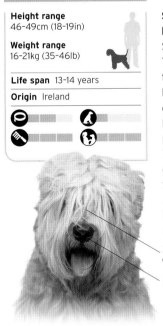

Topknot falls over eyes

Large, black nose

Dark hazel eyes

Tail held up high

Triangular ears

Darker shade gradually fades as dog matures

Longer hair on muzzle forms beard

Soft, silky, wheaten coat forms loose waves

Black toenails

DUTCH SMOUSHOND

AN EASY TO LOOK AFTER, ADAPTABLE, INTELLIGENT, AND COMPANIONABLE DOG

FCI

Height range
35–42cm (14–17in)

Weight range
9–10kg (20–22lb)

Life span 12–15 years

Origin The Netherlands

This former "coachman's dog" is strong enough to follow a horse and carriage and is also a keen rat-catcher. During the 1970s this breed almost became extinct; it is still rare but is now regaining popularity. This dog makes a good watchdog, gets on well with children, and will even accept the family cat. It needs plenty of exercise.

Forelock falls forward giving a dishevelled appearance

Darker drop ears covered in shorter hair

Thin, black-rimmed lips

Unkempt, coarse, wiry, yellow coat, with weatherproof undercoat

Legs slightly less hairy than body

Cat-like feet with black nails

BEDLINGTON TERRIER

LOOKS DECEIVE IN THIS KEEN, SWIFT, AND TENACIOUS BREED

KC

Height range
40-43cm (16-17in)

Weight range
8-10kg (18-22lb)

Life span 14-15 years

Origin UK

Other colours

Sandy   Liver

All colours may have tan markings.

The typical terrier spirit lies beneath the sheep-like coat of the Bedlington Terrier. It was bred from the Whippet (see p.128) and other terriers to hunt hare and rabbits above ground. Its sight hound blood has given it not only great speed but a more tolerant temper than some terriers, and it is now kept as a companion. The Bedlington Terrier needs to be sufficiently occupied to avoid behavioural problems developing. If given enough activity, it is an affectionate and dynamic companion. It has a unique show clip.

Show clip leaves tassels on ear tips

Thin, velvety, drop ears

Relatively small eyes

Hair left longer on head

Black nose

Arched, flexible back

Non-shedding, thick, blue coat

Deep chest

Hind legs appear longer than forelegs

BORDER TERRIER

AN ENERGETIC AND CHEERFUL TERRIER WITH A RELAXED PERSONALITY

KC

Height range
25-28cm (10-11in)

Weight range
5-7kg (11-15lb)

Life span 13-14 years

Origin UK

Other colours

Wheaten

Blue and tan

Originally used for hunting foxes and rats, the Border Terrier still excels in trials but is also a highly popular pet. Its temperament, which is unusually cooperative for a terrier, makes it more tolerant of small children and other dogs. The protective wiry coat is easily stripped in summer.

High-set, drop ears

Short, strong muzzle

Dense, grizzled coat has thick undercoat

Short, thick tail

Tan hair on legs

Red coat

LAKELAND TERRIER

THIS ROBUST AND CHEERFUL DOG IS BEST SUITED TO AN EXPERIENCED OWNER

KC

Height range
33-37cm (13-15in)

Weight range
7-8kg (15-18lb)

Life span 13-14 years

Origin UK

Other colours

Variety of colours

This determined, agile little terrier was bred to chase foxes over hilly terrain and into their burrows, and it retains the tendency to chase anything that moves - regardless of size - and to be aggressive with other dogs. With training, it makes a fearless guard dog and an enthusiastic companion.

Small, V-shaped, button ears carried alertly

Long thighs

Tail carried high but not curled

Back strong and moderately short

Broad, strong muzzle hidden by beard

Wiry, wheaten coat

Tail carried erect

Tan markings on face

Very slight stop

Head and muzzle of equal length

Small, V-shaped, semi-erect ears

Wiry, tricolour coat with white predominant

Dark, circular eyes

Black nose

Chest deep but not broad

Black patch on back

Long, powerful thighs

Round, compact feet

FOX TERRIER

THIS CHEERFUL, FRIENDLY DOG IS GOOD WITH CHILDREN AND ENJOYS LONG WALKS
KC

Height range
Up to 39cm (Up to 15in)

Weight range
Up to 8kg (Up to 18lb)

Life span 10 years

Origin UK

Other colours

White

May have tan or black markings.

An energetic and sometimes vocal
companion, the Fox Terrier from England
was originally kept to kill vermin, hunt rabbit,
and tackle foxes that had been run to ground.
Its bold and fearless nature and love of
digging make early socialization and
training essential to prevent snappiness
and curb any tendency to dig. If this is
done, the Fox Terrier makes a wonderful
family pet that loves to play and readily
reciprocates any affection it receives.

The Wire Fox Terrier's coat needs regular
grooming and "plucking" to remove any
shed hair, and more extensive stripping three
or four times a year. The coat should never
be clipped because this does not remove
shed hair and may cause irritation, and also
leads to deterioration in coat texture and
colour. The Fox Terrier is ancestral to several
other dog breeds, including the Parson
Russell Terrier (see p.195), the Jack Russell
Terrier (see p.196), the Toy Fox Terrier (see
p.208), the Brazilian Terrier (see p.209), and
the Rat Terrier (see p.211).

SMOOTH FOX TERRIER

Much rarer than its wire-haired cousin, the
Smooth Fox Terrier's shorter coat requires less
grooming. This dog's close-fitting coat clearly
shows its very distinctive wedge-shaped head.

JAPANESE TERRIER

AN ELEGANT AND LIVELY LITTLE DOG WITH A SENSITIVE AND PLAYFUL NATURE

FCI

Height range
30-33cm (12-13in)

Weight range
2-4kg (5-9lb)

Life span 12-14 years

Origin Japan

Other colours

Black, tan, and white

Also known as the Nippon or Nihon Terrier, this rare breed is strong and athletic for its size. Its ancestors are thought to include the English Toy Terrier (see p.210) and the now extinct Toy Bull Terrier. The Japanese Terrier has been kept as a lapdog, ratter, and retriever, and makes an adaptable family pet as well as a good watchdog.

Pronounced stop

High-set, button ears

Strong, slightly arched back

Short, smooth, glossy, white coat, with black markings

Dark, oval-shaped eyes

Typical black markings on head

Small, black nose

Black spots on legs

TOY FOX TERRIER

THIS SMALL DOG IS FUN-LOVING AND BRAVE, BUT CAN BE BOSSY

AKC

Height range
23-30cm (9-12in)

Weight range
2-3kg (5-7lb)

Life span 13-14 years

Origin USA

Other colours

White and tan

White and black

White, chocolate, and tan

Also called the American Toy Terrier, this breed is a cross between the Smooth Fox Terrier (see p.206) and various toy breeds. The result is a dog that is a good ratter but also family-friendly. As with all toy breeds, the Toy Fox Terrier is not recommended as a pet in a home where there are babies and toddlers, but older children will enjoy its zest for life.

Face predominately black with tan markings

Docked tail held upright

Bright, dark, round eyes

Erect, pointed ears

Black patch

Tan markings on cheek

Fine-haired, satin-like, white coat

BRAZILIAN TERRIER

WITH A STRONG TERRIER TEMPERAMENT, THIS FRISKY, SPIRITED DOG IS QUICK TO LEARN

FCI

Height range
33-40cm (13-16in)

Weight range
7-10kg (15-22lb)

Life span 12-14 years

Origin Brazil

Bred from European terriers crossed with local Brazilian farm dogs, this breed has marked hunting instincts and is eager to explore and dig as well as track, chase, and kill rodents. Like its smaller cousin, the Jack Russell Terrier (see p.196), the Brazilian Terrier needs to know who is boss. It rewards a firm owner with devotion and obedience and makes a protective - and vocal - watchdog. Ever active, it thrives on a long, daily walk to keep it mentally and physically stimulated, otherwise it becomes restless. When well trained, the Brazilian Terrier makes an excellent family pet.

Alert expression

Croup slopes to tail

Typical tan markings on head

Black marking

Short, smooth, predominately white coat

Triangular, drop ears

Low-set, short tail

Deep chest

ENGLISH TOY TERRIER

A PERKY, FRIENDLY, AND CONFIDENT LITTLE COMPANION DOG

KC

Height range 25–30cm (10–12in)	
Weight range 3–4kg (7–9lb)	
Life span 12–13 years	
Origin UK	

The oldest British toy breed, the English Toy Terrier used to be called the Miniature Black and Tan Terrier. It differs from its larger cousin, the Manchester Terrier (opposite), only in its size and its erect ears. English Toy Terriers were popular as town pets during Queen Victoria's reign, when toy dogs became fashionable. Before that it was a rat-catcher. Like other terriers, this breed veers from cuddly family pet to voracious rodent-hunter. It bonds with its owner and makes a good watchdog. Because it is small, the English Toy Terrier needs less exercise than the Manchester Terrier and adapts well to city living.

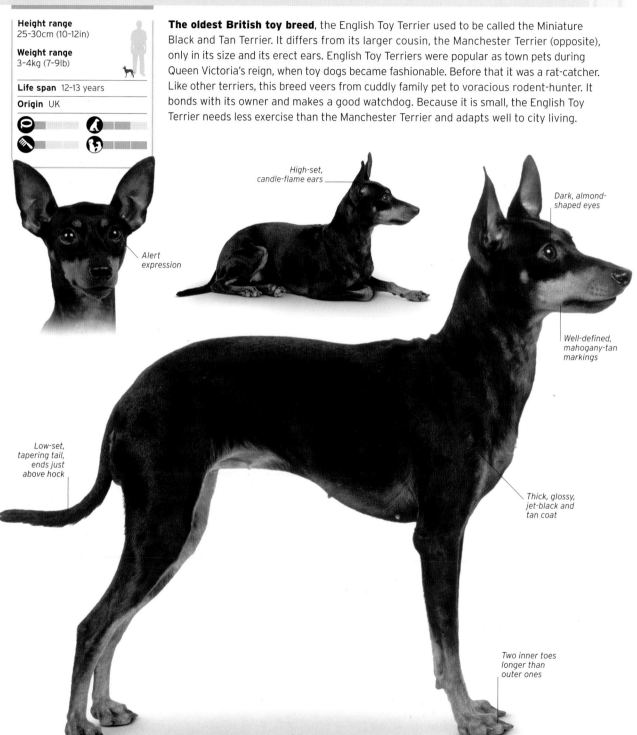

Alert expression

High-set, candle-flame ears

Dark, almond-shaped eyes

Well-defined, mahogany-tan markings

Low-set, tapering tail, ends just above hock

Thick, glossy, jet-black and tan coat

Two inner toes longer than outer ones

MANCHESTER TERRIER

THIS DEVOTED FAMILY PET ADAPTS WELL TO TOWN OR COUNTRY LIFE

KC

Height range
38-41cm (15-16in)

Weight range
5-10kg (11-22lb)

Life span 13-14 years

Origin UK

With its sleek good looks, the Manchester Terrier makes an elegant and lively companion dog, bigger than the related English Toy Terrier (opposite). It takes its name from the weekly rat-killing contests in Manchester that occurred in the 19th century and at which it excelled. Ruthless with vermin, it is gentle with its owners.

Slightly rounded back

Small, V-shaped, button ears

Black nose

Short tail carried low

Smooth, short, glossy, black and tan coat

Well-arched, compact forefeet

Tan markings on legs

RAT TERRIER

AN ENERGY-CHARGED BUNDLE OF FUN FOR HUMANS BUT A TERROR FOR VERMIN

AKC

Height range
Miniature:
25-32cm (10-13in)
Standard:
33-46cm (13-18in)

Weight range
Miniature:
3-4kg (7-9lb)
Standard:
5-16kg (11-35lb)

Life span 11-14 years

Origin USA

Other colours

Variety of colours

Tan markings are common.

This terrier is a phenomenal rat-catcher - one dog is reputed to have rid a barn infested with over 2,500 rats in just seven hours. Popular in the United States, the Rat Terrier was President Theodore Roosevelt's choice of hunting dog. The Miniature makes a good pet; the Standard suits an energetic owner. There are two ear types: erect and button.

Pear-shaped head

Black coat

Erect ears

Inquisitive, alert expression

Sturdy, compact body with tan parts

Standard

White feet

AMERICAN HAIRLESS TERRIER

THIS DISTINCTIVE-LOOKING DOG, WITH TERRIER TRAITS, IS ALERT AND FRIENDLY

AKC

Height range
30-41cm (12-16in)

Weight range
5-7kg (12-15lb)

Life span 12-13 years

Origin USA

Other colours

Any skin colour

The first hairless Rat Terriers (see p.211) were the result of a genetic mutation, but were then bred with each other to produce hairless puppies. Apart from its lack of hair, this is a typical, lively terrier. It needs a coat in winter to stay warm and to avoid sunburn in summer. Ears may be erect, semi-erect, or button.

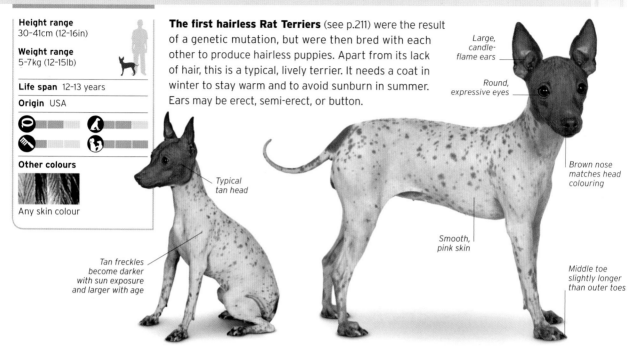

Large, candle-flame ears

Round, expressive eyes

Brown nose matches head colouring

Typical tan head

Smooth, pink skin

Middle toe slightly longer than outer toes

Tan freckles become darker with sun exposure and larger with age

PATTERDALE TERRIER

THIS INDEPENDENT AND TENACIOUS HUNTER-DIGGER NEEDS AN EXPERIENCED OWNER

Height range
25-38cm (10-15in)

Weight range
5-6kg (11-13lb)

Life span 13-14 years

Origin UK

Other colours

Red

Liver or bronze

Black and tan

Coats may be grizzled.

The isolated valleys of the Lake District each had their own terrier – this one originates from the village of Patterdale. It remains popular in the UK but has gained favour in the United States too. It makes an excellent hunting companion as it never gives up on its prey. There are two coat types: smooth and broken.

Eyes set wide apart

High-set, triangular, drop ears

High-set tail

Head reflects its Staffordshire Bull Terrier bloodlines (see p.214)

Coarse, black topcoat

Smooth-coated

KROMFOHRLANDER
THIS EVEN-TEMPERED, LOVABLE TERRIER IS GOOD WITH THE ENTIRE FAMILY

FCI

Height range
38–46cm (15–18in)

Weight range
9–16kg (20–35lb)

Life span 13–14 years

Origin Germany

A recent German breed, only recognized since the 1950s, this dog takes its name from its place of origin in Germany. It was bred from a Wire Fox Terrier (see p.206) and a locally owned dog. The result is a kindly, attractive, low-maintenance, eager-to-please dog, which makes a good watchdog and, like other terriers, is a keen ratter. While wary of strangers, it is gentle and playful with familiar people and dogs. There are two coat types: rough-haired and smooth-haired.

Triangular, drop ears

Thick coat lying close to body

Rough-haired

Oval, brown eyes

White blaze with tan speckles

Typical, symmetrical head markings

Gently sloping stop

Irregular-shaped tan markings

White coat

Feathering on upper thighs

Tan speckling on legs

Forefeet and hind feet similar in shape

Smooth-haired

STAFFORDSHIRE BULL TERRIER

THIS FEARLESS DOG LOVES CHILDREN AND CAN ACHIEVE HIGH LEVELS OF OBEDIENCE

KC

Height range
36–41cm (14–16in)

Weight range
11–17kg (24–37lb)

Life span 10–16 years

Origin UK

Other colours

Variety of colours

Originally bred for pit-fighting in the 19th century, the Staffordshire Bull Terrier was developed from crosses between bulldogs and terriers. The modern "Staffie", as it is often affectionately known, has moved on from its historical background to become a people-loving pet, enormously popular in both town and country. This dog is robust, boisterous, and possesses legendary courage. A Staffordshire Bull Terrier is unlikely to back down if challenged by an unfamiliar dog. Firm handling and early obedience training are essential.

Small, semi-erect ears

Broad head with distinct stop

Dark rims to eyes

Broad chest with white marking

Feet turn out slightly from pasterns

Almost straight, tapering tail

Darker hair on muzzle

Strong neck

Smooth, short, red coat

Powerful, muscular body

White markings on feet

AMERICAN STAFFORDSHIRE TERRIER

A LARGER VERSION OF THE ENGLISH STAFFIE, THIS IS A COURAGEOUS AND COMPANIONABLE DOG

FCI

Height range
43-48cm (17-19in)

Weight range
26-30kg (57-66lb)

Life span 10-16 years

Origin USA

Other colours

Variety of colours

Developed from the Staffordshire Bull Terrier (opposite), this dog was recognized as a separate breed in the United States in the 1930s. Apart from being more heavily built than its English counterpart, the American Staffordshire Terrier shares all the characteristics of the original "Staffie". It is bold and intelligent and makes a loyal family pet.

Very prominent cheek muscles

Powerful, muscular thighs

Dark eyes set low and wide apart

Broad, deep chest

Short, stiff, shiny, blue-fawn coat

Heavy neck, slightly arched

Moderately sized, compact feet

White feet

AMERICAN PIT BULL TERRIER

NOT RECOMMENDED FOR MOST OWNERS, THIS DOG NEEDS SKILLED HANDLING

Height range
46-56cm (18-22in)

Weight range
14-27kg (31-60lb)

Life span 12 years

Origin USA

Other colours

Any colour

Merle colours discouraged.

The ancestors of the American Pit Bull Terrier were dogs brought to the United States in the 19th century by Irish immigrants. Although bred for fighting, this dog became much loved as a working or family dog. The breed has lately acquired a reputation for aggression, which is vigorously refuted by its supporters.

High-set, semi-erect ears

Distinctive wrinkles on forehead

Muscular, heavy neck

Tapering tail

Short, dense, glossy, red coat

Body stockily built, muscular, and agile

Deep, moderately wide chest, with small, white markings

SKYE TERRIER
FULL OF CHARACTER, THIS DOG OFTEN BECOMES DEVOTED TO ONE PERSON

KC

Height range
25-26cm (up to 10in)

Weight range
11-18kg (24-40lb)

Life span 12-15 years

Origin UK

Other colours

Cream

Black

May have white spot on chest.

A very old breed from the Western Isles of Scotland, the Skye Terrier was originally used for fox- and badger-hunting. With a long, low-slung body, the Skye Terrier could easily slip into the narrow underground passages used by its quarry. This elegant little dog is active and good-spirited, and makes an excellent pet, becoming devoted to family and home. The long coat that is characteristic of the breed can take several years to grow to its full adult length. To prevent the hair from matting, a Skye Terrier needs a weekly grooming session.

Erect ears, fringed with long, silky hair

Soft, light grey hair covers brown eyes

Darker hair on face

Black nose

Silky, fawn coat

Adult and two puppies

Hair on ears darker than body hair

Body much longer than leg length

Long, straight, grey coat parts down centre of back

Lighter patches on coat

Long, feathered tail

DANDIE DINMONT TERRIER

THIS LOVEABLE AND AFFECTIONATE DOG IS GOOD WITH OTHER PETS IF SOCIALIZED EARLY

KC

Height range
20–28cm (8–11in)

Weight range
8–11kg (18–24lb)

Life span Up to 13 years

Origin UK

Other colours

Mustard

May have white chest hair.

This terrier comes from the border country between England and Scotland, where it was developed to hunt badger and otter. It was named the Dandie Dinmont Terrier after a character who owned a similar-looking dog in a novel by Sir Walter Scott. Game, sensitive, and intelligent, the Dandie Dinmont Terrier thrives on love and attention.

Large, wide-set, dark hazel eyes

Large, domed head covered in soft, silky, light-coloured hair

Body length greatly exceeds leg length

Pendant ears set well back

Long, tapering tail with feathering on underside

Lighter-coloured lower legs

Pepper coat of dark bluish-black hair

MINIATURE PINSCHER

THIS DOG IS HAPPY TO LIVE IN A SMALL SPACE BUT NEEDS REGULAR EXERCISE

KC

Height range
25–30cm (10–12in)

Weight range
4–5kg (9–11lb)

Life span Up to 15 years

Origin Germany

Other colours

Blue and tan   Brown and tan

Bred in Germany and developed from the much larger German Pinscher (see p.218), this sturdy but graceful dog was once used as a farmyard rat-hunter. The Miniature Pinscher is quick and lively, moving with a characteristic high-stepping, hackney gait. Perfect for a small home, the breed has sharp senses that make it a good watchdog.

Tapering muzzle

Neck arches slightly

Tail carried high

Straight back

High-set, erect ears

Well-defined tan markings

Short, smooth, black and tan coat

Cat-like feet

GERMAN PINSCHER

A GREAT COMPANION AND WATCHDOG FOR A FIRM OWNER

KC

Height range
43-48cm (17-19in)

Weight range
11-16kg (24-35lb)

Life span 12-14 years

Origin Germany

Other colours

Isabella   Blue

Also known as the Standard Pinscher, this tall terrier started out as a general-purpose farm dog. It makes a protective guard dog, but needs to be well trained so that it does not become overprotective, bark for too long, or behave aggressively towards other dogs. With the right training, it is gentle and responsive.

Dark, oval eyes

Tail sweeps
upwards

Triangular,
drop ears

Short, sleek, thick,
stag-red coat

Short,
round feet

MINIATURE SCHNAUZER

THIS CHEERFUL, FRIENDLY, FUN-LOVING DOG IS RELIABLE WITH ALL THE FAMILY

KC

Height range
33-36cm (13-14in)

Weight range
6-7kg (13-15lb)

Life span 14 years

Origin Germany

Other colours

White   Black

Black and silver

Popular in North America, as well as in its native Germany, the Miniature Schnauzer is named for its distinctive muzzle (*schnauze* means snout in German). An intelligent little dog, it responds well to obedience training. Despite its small size, it is energetic and needs play off the lead as well as a brisk daily walk to keep it healthy and happy.

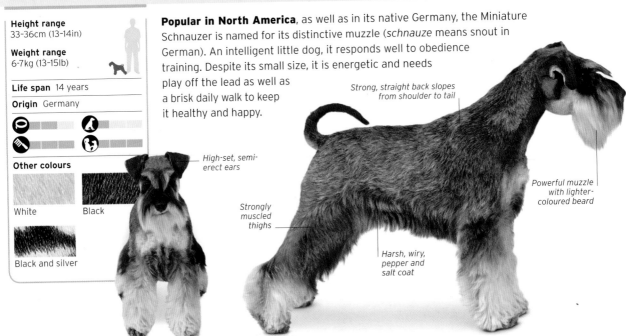

Strong, straight back slopes
from shoulder to tail

High-set, semi-
erect ears

Powerful muzzle
with lighter-
coloured beard

Strongly
muscled
thighs

Harsh, wiry,
pepper and
salt coat

AUSTRIAN PINSCHER

THIS ALERT AND FAITHFUL WATCHDOG IS SUITABLE FOR A RURAL OWNER

FCI

Height range
42–50cm (17–20in)

Weight range
12–18kg (26–40lb)

Life span 12–14 years

Origin Austria

Other colours

Russet gold or brownish yellow

Black and tan

Bred as an all-purpose guard and herding farm dog in its native Austria, this breed rewards a confident owner with complete loyalty and devotion. Barking at anything suspicious, it makes an excellent watchdog for isolated locations, but its protective instincts and fearlessness can lead to aggression.

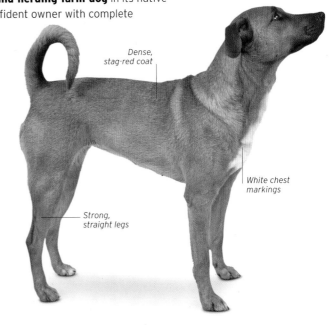

Dense, stag-red coat

White chest markings

Strong, straight legs

Triangular, drop ears

Darker-coloured muzzle

AFFENPINSCHER

THIS MISCHIEVOUS, MONKEY-LIKE LITTLE DOG CAPTIVATES WITH ITS AMUSING ANTICS

KC

Height range
24–28cm (9–11in)

Weight range
3–4kg (7–9lb)

Life span 10–12 years

Origin Germany

Sometimes called the Black Devil, the Affenpinscher is among the oldest of the European toy dogs. It retains its terrier instincts though, and is a brave watchdog and ratter despite its size. With its bright, sometimes stubborn personality, this dog learns easily but needs to know who is boss. It loves to play and gets on well with children who handle it considerately.

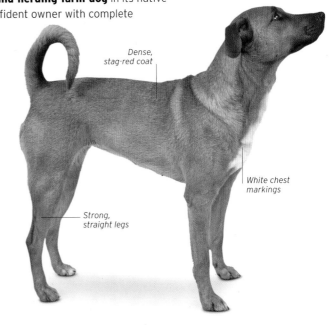

Domed, broad forehead

Black coat

Lighter, greyish beard

Straight forelegs

Blunt muzzle with wide nostrils

Small, round, dark feet

SOFT MOUTH
Gundogs used for retrieving, like this dual-purpose English Springer Spaniel, are trained to carry game without crushing it.

GUNDOGS

Before the advent of firearms, hunters used dogs to help them locate and chase game. With the introduction of guns, a different type of dog was required. Gundogs were developed to carry out specific tasks and to work more closely with the hunters. The breeds fall into several categories based on the type of work they were bred to perform.

The Lagotto Romagnolo is bred for retrieving from water

The dogs in the gundog group, which hunt by scent, are classified broadly in three main divisions: the pointers and setters, which locate prey; the spaniels, which flush game out of cover; and the retrievers, which collect fallen prey and bring it back to the hunter. Breeds that combine these functions are known as HPR (hunt/point/retrieve) dogs and include the Weimaraner, German Pointer, and the Hungarian Vizsla.

Pointers have been used as hunting dogs since the 17th century. They have the extraordinary ability to indicate the location of prey by "pointing" – freezing into position with nose, body, and tail aligned. A pointer remains motionless until the hunter either flushes out the game or instructs the dog to do so. The English Pointer, which features in many old sporting portraits alongside hunting squires and their "bags" of game birds, is a classic example of the type.

Setters also direct attention to game by freezing. Typically used to hunt quail, pheasant, and grouse, these dogs crouch, or "set", when they pick up a scent. Originally, setters were trained to work with hunters who caught game with nets while their dogs prevented the prey from making an escape on the ground.

Spaniels drive out, or flush, game birds, forcing them to take wing into the line of the guns. They watch where a bird falls and are usually sent to retrieve it. This division includes small, silky-coated, long-eared dogs, such as the Springer Spaniel and Cocker Spaniel, used for finding game on land, and less familiar breeds, such as the Barbet and the Wetterhoun, which specialize in flushing waterbirds.

The retrievers were bred specifically for retrieving waterfowl. In common with some breeds of the spaniel division, these gundogs often have water-resistant coats. They are renowned for their "soft" mouths, and quickly learn to carry game without damaging it.

VERSATILE VIZSLA
The Hungarian Vizsla is one of various gundog breeds that are skilled at multi-tasking and combine several functions.

FAMILY RETRIEVER
The water-loving Golden Retriever is a popular bird dog that, because of its gentle, calm, and lovable temperament, has also become a firm family favourite.

AMERICAN COCKER SPANIEL

A SMALL GUNDOG WITH A HAPPY DISPOSITION

KC

Height range
34–39cm (13–15in)

Weight range
7–14kg (15–31lb)

Life span 12–15 years

Origin USA

Other colours

Any colour

Known for its sweet, playful nature, the American Cocker Spaniel is suited to life as a pet or a working gundog; the breed has speed and stamina and needs plenty of exercise. It also has a tendency towards shyness, so early and regular socialization is important.

Pronounced stop

Conspicuously rounded head

Sturdy, compact body

Low-set ears, fringed with long, silky hair

Large, round eyes

Red coat with lighter underparts

Long, wavy, jet-black coat

ENGLISH COCKER SPANIEL

THIS GUNDOG IS GENTLE, AFFECTIONATE, AND INTELLIGENT

KC

Height range
38–41cm (15–16in)

Weight range
13–15kg (29–33lb)

Life span 12–15 years

Origin UK

Other colours

Any colour

Solid colours should have no white markings.

Originally known as the "cocking spaniel" and used for flushing woodcock and grouse, the English Cocker Spaniel is one of the most popular spaniel breeds. Smaller than the English Springer Spaniel (see p.226), this dog was developed to work in dense undergrowth. Show dogs are sturdier and heavier than working dogs, but both make excellent pets.

Square muzzle with moderate flews

Black saddle

Ears fringed with long, wavy hair

Feathering on tail

Long, silky, blue-roan coat

Red coat with feathering on chest and legs

GERMAN SPANIEL

THIS GREAT FAMILY DOG IS NOT FOR THE INEXPERIENCED OWNER OR CITY DWELLER

FCI

Height range
44–53cm (17–21in)

Weight range
18–25kg (40–55lb)

Life span 12–14 years

Origin Germany

Other colours

Red

Brown

Red roan

An excellent retriever, this dog loves the water. The German Spaniel has masses of stamina and is happiest working, although long, brisk walks will keep it content. This breed will live outdoors, but thrives indoors with a family, and makes a good working gundog and pet.

Brown saddle

Short, fine, brown coat on head

Medium-brown eyes with kind expression

Lightly feathered, drop ears

Dense, wavy, brown-roan coat

Spoon-shaped feet

FIELD SPANIEL

A HIGH-ENERGY WORKING GUNDOG SUITABLE FOR THE COUNTRY DWELLER

KC

Height range
44–46cm (17–18in)

Weight range
18–25kg (40–55lb)

Life span 10–12 years

Origin UK

Other colours

Black

Roan

May have tan markings.

Originally a cross between the English Cocker Spaniel (opposite) and the Sussex Spaniel (see p.224), the Field Spaniel was used for retrieving from water and heavy cover. This docile but high-energy, medium-sized gundog needs to be kept busy and makes the perfect hunting companion for an active family living in the country.

Moderate stop

Long body relative to leg length

Light feathering on underside of tail

Liver-coloured nose

White mark on chest

Moderately long, liver coat

Feathering on back of legs

BOYKIN SPANIEL

THIS CHEERFUL, ENERGETIC SPANIEL MAKES A LOYAL AND INTELLIGENT COMPANION

AKC

Height range
36–46cm (14–18in)

Weight range
11–18kg (24–40lb)

Life span 14–16 years

Origin USA

Other colours

Liver

May have white hair
on chest and toes.

The official state dog of South Carolina, the Boykin Spaniel is a devoted companion and gets on well with other dogs and children. Its easy-going nature and willingness to work make it an ideal gundog or pet for an active family. The Boykin Spaniel's curly coat requires regular grooming.

Shorter hair
on face

Traditionally
docked tail

Distinctive,
oval, brown
eyes

Curly, dark
chocolate coat

Compact,
round feet

SUSSEX SPANIEL

A KINDLY DOG WITH A FROWNING FACE THAT BELIES AN EASY-GOING, ENTHUSIASTIC NATURE

KC

Height range
38–41cm (15–16in)

Weight range
18–23kg (40–51lb)

Life span 12–15 years

Origin UK

Although active by nature, this English gundog from Sussex will adapt to life in a smaller household provided it is exercised sufficiently. Unlike other gundogs, the Sussex Spaniel will bark, or "give tongue", while working – a trait frowned upon in all other gundog breeds; also distinctive is the rolling action to its gait.

Hazel
eyes under
wrinkled brow

Long, rich,
golden-liver coat

Body length exceeds
leg length

Shorter
hair
on face

Feathering
on chest

Pendant ears
covered with
long, silky hair

Round feet
with feathering
between toes

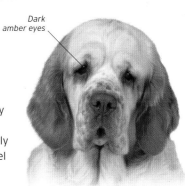

CLUMBER SPANIEL

THIS BIG, GOOD-TEMPERED DOG ENJOYS FAMILY LIFE AND A COUNTRY HOME

KC

Height range
43–51cm (17–20in)

Weight range
25–34kg (55–75lb)

Life span 10–12 years

Origin France

Although its history has been romanticized, this dog is thought to have originated in 18th-century France, where it was favoured by the aristocracy. During the French Revolution Clumber Spaniels may have been brought to England and further developed at Clumber Park in Northumberland, home of the Duke of Newcastle. Muscular and low to the ground, this dog is the most solidly built of all the spaniels. Its calm and steady nature made the breed popular as a gundog but it is now more commonly kept as a pet. Gentle and well behaved, the Clumber Spaniel is easy to train as a companion dog.

Dark amber eyes

Broad head

Wide, deep chest

Broad, deep muzzle with well-defined stop

Large, drop ears

Heavy-boned, firm body, low to the ground

Well-feathered tail

Feathering at throat

Short legs

Long, plain white coat with orange markings

Large, round feet

Pronounced stop

Almond-shaped,
dark hazel eyes
express kind nature

Pendant ears,
set at eye-level

Weather-resistant,
thick, straight, liver
and white coat

Well-feathered
tail, carried below
level of back

Heavily
feathered
chest

Liver
freckling
on legs

Body moderately
feathered all over

Well-rounded,
compact feet

ENGLISH SPRINGER SPANIEL

FULL OF ENTHUSIASM AND AFFECTION, THIS IS A SOCIABLE WORKING OR COMPANION DOG

KC

Height range
46–56cm (18–22in)

Weight range
18–23kg (40–51lb)

Life span 12–14 years

Origin UK

Other colours

Black and
white

May have tan markings.

This classic gundog is so called because it was originally used to "spring" game – startle birds into the air. Spaniels used as gundogs were once classified according to their size: the larger dogs (called Springers, see pp.226–28) were used for flushing game, and the smaller ones (called Cockers, see pp.222–23) for flushing woodcock. Until the beginning of the 20th century the English Springer Spaniel was not recognized as an official breed, although it had developed into a distinct type known as the Norfolk Spaniel.

The English Springer Spaniel will work with hunters in the field all day, undeterred by rough terrain or adverse weather conditions, even jumping into freezing water when necessary. This breed is a popular choice with game shooters but its friendly, biddable disposition makes it an excellent family dog too. It likes company, including children, other dogs, and the household cat. If left alone for too long, it may resort to excessive barking. A non-working dog needs long, energetic daily walks and will enjoy having a stream to splash in, mud to roll in, or toys thrown for it to retrieve. This breed is bright and willing to learn, and will respond to calm authority. It is highly sensitive, so giving harsh or loud commands is likely to be counterproductive.

The English Springer Spaniel's love of the outdoors means that it needs weekly grooming to prevent its thick coat from becoming matted and dirty, and regular trimming, especially of the long feathering on the ears and legs.

There are two types of English Springer Spaniel: working and show. Dogs bred specifically to work in the field tend to have their tails docked and be slightly smaller and of lighter build than dogs produced for showing. Both types make equally good companion dogs.

WELSH SPRINGER SPANIEL

THIS GREAT WORKING DOG LOVES TO BE INCLUDED IN FAMILY ACTIVITIES

KC

Height range
46-48cm (18-19in)

Weight range
16-23kg (35-51lb)

Life span 12-15 years

Origin UK

A close cousin of the English Springer Spaniel (see p.226) and the English Cocker Spaniel (see p.222), this medium-sized Welsh gundog has a jolly disposition and makes a fine family dog and hunting companion. It is inclined to wander, so early and consistent training is imperative.

Finer head than English Springer Spaniel (see p.226)

Low-set, lightly feathered, vine-leaf-shaped ears

Brown nose

Long, muscular neck

Feathering on chest

Feathering above hock

Naturally straight, soft, rich red and white coat

Round, cat-like feet

IRISH WATER SPANIEL

THE CLOWN OF THE SPANIEL FAMILY, THIS DOG NEEDS AN ACTIVE LIFE

KC

Height range
51-58cm (20-23in)

Weight range
20-30kg (44-66lb)

Life span 10-12 years

Origin Ireland

This tireless dog is an ideal companion for hikers. Its dark liver coat is virtually waterproof, and the breed's enthusiasm for plunging into ice-cold water earned it the nickname of "Bogdog". Although gentle and faithful, it is slow to mature and can be headstrong, so needs thorough training when young.

Broad, level back

Nose matches coat colour

Smoother hair on face

Smooth hair on throat forms V-shaped patch

Naturally oily, dense coat

Smooth tail except at base

Puce-liver coat forms dense ringlets

Large, round feet well covered with hair

AMERICAN WATER SPANIEL
THIS DOG IS EAGER TO PLEASE AND EASY TO CARE FOR

KC

Height range
38-45cm (15-18in)

Weight range
12-21kg (26-46lb)

Life span 10-12 years

Origin USA

Other colours

Chocolate

May have a few white hairs on chest and toes.

Originally bred as an all-round hunting and water dog in the Great Lakes region of the United States, the American Water Spaniel's moderate size and lean build allowed it to work from boats as well as on shore. The breed is still used to flush and retrieve waterfowl, but also makes an easy-going companion for an active family. Its dense, curly coat is inherited from ancestors that include the Irish Water Spaniel (opposite) and the Curly Coated Retriever (see p.259). Some dogs have a less tightly curled coat, called the Marcel coat.

Broad head

Ears covered with curly hair

Adult and puppy

Light brown eyes

Tight, liver curls, oily to touch

Smooth hair on face

Moderate feathering along tail

Moderately feathered legs

SPANISH WATER DOG

AN ADAPTABLE WORKING DOG WITH A NO-NONSENSE ATTITUDE

KC

Height range
40–50cm (16–20in)

Weight range
14–22kg (31–49lb)

Life span 10–14 years

Origin Spain

Other colours

White

Black

Brown and white

Black and white

This distinctive breed has had many roles and names in its homeland, where it is now called the Perro de Agua. Merchants from North Africa or Turkey may have brought this type of dog to Andalusia, where it is most likely to be found today. The Spanish Water Dog has been used for herding, hunting, and towing boats in ports. It is a biddable, generally level-headed companion but can be impatient with children. Until the 1980s the breed was known only in southern Spain, and it remains rare today.

Brown nose matches colour of coat

Light chest markings

Tail barely reaches hocks

Back slopes gently down towards tail

Woolly, brown coat forms cords if left unclipped

Legs slightly shorter than body length

Round feet covered in hair

PORTUGUESE WATER DOG

ACTIVE AND INTELLIGENT, THIS DOG NEEDS AN OWNER TO MATCH

KC

Height range
43–57cm (17–22in)

Weight range
16–25kg (35–55lb)

Life span 10–14 years

Origin Portugal

Other colours

White

Brown

Black and white

Brown and white

Black and brown dogs may have white markings.

Although classed as a gundog, this dog was used to retrieve fishermen's nets as often as hunters' game. The breed's adaptability springs from a lively mind and desire to please, but if not kept busy it can be destructive. There are two coat types: long and wavy or short and curly.

Round eyes, set well apart

Curved tail with plume at tip

Forehead has central furrow

Hind quarters clipped for work and showing

Long, wavy, black coat

Round feet

Long and wavy coat

STANDARD POODLE

THIS INTELLIGENT RETRIEVER DOG MAKES AN EASY FAMILY COMPANION

KC

Height range
Over 38cm (Over 15in)

Weight range
21–32kg (46–71lb)

Life span 10–13 years

Origin Germany

Other colours

Any solid colour

Claimed by France but probably from Germany, this breed was originally a water dog, and the standard size remains closest to those roots. It is popular for crossbreeding because it is robust, clever, and good-tempered. A simple all-over clip is easiest to maintain.

Head carried high

Long, wide, pendant ears

Dark, almond-shaped eyes

Strong, well-chiselled face and jaw

Profuse, dense, curly, black coat

Small, oval feet, with arched toes

BARBET
THIS RELAXED, AFFECTIONATE DOG NEEDS DAILY GROOMING

KC

Height range
53–65cm (21–26in)

Weight range
16–27kg (35–60lb)

Life span 12–14 years

Origin France

Other colours

Variety of colours

One of Europe's oldest water dogs, with ancestors dating back to the Middle Ages, the Barbet has contributed to many other breeds. Its coat is perfect protection for a working dog but its high maintenance may be one reason why this breed is no longer popular, despite its tolerant, friendly attitude to children and to other dogs.

Low-set, drop ears covered by long hair

Face profusely covered with hair

Grey hairs on chin

Long, woolly, curly, solid black coat

Tail has slight hook at tip

Round, broad feet

FRISIAN WATER DOG
THIS CAPABLE, RESERVED BREED DOES BEST WITH A FIRM OWNER

FCI

Height range
55–59cm (22–23in)

Weight range
15–20kg (33–44lb)

Life span 12–13 years

Origin The Netherlands

Other colours

Dark brown

Also known as the Dutch Spaniel or Wetterhoun, this breed was originally used by fishermen to control otters. It is still used for flushing and retrieving, but also as a guard and farm dog. Its independent, slightly suspicious character makes it unsuitable for city living, but it is a reliable and rugged dog for a rural home.

Low-set ears hang flat against head

Rounded top to head

Long tail curled into a ring

White chest markings

Solid black coat

Round, arched feet

CORDED POODLE
SMART AND FRIENDLY, THIS DOG IS WRAPPED IN EASY-CARE DREADLOCKS

Height range
24–60cm (9–24in)

Weight range
21–32kg (46–71lb)

Life span 10–13 years

Origin France

Other colours

Any colour

Like other poodles, this is a friendly, intelligent, and level-headed dog that makes a good guard or companion. Corded Poodles have been bred from separate lines of the well-known Standard Poodle (see p.231) for many years but as yet are not recognized as a breed in their own right. Their look was popular in the 19th century but today is rarely seen – even in France. This kind of cording is more often found on herding breeds, offering protection against both weather and predators. Most poodle coats will cord with a little encouragement, and once the cords have formed, are fairly easy to look after.

Muzzle has straight bridge

Black, corded coat

Long, elegant, narrow head

Oblique, almond-shaped eyes

Ears covered with many cords

Level back

Fine, dense, corded, white coat

BRITTANY
THIS ADAPTABLE AND RELIABLE DOG IS IDEAL FOR AN ACTIVE OWNER

KC

Height range
47–51cm (19–20in)

Weight range
14–18kg (31–40lb)

Life span 12–14 years

Origin France

Other colours

Liver and white

Black and white

Black, tan, and white

Colours may be merged and not clearly defined (roan).

Also known as the Brittany Spaniel, and as the Epagneul Breton in its native France, this versatile gundog flushes and retrieves game but is best at simply locating game birds. An old-established breed, the Brittany almost disappeared in the 19th century but today has regained popularity both as a sporting dog and a good-natured family companion.

Oval, dark eyes

High-set tail carried just below back level

Triangular, drop ears

Muzzle tapered but not pointed

Orange flecking

Dense, fairly fine, slightly wavy, orange and white coat

Feathering on forelegs

Compact, round feet

LAGOTTO ROMAGNOLO
THIS AFFECTIONATE AND BOISTEROUS DOG IS BEST SUITED TO A COUNTRY LIFE

KC

Height range
41–48cm (16–19in)

Weight range
11–16kg (24–35lb)

Life span 12–14 years

Origin Italy

Other colours

Orange

Brown

Roan

Orange and roan coats may have a brown mask.

This breed originally worked as a retriever in the marshland of northern Italy, then later as a truffle hound. Today, it is bred as often for companionship as for work. The Lagotto Romagnolo is good-natured and likes to be kept busy. Its characteristic ringlet coat needs weekly combing and annual clipping.

Moderately large, triangular, drop ears with rounded tips

Liver-coloured nose

Woolly, off-white coat forms tight ringlets

Curly, white coat with brown markings

Deep chest

Rounded, compact feet

PONT-AUDEMER SPANIEL

THIS ENGAGING BREED IS ENERGETIC OUTDOORS BUT RELAXED IN THE HOME

FCI

Height range
51–58cm (20–23in)

Weight range
18–24kg (40–53lb)

Life span 12–14 years

Origin France

Other colours

Brown

This French pointer and retriever is a specialist at hunting in water and swampland. The breed is thought to have been developed in the 19th century, and may include the Irish Water Spaniel (see p.228) in its ancestry. The Pont-Audemer Spaniel has never been well known, even in France, and by the 20th century was nearly extinct. It survived in small numbers and is still used for hunting but also makes a gentle house dog. The curly, slightly ruffled-looking coat is not particularly difficult to maintain, though it does need regular care.

Drop ears covered with long, silky hair

Rounded skull with topknot of curly hair

Long, slightly pointed muzzle

Small, dark amber eyes

Deep, broad chest reaches elbows

Tail slightly curved with lighter-coloured tip

Curly, dishevelled-looking, brown coat with grey and brown mottlings

Round feet with long, curly hair between toes

SMALL MUNSTERLANDER
A LIVELY, INTELLIGENT DOG STILL USED MAINLY FOR HUNTING

KC

Height range
52-53cm (20-21in)

Weight range
18-27kg (40-60lb)

Life span 13-14 years

Origin Germany

One German name for the breed, Heidewachtel or "heath quail dog", describes this dog's first purpose of flushing game birds. Although it is a cheerful and affectionate companion, hunters quickly snap up almost all of the small numbers that are bred each year. Despite its name, this breed is not directly related to the Large Munsterlander (below).

Well-feathered, broad ears

Silky, brown coat

White legs with brown mottling

White blaze on head

Medium-length, well-feathered tail

LARGE MUNSTERLANDER
THIS HUNTING DOG IS HAPPIEST IN THE HOME

KC

Height range
58-65cm (23-26in)

Weight range
29-31kg (65-68lb)

Life span 12-13 years

Origin Germany

The Grosser Munsterlander, as it is called in Germany, is more closely related to the German pointers than the Small Munsterlander (above). It is slow to mature, but makes a calm, highly trainable, and versatile gundog. It positively thrives on close human company and is good with children.

Black mantle

Long, dense coat provides insulation

Legs are well feathered

Solid black head

White hairs at tip of snout

White coat with black flecking

FRISIAN POINTING DOG

THIS ADAPTABLE, ROBUST FARM DOG IS EASY TO LIVE WITH

FCI

Height range
50–53cm (20–21in)

Weight range
19–25kg (42–55lb)

Life span 12–14 years

Origin The Netherlands

Other colours

Orange with white markings.

Bred by farmers, this dog, also known as the Stabyhoun, tracks, points, and retrieves alongside hunters. It makes an active and even-tempered family companion, and is excellent with children. This breed, despite efforts to improve its numbers, remains rare even in its native land.

Long, straight, smooth, black coat with white markings

Pronounced stop

Black ticking

Long, level back

Feathered, curving tail

Back of front legs well feathered

DRENTSCHE PARTRIDGE DOG

A DEDICATED HUNTING DOG, BUT CALM ENOUGH FOR CITY LIFE

FCI

Height range
55–63cm (22–25in)

Weight range
20–25kg (44–55lb)

Life span 12–13 years

Origin The Netherlands

Somewhere between a pointer and a retriever, the Drentsche Partridge Dog, or Patrijshond, is a typically versatile European hunting dog related to the Small Munsterlander (opposite) and the French Spaniel (see p.240). It makes a reliable and relaxed family companion as long as it has enough activity.

Oval, amber eyes

Brown markings

Well-feathered tail

Wavy, white coat

Brown spots on legs

Drop ears covered with long, silky hair

KOOIKERHONDJE

THIS CHEERFUL, ENERGETIC DOG IS NOT SUITED TO CITY LIFE

KC

Height range
35-42cm (14-17in)

Weight range
9-11kg (20-24lb)

Life span 12-13 years

Origin The Netherlands

This breed goes by several other names, including Dutch Decoy Spaniel, which describes its original and unusual role. Romping and waving its flag-like tail, never barking, it was used for centuries to lure and drive curious waterfowl into tunnel traps or "kooien" for hunters to catch alive – a task it still performs today for researchers wanting to tag and release birds. It is a rare breed, but its working history makes it a playful, good-natured dog that is dedicated to its owners, although can be aloof with strangers.

Sleek, slightly wavy, white coat with orange-red patches

White blaze on face

Shorter hair on face

Drop ears covered in long, silky hair

Alert, almond-shaped, deep brown eyes

Well-feathered tail

Long hair on neck forms ruff

Feathering on back of front legs

Small, hare-like feet

PICARDY SPANIEL

THIS DOG LOVES OPEN SPACES BUT MAKES A CALM COMPANION AT HOME

FCI

Height range
55–60cm (22–24in)

Weight range
20–25kg (44–55lb)

Life span 12–14 years

Origin France

One of the oldest spaniel breeds, the Picardy Spaniel is still used in France to flush birds in woodland and wetland areas. An enthusiastic swimmer, it makes a placid, reliable, and affectionate family dog, which will even adapt to city life if given a reasonable amount of exercise.

Long, low-set, drop ears

Oval head with well-defined stop

Back slopes down towards tail

Dense coat has slight wave and grey mottling

Curved tail with feathering

Squarely built body

Brown patch

Large feet are round, with feathering between toes

Rich tan markings

BLUE PICARDY SPANIEL

THIS PLAYFUL, GENTLE SPANIEL LOVES PLENTY OF ATTENTION AND EXERCISE

FCI

Height range
57–60cm (23–24in)

Weight range
20–21kg (44–46lb)

Life span 11–13 years

Origin France

Mainly used as a water dog for pointing and retrieving snipe in marshland, this quiet and easy-going breed is a fun-loving companion and good with children. However, the Blue Picardy Spaniel's friendly temperament means that it is of little use for guarding.

Well-defined stop

Slightly wavy coat with black patches

Pendulous flews

Lighter-coloured blaze

Tail about hock length

Long, drop ears are covered with wavy hair

Grey-black speckling gives bluish shade to coat

Tight, round feet have plenty of hair between toes

FRENCH SPANIEL

THIS FRIENDLY, ELEGANT GUNDOG IS HAPPY ON CITY STREETS OR IN WIDE OPEN SPACES

FCI

Height range
55-61cm (22-24in)

Weight range
20-25kg (44-55lb)

Life span 12-14 years

Origin France

In its native land the French Spaniel is claimed to be the original of all hunting spaniels. It is still used for hunting at home and abroad, but because it is level-headed and not inclined to bark, it also makes a good city dog, as long as it is given enough exercise and affection.

Large, oval eyes match brown of coat

Tail curves upwards towards tip

Pendant ears set quite far back on the head

Straight top to muzzle

Brown spotting on chest

Silky, white and brown coat

ENGLISH SETTER

THE PERFECT COUNTRY-HOUSE DOG IN BOTH LOOKS AND CHARACTER

KC

Height range
61-64cm (24-25in)

Weight range
25-30kg (55-66lb)

Life span 12-13 years

Origin UK

Other colours

Orange or lemon belton

Liver belton

Liver beltons may have tan markings.

Developed to track, set, and retrieve birds, this breed is still worked today, although different bloodlines are used for hunting or home life. Elegant in appearance, the English Setter is a cheerful and tireless companion that needs a good deal of space and activity, but has a calm and reliable temperament.

Low-set, pendant ears

Blue belton coat

Well-feathered tail

Light tan marks on face

Square muzzle with slightly pendulous flews

IRISH SETTER

AN EXUBERANT, ENTHUSIASTIC BREED FOR A PATIENT AND ACTIVE OWNER

KC

Height range
64–69cm (25–27in)

Weight range
27–32kg (60–71lb)

Life span 12–13 years

Origin Ireland

The red dog, or Modder Rhu, of Ireland started out as a hunting dog and is still an effective worker, but today is more commonly kept as a striking and spirited companion. Slow to mature, it needs firm training from an early age. The breed's devil-may-care attitude and tendency to get into scrapes when young can try an owner's patience, but its sociable nature and zest for life make it worth the extra effort. It does not simply tolerate other dogs and children, but actively seeks them out to play with.

Silky, drop ears

Deep, square muzzle

Level, almond-shaped eyes have kind expression

Shorter hair on front of lower legs

Well-feathered tail

Long, glossy, red coat

Very deep and narrow chest

Longer hair on underside of body

Feathering on back of legs

IRISH RED AND WHITE SETTER

THIS PLAYFUL DOG IS SLOW TO MATURE, BUT IT IS WORTH THE WAIT

KC

Height range
64–69cm (25–27in)

Weight range
25–34kg (55–75lb)

Life span 12–13 years

Origin Ireland

This setter has the red and white colouring that is typical of many hunting dogs, but today it is more often kept for company. Long overshadowed by the related Irish Setter (see p.241), this intelligent if impulsive breed is slowly gaining the popularity it deserves. Cheerful and energetic, it thrives on attention and firm guidance.

Broad, domed head

Clear, crisp coloured areas

Ears level with eyes and set well back

Red mottling on face

Strong body with deep chest

Fine, wavy, red and white coat

GORDON SETTER

AN OUTGOING BUT OBEDIENT CHARACTER BRED FOR WIDE OPEN SPACES

KC

Height range
62–66cm (24–26in)

Weight range
26–30kg (57–66lb)

Life span 12–13 years

Origin UK

Originally employed in Scotland to track game birds and then freeze once it had located them, changes in hunting fashions have seen this breed move from field to fireside. It brings with it a level-headed and loyal nature, but also a need for daily, vigorous exercise and a good deal of space.

Lean, long neck

Deep head with slightly rounded skull

Shiny, coal-black coat

Fringe on belly may extend to throat

Full feathering on long, muscular thighs

Typical chestnut-red marking on feet and lower legs

NOVA SCOTIA DUCK TOLLING RETRIEVER

THIS GUNDOG HAS ADAPTED WELL TO THE FAMILY ENVIRONMENT

KC

Height range
45–53cm (18–21in)

Weight range
17–23kg (37–51lb)

Life span 12–13 years

Origin Canada

This breed takes its name from its role in an unusual form of duck and goose hunting. The dog used to retrieve sticks – thrown by hunters in a hide – with a great show of activity but no barking, and this would lure in, or "toll", inquisitive birds. Once the birds were in range, the hunters could shoot them and the dog would retrieve them. The ideal dog for this role, its playful, quiet, and obedient qualities make it an excellent companion breed. It is also tireless, so needs plenty of exercise.

Almond-shaped eyes have alert expression

Triangular drop ears held slightly erect

Tapering muzzle with slightly wedge-shaped head

Level back

Close-fitting lips

Typical white chest markings

Water-repellent, red coat with dense undercoat

Well-feathered tail, broad at base

Typical white markings on feet

GERMAN POINTER

THIS INTELLIGENT BREED IS GENIAL AND GENTLE IF KEPT BUSY

KC

Height range
53–64cm (21–25in)

Weight range
20–32kg (44–71lb)

Life span 10–14 years

Origin Germany

Other colours

Liver

Brown

Black

A superlative hunting dog, which tracks, points, and retrieves over any terrain from heathland to marshland, the German Pointer or Deutsch Kurzhaar is a loyal, obedient breed. In its homeland it has always been kept for the home as well as the hunt, and the breed is generally level-headed and reliable. This is an energetic dog, and individuals can become hyperactive and destructive if they are not given enough exercise. There are three coat types: wire-haired, long-haired, and short-haired. By far the best known is the German Short-haired Pointer, called GSP by hunters in the UK.

Brown nose

Short-haired

Broad, drop ears, rounded at tips

Medium-sized, brown eyes

Well-defined stop

Wire-haired

Liver coat with white ticking, coarse to touch

Liver patch

Tapering tail with white tip, carried low

Tucked-up belly

Spoon-shaped, compact feet

Short-haired

CESKY FOUSEK

THIS RURAL BREED IS INTELLIGENT AND ROBUST BUT MAY BE HEADSTRONG

FCI

Height range
58-66cm (23-26in)

Weight range
22-34kg (49-75lb)

Life span 12-13 years

Origin Czech Republic

Other colours

Brown

Brown coats may have ticked markings on chest and lower limbs.

This breed, variously claimed to be of Czech, Slovakian, or Bohemian descent, is still a popular hunting dog in these areas but is rare elsewhere. It is loyal and trainable, and usually gentle around people, but is a natural hunter and so may be unreliable with other pets.

Distinctive, bushy eyebrows

Large, drop ears

Beard of soft hair

Tail traditionally docked to two-fifths of length

Deep-set, amber eyes with kind expression

Brown nose

Hard, protective, dark roan coat with brown patches

Compact, spoon-shaped feet

KORTHALS GRIFFON

THIS RUGGED AND RELIABLE BREED IS A FRIENDLY TOWN OR COUNTRY COMPANION

KC

Height range
50-60cm (20-24in)

Weight range
23-27kg (51-60lb)

Life span 12-13 years

Origin The Netherlands

Other colours

Liver

White and orange

Roan, white, and brown

Related to the German Pointer (opposite), bred by Dutchman Edward Korthals, and adopted by French hunters, this is a versatile and easy-going breed. It is not the fastest gundog but is popular for hunting where obedient, close-working dogs are needed – qualities that also make it a valuable companion.

Body length exceeds leg length

Hairy eyebrows

Shorter, liver hair on ears

Long muzzle with hairy beard and moustache

Harsh, coarse, steel-grey coat, with dense undercoat

Deep chest

Round feet with tight, arched toes

WEIMARANER

THIS BEAUTIFUL, INTELLIGENT DOG NEEDS PLENTY OF SPACE

KC

Height range
56–69cm (22–27in)

Weight range
25–41kg (55–90lb)

Life span 12–13 years

Origin Germany

Created as an all-purpose hunting, pointing, and retrieving gundog, this 19th-century breed, nicknamed the "Grey Ghost", is a careful, almost stealthy dog in the field. While the Weimaraner may be reserved with strangers, it is a bouncy family companion and can be too boisterous for small children. Elegant lines, striking colour, and grace in movement have contributed to this breed's popularity both as a pet and working dog, but it can stay active for hours, and needs an owner with similar stamina. There are two coat types: long-haired and short-haired.

Feathering
on legs

Long-haired

Striking, pale
blue-grey eyes

Large, high-set ears
have slight fold

Grey nose

Body as long as
height at the withers

Tail reaches hocks

Silky, silver-grey coat

Moderately
tucked-up belly

Firm, compact feet

Short-haired

HUNGARIAN VIZSLA
THIS LOYAL AND GENTLE DOG IS HIGH-ENERGY BUT LOW MAINTENANCE

KC

Height range
53–64cm (21–25in)

Weight range
20–30kg (44–66lb)

Life span 13–14 years

Origin Hungary

A typical European hunting dog thought to date back to the 16th century, this breed is also known as the Hungarian Short-haired Pointer. It is extremely affectionate and intelligent, and responds well to training. Popular with both hunters and families, the dog has almost boundless energy and will seek and retrieve sticks as readily as it will game – all day if allowed.

Strong, muscular back

Nose colour matches coat

Eyes slightly darker than coat colour

Smooth, arched neck is muscular

Slightly curved tail tapers to pointed tip

Distinctive, sleek, golden-russet coat lacks insulating undercoat

Long forearms

Tight, arched, round, cat-like feet

HUNGARIAN WIRE HAIRED VIZSLA
BRED TO HUNT, BUT ALSO MAKES AN OBEDIENT AND AFFECTIONATE COMPANION

KC

Height range
53–62cm (21–24in)

Weight range
20–30kg (44–66lb)

Life span 12–14 years

Origin Hungary

The wire-haired variety of Hungarian Vizsla, which was developed in the 1930s, has a stronger build than the smooth-haired variety, probably because it originated from a cross between a smooth coated Vizsla and a German Wire-haired Pointer. Its characteristic dense wiry coat is ideal for hunting in cold conditions, while its shaggy beard and eyebrows give it an alert but gentle expression.

Rounded V-shaped ears

Golden sand-coloured coat

Eyes slightly darker than coat

Low set, slightly curved tail

Deep chest reaching down to elbows

Straight forelegs

PORTUGUESE POINTER
THIS TIRELESS AND ADAPTABLE HUNTING DOG IS BEST SUITED TO A WORKING LIFE

KC

Height range
50–58cm (20–23in)

Weight range
16–27kg (35–60lb)

Life span 12–14 years

Origin Portugal

Locally known as the Perdigueiro Português, which literally means the Portuguese Partridge Dog, this breed was used as a pointer for hunters with falcons or nets. Still worked today, the Portuguese Pointer is level-headed and biddable and so, also makes an amenable companion. However, this tenacious hunter needs considerable mental and physical activity every day.

Triangular, drop ears

Moderately developed flews

Deep chest

Dark eyes with dark rims

Short, red-yellow coat

Slightly tucked-up belly

White markings on feet

Square muzzle

Slight dewlap

BRACCO ITALIANO
THIS RARE BREED IS ATHLETIC AND GOOD WITH CHILDREN

KC

Height range
55–67cm (22–26in)

Weight range
25–40kg (55–88lb)

Life span 12–13 years

Origin Italy

Other colours

White

White with orange, amber, or brown markings

Dogs similar to the Bracco Italiano, or Italian Pointer, can be seen in paintings from the 14th century, when they were used to drive game birds into nets. Still used as a working dog today, this breed also makes a level-headed and gentle companion, though it can be stubborn at times.

Slightly arched muzzle

Pendant ears with rounded tips

Well-developed flews

Nose matches coat colour

Powerful neck has soft dewlap

Smooth, roan coat with chestnut markings

Oval-shaped feet

Tail tapers slightly

ITALIAN SPINONE

THIS EASY-GOING AND RELAXED COMPANION IS NOT IDEAL FOR HOUSE-PROUD OWNERS

KC

Height range
58-70cm (23-28in)

Weight range
29-39kg (65-85lb)

Life span 12-13 years

Origin Italy

Other colours

White

Orange roan

White and brown
or brown roan

This versatile tracker and retriever from northern Italy was the region's most popular hunting breed until the 20th century, and is still worked – its shaggy coat is useful protection in heavy undergrowth. More recently it has become a popular companion breed, prized for its gentle temperament and loyalty. An inclination to move at a slightly slower pace than many gundogs makes the Italian Spinone a comfortable walking companion. This breed is for those who love the "doggy" nature of dogs: the coarse coat may not be high maintenance but does retain smells, and the breed has a tendency to drool.

Large, round, ochre eyes with kind expression

Broad, deep chest

Light-coloured nose

Back curves gently

Triangular, pendant ears

Long moustache blends into beard

Thick tail carried low

Coarse, dense, white and orange coat

Slightly tucked-up belly

Large, round feet

FRENCH PYRENEAN POINTER

FCI

Height range
47–58cm (19–23in)

Weight range
18–24kg (40–53lb)

Life span 12–14 years

Origin France

Other colours

Chestnut-brown

Chestnut-brown
dogs may have
tan markings.

The most popular of the French pointers, the French Pyrenean Pointer
is still rare and mostly used for hunting. A swift and tireless breed, it
was created in southwest France to work in mountain terrain.
It is gentle and affectionate at
home, and makes an ideal
companion for the more
active owner.

Broad, straight back,
may be quite long

Nose matches
coat colour

Typical,
chestnut-
brown head

Very short, fine,
chestnut-brown
and white coat

Belly moderately
tucked up

Area of speckling denser
than French Gascony
Pointer (see p.253)

SAINT GERMAIN POINTER

FCI

Height range
53–62cm (21–24in)

Weight range
18–26kg (40–57lb)

Life span 12–14 years

Origin France

Also known as the Braque Saint-Germain, this is a fleet-footed pointer and
retriever of birds in field, woodland, and marshland. However, its coat is not
sufficiently insulated to make it an all-weather dog. The Saint Germain
Pointer is affectionate but sensitive, needing firm yet gentle handling,
and adapts surprisingly well to
urban family life.

Pink nose

Smooth, dull
white coat with
orange markings

Golden-yellow eyes

Tapering, hock-length
tail carried horizontally

Flews cover
lower jaw

Long, deep chest

Long feet
with light-
coloured nails

BOURBONNAIS POINTING DOG

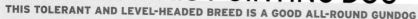

THIS TOLERANT AND LEVEL-HEADED BREED IS A GOOD ALL-ROUND GUNDOG

FCI

Height range
48–57cm (19–22in)

Weight range
16–26kg (35–57lb)

Life span 12–14 years

Origin France

A versatile tracker, pointer, and retriever, the Bourbonnais Pointing Dog is the oldest and perhaps the most level-headed of all the French gundog breeds. Robust in build, giving an impression of power, this dog is full of stamina when working but relaxed and affectionate when off duty.

Brown, drop ears with rounded tips

Slightly tapered muzzle

Pear-shaped head

Nose colour matches brown of coat

Line of belly rises steadily

Fine, dense, white coat with brown ticking and markings

Round feet

PUDELPOINTER

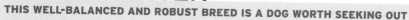

THIS WELL-BALANCED AND ROBUST BREED IS A DOG WORTH SEEKING OUT

FCI

Height range
55–68cm (22–27in)

Weight range
20–30kg (44–66lb)

Life span 12–14 years

Origin Germany

Other colours

Dead leaf

Black

Developed for both the field and home, this cross of poodle and pointer aims to be the best of both: intelligent, hardy, and sociable, with excellent all-round working abilities. Most popular with hunters, the Pudelpointer is an amenable and cheerful rural companion.

Curling forelock

Drop ears lie close to head

Large, dark, amber eyes

Beard and moustache lighter in colour

Sabre-like tail

Hard, rough, brown coat, with dense undercoat

White markings on chest

Slightly tucked-up belly

Oval feet

BRAQUE D'AUVERGNE

A GOOD-NATURED, OBEDIENT DOG WITH LOTS OF STAMINA

KC

Height range
53–63cm (21–25in)

Weight range
22–28kg (49–62lb)

Life span 12–13 years

Origin France

The Braque d'Auvergne, or Auvergne Pointer, was bred in central France by and for hunters, and it remains a tenacious all-purpose hunting dog that can work all day over long distances. Friendly and intelligent, this is a lively, affectionate breed that is easily trained and loves company. The Braque d'Auvergne will thrive in any active household.

Black nose

Level topline

Shiny, short, white coat with black markings

Black flecking over white gives coat blue appearance

Oval, dark hazel eyes

Typical black markings on face and ears

Tail reaches hock

Flews neatly overlap lower lip

ARIEGE POINTING DOG

AN ELEGANT BREED BEST SUITED TO A HIGHLY ACTIVE, DISCIPLINED LIFE

FCI

Height range
56–67cm (22–26in)

Weight range
25–30kg (55–66lb)

Life span 12–14 years

Origin France

Rare even in its homeland in southwest France, the Ariege Pointing Dog, or Braque de l'Ariège, is used for pointing and retrieving, and has some tracking ability. It is almost exclusively owned by hunters, and needs patient training to settle an enthusiastic nature that can spill over into wildness, and plenty to do if it is not to become destructive.

Oval eyes have gentle expression

Flesh-coloured nose

Fine, folded, tan ears

Short, glossy, white coat with fawn ticking

Tapering tail

Long, straight muzzle

Compact feet with well-arched toes

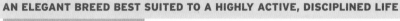

FRENCH GASCONY POINTER

THIS DOG IS GENTLE AND INTELLIGENT AT HOME BUT AN AVID HUNTER OUTDOORS

FCI

Height range
56–69cm (22–27in)

Weight range
25–32kg (55–71lb)

Life span 12–14 years

Origin France

Other colours

Chestnut-brown

Chestnut-brown dogs may have tan markings.

One of the oldest pointer breeds, the French Gascony Pointer, from southwest France, is still kept as a hunter's dog as well as a household companion. Loyal and affectionate, it has a sensitive nature that responds best to gentle, consistent training. It is a determined and enthusiastic tracker in the field.

Drop ears with rounded tips

Broad, straight back

Chestnut-brown eyes

Compact, almost round feet

Slightly tucked-up belly

Very fine, short, chestnut-brown and white coat

Chestnut-brown flecking less dense than on French Pyrenean Pointer (see p.250)

SLOVAKIAN ROUGH-HAIRED POINTER

THIS LOYAL, OBEDIENT, AND LEVEL-HEADED BREED LOVES TO WORK

KC

Height range
57–68cm (22–27in)

Weight range
25–35kg (55–77lb)

Life span 12–14 years

Origin Slovakia

This breed is found under a variety of names, from Slovensky Pointer to Wire-haired Slovakian Pointer, and Slovenský Hrubosrstý Stavač in its homeland. It is probably descended from German hunting dogs, and shows their typical intelligence, good humour, and energy. Not a breed to leave alone at home, it thrives on company and activity.

Long, lean head

Straight, solid back slopes slightly down towards tail

Longer, softer, lighter-coloured hair on muzzle

Drop ears with short, soft hair

Almond-shaped, amber eyes

White markings on chest

Harsh, flat, grey (brown-shaded sable) coat

Rounded feet with well-arched toes

ENGLISH POINTER

THIS ATHLETIC DOG NEEDS PLENTY OF EXERCISE IF KEPT AS A PET

KC

Height range
61-69cm (24-27in)

Weight range
20-34kg (44-75lb)

Life span 12-13 years

Origin UK

Other colours

Variety of colours

Simply known as the Pointer in the UK, this breed is swift and keen when tracking and pointing, tasks for which it has long been used; however, it does not retrieve particularly well. In character, English Pointers are gentle, loyal, and obedient. They are good-natured family companions and reliable with children but can be too boisterous with toddlers. They retain their hunting stamina and need plenty of outdoor space.

White blaze on head

Liver and white coat

Well-developed, soft flews

Very well-defined stop

Bright, hazel eyes

Drop ears

Back slopes gently towards tail

Medium-length tail carried level with back

Fine, hard, short, orange and white coat

Oval feet with well-arched toes

SPANISH POINTER

GENTLE AND INTELLIGENT, THIS BREED IS NIMBLER THAN IT LOOKS

FCI

Height range
59–67cm (23–26in)

Weight range
25–30kg (55–66lb)

Life span 12–14 years

Origin Spain

Also known as the Perdiguero de Burgos, this dog was bred to track deer, but is now mostly used for smaller game. It is a reliable, easy-going breed that fits well into family life. Nonetheless, it is a keen hunter – halfway between a scent hound and a pointer – and thrives on work.

White patch on head

Liver-coloured patch

Tail traditionally docked to one-third of natural length

Dark hazel eyes have soft, sad expression

Well-developed flews cover lower lip

Large, drop ears

Well-defined dewlap on neck

White and liver hairs give coat marbled appearance

Point of sternum prominent

Round, cat-like feet

OLD DANISH POINTER

THIS ADAPTABLE AND ROBUST DOG MAKES A GENTLE, PATIENT COMPANION

FCI

Height range
50–60cm (20–24in)

Weight range
26–35kg (57–77lb)

Life span 12–13 years

Origin Denmark

Its local name, Gammel Dansk Hønsehund, also translates as Old Danish Chicken Dog or Bird Dog. This breed is still used as a determined tracker, pointer, and retriever, and even as a sniffer dog, but it also makes an even-tempered family dog for those willing to give it plenty to do.

Moderate stop

Firm, muscular back slopes slightly towards tail

Tapering tail almost reaches hock

Muscular, slightly "throaty" neck

Liver patch

Broad, drop ears with rounded tips

Liver flecking

Dense, white coat with liver markings

Drop ears set
well back

Moderate
stop

Broad
head

Medium-sized,
hazel eyes

Powerful neck

Level topline

Black nose
fades to light
brown with age

Characteristic
"otter" tail, round
and well haired

Broad chest

Weatherproof,
short, yellow coat

Round,
compact feet

LABRADOR RETRIEVER

THIS KIND AND INTELLIGENT FAMILY FAVOURITE LOVES SPORT AND SWIMMING

KC

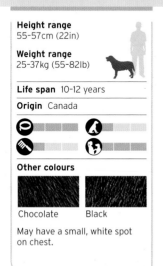

Height range
55–57cm (22in)

Weight range
25–37kg (55–82lb)

Life span 10–12 years

Origin Canada

Other colours

Chocolate   Black

May have a small, white spot
on chest.

One of the most familiar dogs, the Labrador Retriever has been topping "popular dog" lists for at least two decades. The dogs from which the present-day Labrador Retriever descended were not from Labrador, as is commonly supposed, but from Newfoundland. Here, from the 18th century onwards, black dogs with waterproof coats were bred by local fishermen and used to help tow in catches and retrieve escaping fish. Dogs of this early type no longer exist, but a few were brought to England in the 19th century and these led to the development of the modern Labrador Retriever. By the early 20th century the breed was officially recognized and continued to be much admired by field sportsmen for its excellent retrieving skills.

Today, the Labrador Retriever is still widely used as a gundog and has proved efficient at other types of work, such as tracking for police forces. In particular, its steady character makes it a superb guide dog for the blind. However, it is as a family dog that this breed has gained great popularity. The Labrador Retriever is loving and lovable, easy to train, anxious to please, and reliable with children and household pets – but it has too amiable a character to make a good guard dog.

This breed has energy to burn and needs to be kept mentally as well as physically active. Long daily walks are essential, preferably with the chance to have a swim along the way. If this dog sees water, it will plunge straight in. Under-exercised and left to its own devices, a Labrador Retriever may be given to excessive barking or become destructive. It tends to gain weight quickly, and lack of exercise combined with its insatiable appetite can lead to weight problems.

GOLDEN RETRIEVER

Height range
51-61cm (20-24in)

Weight range
25-34kg (55-75lb)

Life span 12-13 years

Origin UK

Other colours

Cream

Bred as a powerful retriever for long-distance work, the Golden Retriever is used by hunters and in field trials. It is also used as a guide dog and kept as a gregarious pet. Responsive and even-tempered, this dog's main aim in life is to please. Its friendly nature means it does not make a good guard dog.

Powerful but well-chiselled head

Long tail without a curl

Drop ears

Long, silky, golden coat

Dark brown eyes

Dense, water-resistant, lighter undercoat

Round, cat-like feet

FLAT COATED RETRIEVER

Height range
56-61cm (22-24in)

Weight range
25-36kg (55-80lb)

Life span 11-13 years

Origin UK

Other colours

Liver

One of the earliest retriever breeds, this was once a favourite among gamekeepers. Today, it is still worked but is more often found as a good-natured and handsome pet. Lively and brimming with enthusiasm, the Flat Coated Retriever is also level-headed and obedient. It has a deep bark so can make a good guard dog.

Dense, black coat

Shallow stop

Triangular, drop ears with rounded tips

Well-feathered tail

Feathering on chest

Round, close-knit feet

CHESAPEAKE BAY RETRIEVER

THIS EVEN-TEMPERED DOG IS SUITED TO COUNTRY LIFE

KC

Height range
53–66cm (21–26in)

Weight range
25–36kg (55–80lb)

Life span 12–13 years

Origin USA

Other colours

Straw bracken   Red-gold

May have small, white markings.

This retriever originated in the northeastern United States and has much in common with the Curly Coated Retriever (below). A superb water dog, the Chesapeake Bay Retriever has typical retriever gentleness but an alert and determined personality. For those who can provide enough activity, this is an intelligent and biddable companion.

Colour of nose matches coat

Moderate stop

Oily, brown double coat

Medium-length, slightly curved tail

Deep chest

Hare-like feet

Leg length equal to depth of body

Wavy coat

CURLY COATED RETRIEVER

THIS ROBUST, ENERGETIC WORKING DOG DOES NOT LIKE TO BE LEFT ALONE

KC

Height range
64–69cm (25–27in)

Weight range
27–32kg (60–71lb)

Life span 12–13 years

Origin UK

Other colours

Liver

Bred for hunting waterfowl, this rare retriever is worked and used as an assistance dog, as well as kept as an affectionate and level-headed companion. High energy levels and a need for company make this dog more suited to a rural life than to an urban home.

Small, triangular, drop ears

Thick, tightly curled, black coat

Tail almost reaches hock

Oval, black eyes match coat colour

Smooth, short hair on head

Round feet with well-arched toes

A Chihuahua may fit into a
handbag but it is not a fashion
accessory. This little breed from
Mexico needs exercise as much
as any larger dog.

COMPANION DOGS

Almost any dog can provide companionship. Many dogs once used for outside duties, such as herding, have moved indoors with the family. Usually, these breeds have been developed for specific tasks and so are traditionally grouped according to their primary function. With a few exceptions, the companion dogs included here are bred solely as pets.

The Pug's flat face and round eyes are designed to appeal

Most companion dogs are small breeds, created primarily to sit on laps, look decorative, and entertain their owners without taking up much room. Some of them are toy versions of larger working breeds. The Standard Poodle, for example, once used for herding or for retrieving waterfowl, was bred down in size to a toy dog that could no longer perform any practical function. Other, larger, dogs sometimes grouped with companion breeds include the Dalmatian, whose career included a short-lived spell as a carriage escort, as much for prestige as guard duty. Now that this job no longer exists, Dalmatians are rarely used for any working purpose.

Companion dogs have a long history. A number of them originated thousands of years ago in China, where small dogs were kept in the imperial courts as ornaments and a source of comfort. Until the late 19th century, companion dogs everywhere were almost exclusively the pampered pets of the wealthy. As such, they often featured in portraits, depicted sitting prettily in the drawing room or with children as a nursery plaything. Some, such as the King Charles Spaniel, owe their enduring popularity to the former patronage of royalty.

Appearance has always mattered in the breeding of companion dogs. Over the centuries, selective breeding has produced characteristics, some bizarre, that serve no useful function but are designed to appeal – for example, the human-like flat faces and large, round eyes of the Pekingese and the Pug. Some have extravagantly long coats, curly tails, or – in the case of the Chinese Crested Dog – no hair at all apart from a few strategically placed tufts on the head or legs.

In modern times, companion dogs are no longer a symbol of class. They find a place with owners of all ages and circumstances, in small apartments as well as large country homes. Although still chosen for their looks, these dogs are also sought after as friends that give and demand affection and adapt happily to family activities.

LIVELY COMPANION
Although Dalmatians have great energy and stamina, they are nearly always kept as pets rather than for practical uses.

SMALLEST DOG
Few companion breeds come smaller than the diminutive and delightful Russian Toy.

GRIFFON BRUXELLOIS

A LIVELY, ALERT, WELL-BALANCED DOG WITH A TERRIER-LIKE DISPOSITION

KC

Height range
23-28cm (9-11in)

Weight range
3-5kg (7-11lb)

Life span Over 12 years

Origin Belgium

Other colours

Black and tan

This cobby little dog originated in Belgium, where it was kept as a stable dog and rode in hansom cabs. With traces of the Affenpinscher (see p.219) in its ancestry, there is a smooth-haired variety (known as the Petit Brabançon) and a rough-haired variety with a distinctive beard. In some countries the rough-haired type is also differentiated by colour – black-coated dogs are known as Belgian Griffons, all other colourings as Griffon Bruxellois. Totally fearless, but very adaptable and affectionate, the breed enjoys a good walk and being pampered. It is not recommended for households with very young children.

Large, dark eyes

Smooth, red coat

Smooth-haired (Petit Brabançon)

Semi-erect, high-set ears with shorter hair

Wiry, red coat

Rough-haired (Griffon Bruxellois)

Round head with upturned nose

High-set tail curves over back when active

Distinctive, bearded chin

Coarse, wiry, black coat

Compact, square body

Rounded, cat-like feet

Rough-haired (Belgian Griffon)

AMERICAN BULLDOG

THIS LOYAL, RELIABLE, AND BRAVE DOG HAS STRONG PROTECTIVE INSTINCTS

Height range
51–69cm (20–27in)

Weight range
27–57kg (60–125lb)

Life span Up to 16 years

Origin USA

Other colours

Variety of colours

Early English settlers brought the Bulldog (see p.94) with them to America. Two breeders, John D. Johnson and Alan Scott, used the English variety to develop the American Bulldog, which is taller, more active, and more versatile than its English counterpart. Male dogs are significantly heavier than females.

Small, button ears

Characteristic dip between shoulders and tail

Large, broad head

Black nose

Well-developed flews

Short, white coat

Short, red coat

Broad, white chest

OLDE ENGLISH BULLDOGGE

AN EXTREMELY STRONG BUT FRIENDLY AND LOVING COMPANION DOG

Height range
41–51cm (16–20in)

Weight range
23–36kg (51–80lb)

Life span 9–14 years

Origin USA

Other colours

Variety of colours

This muscular dog is a re-creation of the original 19th-century Bulldog. It was developed in the United States during the 1970s by David Leavitt to eliminate some of the health problems that are now seen in the modern Bulldog (see p.94). Confident and courageous, these intelligent dogs are excellent family companions. However, they benefit from early socialization and training.

Very pronounced stop

Wide, muscular back

Button ears

Round, brown eyes, set wide apart

Lower jaw is longer than upper jaw (undershot)

Broad chest

Short, glossy, white and tan coat

Rounded, cat-like feet

FRENCH BULLDOG

THIS AFFECTIONATE AND INTELLIGENT CLOWN-LIKE DOG THRIVES ON HUMAN COMPANY

KC

Height range
28-33cm (11-13in)

Weight range
11-13kg (24-29lb)

Life span Over 10 years

Origin France

Other colours

Black brindle

A sturdy, compact little dog, the French Bulldog makes an excellent companion, but has few boundaries and will want to share its owner's favourite chair. Always ready for fun, kind but firm direction may be needed. This breed is a descendent of the British Toy Bulldog taken to France in the 19th century.

Wide-set, dark eyes

Distinctive, erect "bat" ears, wide at base, rounded at top

Short, pied coat with white predominant

Strong, thickset neck

Fawn coat

PEKINGESE

DIGNIFIED AND COURAGEOUS YET SENSITIVE, THIS GOOD-NATURED DOG HAS A MIND OF ITS OWN

KC

Height range
15-23cm (6-9in)

Weight range
5kg (11lb)

Life span Over 12 years

Origin China

Other colours

Variety of colours

An aristocrat, whose ancestors can be traced back to the Tang Dynasty (618-907 CE), the Pekingese was considered sacred in China and could only be owned by royalty. The perfect dog for an apartment, it loves exercise but not long walks. Intelligent and fearless, it makes a loyal companion but can be hard to train.

Coarse, straight, long, gold topcoat

Very short muzzle

Lion-like mane around face

Lighter-coloured undercoat

PUG
THIS PLAYFUL AND INTELLIGENT DOG LOVES PEOPLE BUT IS SOMETIMES WILFUL

KC

Height range
25-28cm (10-11in)

Weight range
6-8kg (13-18lb)

Life span Over 10 years

Origin China

Other colours

Silver

Apricot

Black

This breed, with a long history, originated in China and its ancestors were brought to Europe in the 16th century by the East India Company traders. In Europe, it became popular with royalty and aristocracy. The Pug is a small, sturdy, square dog whose stern appearance belies its cheerful personality and great character. It is highly intelligent, outgoing, has a loving disposition, and makes a loyal companion. The Pug is suitable for a novice dog owner and is good with children as well as other pets. This breed needs regular exercise but not a lot of space - so is ideal for apartment life.

Large, round eyes

Thick neck

Broad chest

High-set, tightly curled tail

Button ears with flap folding forward

Very short muzzle

Smooth, glossy, fawn coat

LHASA APSO

HARDY, INDEPENDENT, AND FRIENDLY, THIS DOG IS NATURALLY SUSPICIOUS OF STRANGERS

KC

Height range
Up to 25cm (Up to 10in)

Weight range
6–7kg (13–15lb)

Life span 15–18 years

Origin Tibet

Other colours

Variety of
colours

First bred in Tibet as a watchdog for temples and monasteries, the Lhasa Apso was brought to Europe via India in the 1920s. It is a small, hardy dog that will happily walk for miles. Its long, flowing coat is not difficult to care for. Very affectionate, it can also be quite stubborn.

Dark, medium-sized
eyes covered by hair

Heavily feathered,
pendant ears

High-set,
plumed tail
with kink at end

Cloak of heavy, straight,
wheaten and white hair,
with thick undercoat

SHIH TZU

THIS INTELLIGENT, BOUNCY, AND OUTGOING DOG LOVES BEING PART OF THE FAMILY

KC

Height range
Up to 27cm (Up to 11in)

Weight range
5–8kg (10–18lb)

Life span Over 10 years

Origin Tibet/China

Other colours

Variety of
colours

This sturdy breed is thought to be a cross between the Pekingese (see p.264) and the Lhasa Apso (above). Abundantly but not excessively coated, it sheds little or no hair, making it a good companion for allergy sufferers. Despite its distinctly arrogant carriage, the Shih Tzu makes an affectionate and friendly pet.

Hair grows upwards
around the muzzle

Heavily plumed tail
with white tip

White
blaze on
forehead

Short, muscular
legs hidden
by long coat

Long, dense,
black and white
topcoat

BICHON FRISE

A GENTLE, INTELLIGENT, AND EXTROVERT DOG WITH A NON-SHEDDING COAT

KC

Height range
23-28cm (9-11in)

Weight range
5-7kg (10-15lb)

Life span Over 12 years

Origin Mediterranean

Sometimes known as the Tenerife dog, the Bichon Frise – a descendant of the Poodle (see p.271) and the Barbet (see p.232) – was allegedly taken from Tenerife to France. This is a happy little dog that loves to be the centre of attention, and does not like being left alone. It can be slow to house train.

Round, black eyes

White topcoat is coarser than soft, dense undercoat

Pendant ears

Round foot, exaggerated by cut of coat

COTON DE TULEAR

A LOYAL, BRIGHT, AND HIGHLY SOCIABLE DOG WITH A SOFT, COTTON-TEXTURED COAT

KC

Height range
22-30cm (8-12in)

Weight range
3-7kg (8-15lb)

Life span Over 12 years

Origin Madagascar

This small, long-haired dog is known for its happy temperament. The Coton de Tulear enjoys the company of humans as well as other dogs and does not like to be left alone. It is sometimes called the Royal Dog of Madagascar, where the dog existed for several hundred years before being introduced to France.

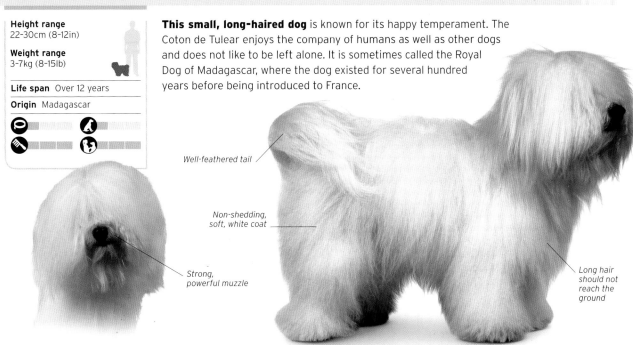

Well-feathered tail

Non-shedding, soft, white coat

Strong, powerful muzzle

Long hair should not reach the ground

LÖWCHEN

Height range
25-33cm (10-13in)

Weight range
4-8kg (9-18lb)

Life span 12-14 years

Origin France/Germany

Other colours

Any colour

The Löwchen, with origins in France and Germany, has existed as a companion dog for at least 400 years. The name Löwchen is German for little lion, hence its other name, the Little Lion Dog. It is a compact little dog with a bright expression and a reputation for agility and quickness. The Löwchen's intelligent, outgoing attitude makes it a pleasure to live with. It is highly recommended as a family pet and its size and non-shedding coat make it an ideal family dog.

Tail carried high over back

Brown coat with lighter underparts and head

Pendant ears with long fringes

Coat often clipped at back, and long at front

Small, round feet covered in hair

Long, wavy, black coat with silver brindling

BOLOGNESE

Height range
26-31cm (10-12in)

Weight range
3-4kg (7-9lb)

Life span Over 12 years

Origin Italy

Slightly more reserved and shy than its relative the Bichon Frise (see p.267), the Bolognese loves people and will form a close relationship with its owner. Like the Bichon Frise, it has a non-shedding coat. The breed originates from northern Italy. Similar dogs were known as far back as Roman times and are represented in many 16th-century Italian paintings.

High-set, drop ears

Body length same as height to withers

Round, black-rimmed eyes

Distinctive, non-shedding, flocked, white coat

MALTESE

A BRAVE, ENERGETIC, AND FEARLESS DOG, BUT ALSO GENTLE MANNERED AND AMIABLE KC

Height range
Up to 25cm (Up to 10in)

Weight range
2-3kg (4-7lb)

Life span Over 12 years

Origin Malta

An ancient dog from the Mediterranean, Maltese-like dogs are mentioned in writings as far back as 300BCE. This is a lively, fun-loving, little dog that belies its chocolate-box appearance. The long, silky coat is a major commitment – it does not shed but requires daily grooming to prevent matting.

Long facial hair tied back with ribbon

Silky, long, white coat

Tail carried over back with hair to one side

Dark brown, oval-shaped eyes with black rims

Well-feathered, long ears hang close to head

Short, cobby - or square - body

HAVANESE

THIS INTELLIGENT, EASY-TO-TRAIN, AND AFFECTIONATE DOG IS THE PERFECT FAMILY PET KC

Height range
23-28cm (9-11in)

Weight range
3-6kg (7-13lb)

Life span Over 12 years

Origin Cuba

Other colours

Any colour

The Havanese is the national dog of Cuba, where it is known as the Habanero. A relative of the Bichon Frise (see p.267), it was probably brought to Cuba by Italian or Spanish traders. The Havanese loves to be at the centre of its family, plays endlessly with children, and is also a good watchdog.

High-set tail carried over back

Pointed, drop ears, set just above eyes

Soft, silky, wavy, wheaten topcoat

Small, hare-like feet hidden by long hair

RUSSIAN TOY

SMALL BUT NOT DELICATE, THIS LOVABLE DOG NEEDS PLENTY OF EXERCISE

KC

Height range
20–28cm (8–11in)

Weight range
Up to 3kg (Up to 7lb)

Life span Over 12 years

Origin Russia

Other colours

Red

Black and tan

Blue and tan

Also known as the Russkiy Toy, this miniature dog, one of the smallest breeds in the world, is descended from the English Toy Terrier (see p.210). The breed became popular in Russia in the second half of the 20th century but is still something of a rarity outside its native country. Despite its tiny size and fragile appearance, the Russian Toy is active, energetic, and usually has robust health. There are two coat types: smooth-haired and long-haired. The long-haired variety is the more recent development.

Round, prominent eyes

Short, close, brown and tan coat

Smooth-haired

Ears fringed with long, silky hair

Black overlay

Long-haired

Pronounced stop

Small, round head

Long, slightly wavy, fawn coat

Well-feathered tail extends to hocks

Slight feathering on back of legs

Long-haired

Small, oval feet

POODLE

A HIGHLY INTELLIGENT, EXTROVERT DOG WITH A NATURAL TALENT TO AMUSE

KC

Height range
Toy:
Up to 28cm (Up to 11in)
Miniature:
28-38cm (11-15in)
Medium:
38-45cm (15-18in)

Weight range
Toy:
3-4kg (7-9lb)
Miniature:
7-8kg (15-18lb)
Medium:
21-35kg (46-77lb)

Life span Over 12 years

Origin France

Other colours

All solid colours

Bred down from the Standard Poodle (see p.231) are three other sizes of Poodle: toy, miniature, and medium (although the medium is not recognized by some kennel clubs). The smaller varieties have always been companion dogs, and were popular in the French court between the reign of Louis XIV and Louis XVI. An elegant dog, the Poodle is energetic, playful, affectionate, and eager to please. It is also very adaptable, equally at home in the city or the countryside. The dog's non-shedding coat makes it popular with allergy sufferers, although it does need regular brushing and clipping.

Dark eyes

White coat

Toy

High-set tail carried away from body

Shorter hair on face

Short but strong back

Dense, grey coat

Long, drop ears

Toy

Strong, muscular hind quarters

Profuse, thick, woolly, black coat

Deep, wide chest

Miniature

Small, oval feet

KYI LEO

THIS ATTRACTIVE, RELAXED, COMPACT BREED NEEDS PLENTY OF ACTIVITY

Height range
23-28cm (9-11in)

Weight range
4-6kg (9-13lb)

Life span 13-15 years

Origin USA

Other colours

Variety of colours

May have tan markings.

A playful, affectionate breed that is gaining popularity, the Kyi Leo is named after its parents: Kyi, Tibetan for dog, after its Lhasa Apso parent from Tibet; and Leo, Latin for lion, after its Maltese parent, which was once called the Lion Dog. Suited to indoor life, this alert dog makes a good watchdog.

Long hairs cover head

Tail curls over back when alert

Body length exceeds leg length

Long, thick, silky, black and white coat

Heavily feathered, drop ears

Short muzzle with beard

Rounded feet, with hair between toes

CAVALIER KING CHARLES SPANIEL

OUTGOING, SPORTING, AND ABSOLUTELY FEARLESS, THIS DOG IS EAGER TO PLEASE

KC

Height range
30-33cm (12-13in)

Weight range
5-8kg (11-18lb)

Life span Over 12 years

Origin UK

Other colours

King Charles

Prince Charles

A relative of the King Charles Spaniel (opposite), this breed dates back centuries. With large, dark eyes, a melting expression, and an ever-wagging tail, the Cavalier King Charles Spaniel is game, easy to train, and loves children – making it the perfect family pet. Its silky coat requires regular grooming.

Short muzzle

White lozenge mark on head

High-set, pendant ears

Long, silky, well-feathered, Blenheim-coloured coat with slight wave

Well-defined stop

Feathering on back of legs

Ruby-coloured coat

KING CHARLES SPANIEL

NATURALLY WELL BEHAVED, THIS DOG MAKES A GENTLE AND AFFECTIONATE COMPANION

KC

Height range
25-27cm (10-11in)

Weight range
4-6kg (9-13lb)

Life span Over 12 years

Origin UK

Other colours

Ruby

King Charles

A very popular, compact little dog, this breed is also known as the English Toy Spaniel. It is related to the Cavalier King Charles Spaniel (opposite), and found in the same colour variations, but it is a separate breed. Its ancestors were a favourite of King Charles II of England (1630-85), and often accompanied him on state occasions. A long, silky coat gives this spaniel an aristocratic look. Happy living in an apartment or house, it loves company and makes an excellent family pet, but does not like being left alone for long periods.

Very pronounced stop

Pendant ears

Characteristic domed head

Short, upturned muzzle with large, wide nostrils

Slightly undershot jaw (lower jaw longer than upper)

Blenheim-coloured coat

Large, wide-set eyes

Prince Charles-coloured, long, silky coat

Tan markings on legs

Well-padded feet

Fine-grained, smooth, blue skin

Long, flowing crest extends from stop to neck

Large, erect ears

Plume of hair on lower section of tail

Sock of white hair encircles long, narrow feet

CHINESE CRESTED

THIS ELEGANT, INTELLIGENT DOG ALWAYS ATTRACTS ATTENTION

KC

Height range
23-33cm (9-13in)

Weight range
Up to 5kg (Up to 11lb)

Life span 12 years

Origin China

Other colours

Any colour

Hairlessness is a feature of several dog breeds around the world. It is the result of a genetic mutation that was initially considered a curiosity but then became desirable as the breed did not harbour fleas, shed hair, or have body odour. Although the Chinese Crested requires little grooming, its bare skin is sensitive: in winter it needs a coat to keep it warm, and in summer requires protection from the intense heat of the sun, which can burn and dry out its skin. This delicate skin, combined with the fact that the Chinese Crested needs little exercise and activity, makes it unsuitable for families that spend a lot of time outdoors. However, it is an ideal companion dog for older people due to its happy and friendly nature and playful personality.

Some Chinese Crested dogs are more lightly built than others. These fine-boned individuals are referred to as the deer type, while Chinese Crested dogs that have a heavier build are known as the cobby type.

POWDERPUFF VARIETY

Unlike the hairless variety, the Powderpuff Chinese Crested has a long, soft coat, which needs regular grooming to prevent matting. Both coat varieties can occur in the same litter.

CHIHUAHUA

A COMPANIONABLE, CLEVER, TINY DOG WITH A LARGE-DOG PERSONALITY

Height range
15–23cm (6–9in)

Weight range
2–3kg (4–7lb)

Life span Over 12 years

Origin Mexico

Other colours

Any colour

Always a single colour – never dappled or merle.

The smallest dog breed in the world, the Chihuahua is a highly intelligent, easily trained dog that makes a delightful companion. The breed is thought to have originated in China, but it is named after the Mexican state of Chihuahua, where it first came to prominence in the 1890s. The Chihuahua's size means it can be taken anywhere, making it the perfect lap dog. Possessive by nature, the Chihuahua is also an excellent watchdog and is ready to stand up for itself even if the opposition is far bigger. It is not suitable for a family with young children.

Distinctive apple-shaped head

Large, round eyes

Large, triangular, bat-like ears

Fawn coat with lighter underparts

Short-haired

Medium-length tail carried high over back

Smooth, glossy, red topcoat

Long-haired

Small, dainty feet

TIBETAN SPANIEL

THIS FUN-LOVING, INTELLIGENT, PLAYFUL DOG THRIVES ON HUMAN COMPANY

KC

Height range
25cm (10in)

Weight range
4-7kg (9-15lb)

Life span Over 12 years

Origin Tibet

Other colours

Any colour

This small dog has a delightful, easy-going temperament. Bred and owned by the monks of Tibet, the Tibetan Spaniel has a long history and was first brought to the UK around 1900, by returning medical missionaries. In spite of its slightly haughty expression, this dog is only too happy to run around a garden and play.

Head small in proportion to body

Pendant, feathered ears

Dark brown, expressive, oval eyes

Sleek, sable coat

TIBETAN TERRIER

AN ATHLETIC, BRIGHT, SURE-FOOTED DOG PACKED WITH ENERGY AND ENTHUSIASM

KC

Height range
36-41cm (14-16in)

Weight range
8-14kg (18-31lb)

Life span Over 10 years

Origin Tibet

Other colours

Variety of colours

Resembling a miniature Old English Sheepdog (see p.49), the Tibetan Terrier was originally bred for herding and was also used as a guard dog, for traders journeying to and from China. This medium-sized dog requires a firm hand, but the reward is a loyal, devoted companion. The long coat needs daily grooming to prevent matting.

Silky, caramel and white topcoat

Feathered tail curls over back

Long hair falls over eyes

Feathering covers round, snow-shoe-like feet

JAPANESE CHIN

THIS EXTROVERT, STYLISH, LIVELY DOG IS DAINTY BUT DEFINITELY NOT DELICATE

KC

Height range
20-28cm (8-11in)

Weight range
2-3kg (5-7lb)

Life span Over 10 years

Origin Japan

Other colours

Red and white

Ancestors of the Japanese Chin are thought to have been a royal gift from China to the Emperor of Japan. This dog was bred especially to warm the laps and hands of the ladies of Japan's Imperial Palace. Happy living in a small space, it makes an ideal apartment dog but its profuse coat sheds heavily.

Short, wide muzzle with upturned nose

Compact, square body

White marking on domed head

Feathered tail curves over back

Long, straight, silky, black and white coat

Short hair on front of legs

DANISH-SWEDISH FARMDOG

ALERT, ATTENTIVE, AND FRIENDLY, THIS DOG NEEDS A LOT OF EXERCISE

FCI

Height range
32-37cm (13-15in)

Weight range
7-12kg (15-26lb)

Life span 10-15 years

Origin Denmark/Sweden

This working dog has historically been used on farms in Denmark and Sweden as a herder, watchdog, and ratter, as well as a companion. Always eager to play, the Danish-Swedish Farmdog is good with children, so can make a great family dog, but it does have a tendency to chase small animals.

High-set, button ears

Rounded croup

Rose ear

Triangular-shaped head is small in relation to body

Tan markings on face

White coat

Black patch

Short, smooth, white coat with tan patches

DALMATIAN

THIS PLAYFUL AND EASY-GOING DOG NEEDS PLENTY OF EXERCISE AND PERSISTENT TRAINING

KC

Height range
56-61cm (22-24in)

Weight range
18-27kg (40-60lb)

Life span Over 10 years

Origin Unknown

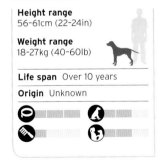

Particularly popular in Britain during the early 19th century, the Dalmatian was known as the "carriage dog", because it was trained to run under or beside horse-drawn carriages and fire engines, often travelling very long distances. The only spotted dog breed, the Dalmatian is intelligent, friendly, and outgoing, and makes an excellent companion. However, it does have a lot of energy and can be stubborn and aggressive with other dogs, so an owner needs to dedicate time to training. The puppies are born pure white, making it difficult to predict whether the spots will be black or liver once mature; this dog's white coat sheds a great deal.

Liver-coloured nose

Liver spots on white coat

Pups develop spots a few weeks after birth

Black spots are round and well-defined

Tail tapers from base to tip

High-set, drop ears taper to rounded point

Short, dense, glossy, white coat

Round, cat-like feet with well-arched toes

MINIATURE AMERICAN SHEPHERD

THIS LOYAL LITTLE DOG RETAINS THE HERDING INSTINCT OF ITS ANCESTORS

AKC

Height range
33–46cm (13–18in)

Weight range
9–18kg (20–40lb)

Life span 12–13 years

Origin USA

Other colours

Liver

Blue merle

Black

Downsized from the Australian Shepherd (see p.63) by American breeders, this dog is sometimes called the Miniature Australian Shepherd. It is highly intelligent, easy to train, and very good with children. The Miniature American Shepherd is eager to please, but can be nervous and quite destructive if left on its own for long periods of time.

High-set ears

Red merle coat

White markings on chest, legs, and muzzle

Tapering muzzle with rounded tip

Oval feet with well arched toes

HIMALAYAN SHEEPDOG

THIS DOG IS RESERVED BY NATURE SO CAN MAKE AN EXCELLENT WATCHDOG

Height range
51–63cm (20–25in)

Weight range
23–27kg (51–60lb)

Life span 10–11 years

Origin Nepal/India

Other colours

Gold

Black

Also known as the Bhotia, this rare dog from the foothills of the Himalayas is related to the larger Tibetan Mastiff (see p.77), but its exact origins and former uses are obscure. This is a powerful dog with a strong herding instinct. Kept as a family pet, it is a good companion and an efficient guard dog.

Thick, bushy tail, loosely turned over back

Drop ears lie close to head

Black and tan coat

White markings

Long, harsh, creamy white topcoat

Cat-like feet

THAI RIDGEBACK
THIS TOUGH, INDEPENDENT-MINDED DOG IS VERY ATHLETIC

FCI

Height range
51–61cm (20–24in)

Weight range
23–34kg (51–75lb)

Life span 10–12 years

Origin Thailand

Other colours

Isabella

Red

Blue

An old breed and unknown outside Thailand until the mid-1970s, the Thai Ridgeback has since gained recognition in other countries. It was used for hunting, to follow carts, and as a guard dog. Its earlier geographic isolation has resulted in most of its original natural instincts and drives remaining, as there were few chances for it to breed with other dogs. Today, it is primarily kept as a companion dog, and is naturally protective of its home and family. It can make a loyal, loving pet, but is often suspicious of other dogs, and can be aggressive or shy if not properly socialized.

Erect ears

Muzzle longer than skull

Ridge of hair on back lies in opposite direction to rest of coat

Short, smooth, black coat

Slightly wrinkled forehead

GOLDENDOODLE
This attractive dog is a cross between a Standard Poodle and a Golden Retriever. The characteristics of the poodle parent are clearly visible.

CROSSBREEDS

Dogs of mixed breeding vary from the so-called designer dogs, with purebred parents of two different recognized breeds, to the bit-of-everything type, the result of accidental, random crosses (see p.290). Some designer hybrids are now extremely fashionable. They are mostly given whimsical combination names, such as Cockapoo (a Cocker Spaniel–Poodle cross).

No pedigree, parents unknown – but an excellent companion

One of the reasons for creating modern designer dogs was to mix the desired characteristics from one breed with the non-shedding, hypoallergenic coat of another. A cross of this type currently enjoying great popularity is the Labradoodle, a mixture of Labrador Retriever and Poodle. However, even when the parents are readily recognized breeds such as these, it may be impossible to predict which side of the family the puppies will favour. Labradoodles, for example, show little consistency from litter to litter, some puppies inheriting the curly poodle coat while others are more obviously influenced by the Labrador parent. Such lack of standardization is common in designer crosses, although occasionally it has proved possible to produce a standard and breed dogs to type. An example of this is the Lucas Terrier, the result of crossing the Sealyham Terrier and the Norfolk Terrier. Currently, it is rare for such crosses to achieve breed recognition.

Deliberate mixing of two specific breeds to produce particular characteristics has proliferated since the end of the 20th century, but is by no means a modern trend. One of the best-known crossbreeds, the Lurcher, has been around for several hundred years. This dog combines the qualities of speedy sight hounds, such as the Greyhound and Whippet, with desirable traits found in other breeds, such as the collie's enthusiasm for work and the tenacity of the terrier.

Prospective owners of a designer dog should take into account the personalities and temperaments of both breeds involved in the mix. These may be very different and either one might predominate. It is also important to consider both parent dogs' requirements for general care and exercise.

All crossbred dogs are commonly believed to be more intelligent than pedigree dogs, but there is no sound evidence for this. Random breeds are often said to be healthier than purebreds, and it is true that they are at much lower risk of the inherited diseases prevalent in some breeds.

GUNDOG CROSS
The Labradinger is a cross between two popular gundogs – the Labrador Retriever and the English Springer Spaniel.

HEALTHY DOG
Random-bred dogs, like this terrier cross, are usually robust and are largely free from inherited disorders.

LURCHER
FLEET-FOOTED OUTDOORS, AT HOME THIS DOG IS LAID-BACK AND RELAXED

Height range
55-71cm (22-28in)

Weight range
27-32kg (60-71lb)

Life span 13-14 years

Origin UK

Other colours

Any colour

Famed as a poacher's dog, and used to hunt rabbit and hare, traditionally Lurchers were first-generation crosses of a sight hound with a terrier or a herding dog. Today, they are also bred with each other and ideally are greyhound size. In the home Lurchers are peaceful and tolerant, and make fine family companions.

Rough, blue merle coat

Fine, pointed muzzle

Round eyes give alert expression

Long, slender legs

Belly distinctly tucked up

Smooth, fawn coat

Slight feathering on tail

Smooth-haired

Rough-haired

COCKAPOO
THIS INTELLIGENT, GREGARIOUS, AND RELAXED DOG MAKES AN EASY COUNTRY OR CITY COMPANION

Height range
Toy:
Up to 25cm (Up to 10in)
Miniature:
28-35cm (11-14in)
Standard:
Over 38cm (Over 15in)

Weight range
Toy:
Up to 5kg (Up to 11lb)
Miniature:
6-9kg (13-20lb)
Standard:
Over 10kg (Over 22lb)

Life span 14-15 years

Origin Mostly USA

Other colours

Any colour

Most Cockapoos are first-generation crosses of a Toy or Miniature Poodle (see p.271) with an American or sometimes English Cocker Spaniel (see p.222). They are particularly valued for their tractable and affectionate characters. Their appearance is a variable mix of the parent breeds, but always with a wavy coat that sheds very little.

Long hair on muzzle

Square and compact body

Large, dark, round eyes

Drop ears covered with long, silky hair

Tail usually feathered

Fine, fawn coat

Large paws covered by hair

Standard

LABRADOODLE

INCREASINGLY POPULAR, THIS DOG IS RELIABLY PLAYFUL, AFFECTIONATE, AND INTELLIGENT

Height range
Miniature:
36–41cm (14–16in)
Medium:
43–51cm (17–20in)
Standard:
53–61cm (21–24in)

Weight range
Miniature:
7–11kg (15–24lb)
Medium:
14–20kg (31–44lb)
Standard:
23–29kg (51–65lb)

Life span 14–15 years

Origin Australia

Other colours

Any colour

The original Labrador-Poodle cross was intended as an assistance dog for allergy sufferers, but the Labradoodle has rapidly gained popularity as a family pet. In Australia, it is on its way to being a breed with a written standard. Elsewhere, this remains a crossbreed, with no official status but in huge demand. The dog's personality attracts owners as much as its appearance. It is consistently level-headed and biddable without becoming serious or reserved.

Large, dark, rounded eyes

Drop, apricot-coloured ears

Long, curved tail

Curly, cream coat has little dander

Tucked-up belly

Body slightly heavier than a Poodle (see p.271)

Medium-sized, round feet

Standard

SCHNOODLE

INTELLIGENT AND PLAYFUL, THIS DOG NEEDS PLENTY OF MENTAL STIMULATION

Height range
25–70cm (10–28in)

Weight range
3–39kg (6–85lb)

Life span 10–15 years

Origin USA

Other colours

Variety of colours

As this dog is a cross between a miniature, standard, or giant Schnauzer (see pp.218 and 40–41) and a toy, miniature, or standard Poodle (see p.271), it can vary widely in size, weight, colour and appearance. Most are small companion dogs, but they still need sufficient exercise to avoid behavioural problems.

High-set ears

Square body with straight back

Soft, wavy coat

Round, dark brown eyes

Long hair on muzzle

BICHON YORKIE

THIS PLAYFUL, SMALL COMPANION DOG IS IDEALLY SUITED TO URBAN LIFE

Height range
23–31cm (9–12in)

Weight range
3–6kg (7–13lb)

Life span 13–15 years

Origin USA

Other colours

Variety of colours

Some crossbreeds are created deliberately, but the first Bichon Frise (see p.267) and Yorkshire Terrier (see p.192) mix was a happy accident that breeders have chosen to repeat. The result is the Bichon Yorkie – a dog that is usually larger than the diminutive Yorkshire Terrier, with the feisty spirit of its terrier parent tempered by the more compliant nature of the Bichon Frise.

Dark nose

Dark, round eyes

High-set ears

Darker, plumed tail carried high when moving

Double-layered, silky, curly, white and orange coat

Round, tight feet

BULL BOXER

THIS FRIENDLY AND BOISTEROUS DOG IS EASIER TO TRAIN THAN OTHER MASTIFF-TYPES

Height range
41–53cm (16–21in)

Weight range
17–24kg (37–53lb)

Life span 12–13 years

Origin UK

Other colours

Any colour

The Bull Boxer is a cross between the laid-back Boxer (see p.88) and bull-baiting dogs, such as, the Staffordshire Bull Terrier (see p.214), which is highly popular but may be difficult with other pets. The Bull Boxer occupies the middle ground in size and character. This dog needs commitment, but rewards its owner well.

Small, semi-erect, drop ears

Powerful build inherited from both parents

Rounded eyes have alert expression

Long, tapering, curved tail

Strong, blunt muzzle with overhanging lip

Broad, deep chest

Smooth, shiny, short, dense, black coat

White markings on feet

Legs longer than Staffordshire Bull Terrier's

LUCAS TERRIER

THIS FRIENDLY, NON-YAPPY TERRIER GETS ON WELL WITH CHILDREN AND OTHER PETS

Height range
23-30cm (9-12in)

Weight range
5-9kg (11-20lb)

Life span 14-15 years

Origin UK

Other colours

White

Tan coats may have a black or badger-grey saddle. White coats may be marked with black, badger-grey, and/or tan.

This rare working terrier was developed in the 1940s by crossing Norfolk Terriers with Sealyham Terriers (see p.191) to produce a small, nimble dog to follow game to ground. Smart and eager to please, it is easy to train and quietly behaved, provided it has a good daily walk. It enjoys play and loves to dig, but is less inclined to bark than other terrier breeds.

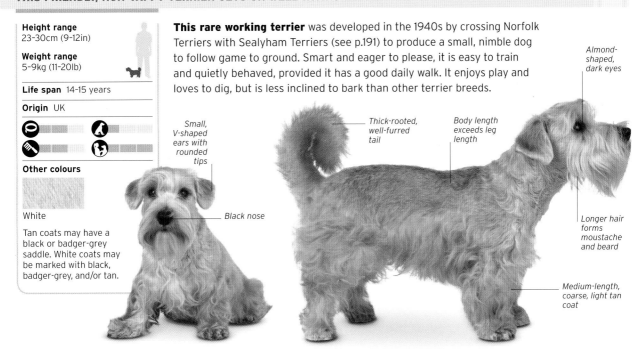

Small, V-shaped ears with rounded tips

Black nose

Thick-rooted, well-furred tail

Body length exceeds leg length

Almond-shaped, dark eyes

Longer hair forms moustache and beard

Medium-length, coarse, light tan coat

MAL-SHI

AN ENDEARING DOG WITH A KIND DISPOSITION THAT LOVES HUMAN COMPANY

Height range
21-51cm (8-20in)

Weight range
2-7kg (5-15lb)

Life span 12-14 years

Origin USA

Other colours

Black and brown | Black

Black and white | Brown and white

May also be brown.

Also known as the Malt-tzu, this small dog is a cross between a Maltese (see p.269) and a Shih Tzu (see p.266). Developed in the 1990s, the Mal-shi has proved popular in many countries especially where there is demand for dogs with low shedding coats. If puppies are well socialized and trained, they are said to be a good choice for first time owners.

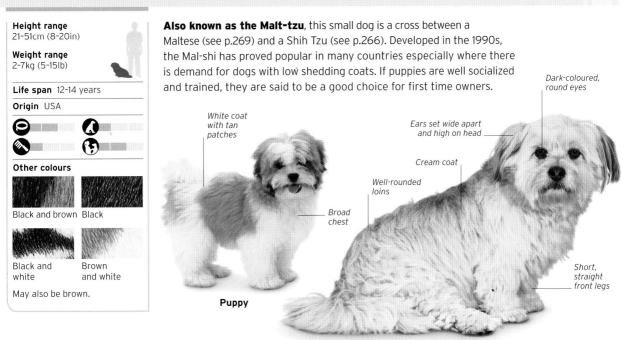

White coat with tan patches

Broad chest

Puppy

Ears set wide apart and high on head

Cream coat

Well-rounded loins

Dark-coloured, round eyes

Short, straight front legs

GOLDENDOODLE

A DELIGHTFUL NEW CROSSBREED, THIS DOG IS SOCIABLE AND EASY TO LIVE WITH

Height range
Up to 61cm (up to 24in)

Weight range
23-41kg (51-90lb)

Life span 10-15 years

Origin USA

Other colours

Any colour

One of the newest "designer dogs", this mixture of the Golden Retriever (see p.258) and the Poodle (see p.271) was first bred in the USA in the 1990s. Since then the Goldendoodle's growing popularity has encouraged breeders elsewhere to continue its development. Most of these dogs are first-generation crosses and vary considerably in appearance – some have curly coats, while others are wavy or straight. The crossbreed's size depends on whether the Poodle parent is a medium, miniature, or toy variety. Although lively and energetic, Goldendoodles have gentle temperaments and are usually easy to train. They get on well with children and other pets.

Brown nose

Drop ears, slightly darker than rest of coat

Well-defined stop

Dark eyes with kind expression

Darker saddle of hair

Slightly tucked-up belly

Thick, curly, apricot coat

Heavily feathered tail

Front feet larger than back feet

LABRADINGER

THIS ATTRACTIVE ALL-ROUNDER IS SUITABLE AS A FAMILY DOG AND AS A GUNDOG

Height range
46-56cm (18-22in)

Weight range
25-41kg (55-90lb)

Life span 10-14 years

Origin USA

Other colours

Yellow

Liver

Chocolate

Also known as the Springador, this Labrador Retriever and English Springer Spaniel cross (see pp.256-57 and 226-27) may result from unplanned breeding on country estates where gundogs were kept. Interest in fashionable crossbreeds has given it popularity, and a name. It is an excellent gundog that can be trained to retrieve and flush game, and also makes a good family pet.

Slight stop

Level back

Deep chest

Thick tail extends to hock

Amber eyes

Drop ears with rounded tips

Soft, wavy, black coat

Compact feet with well-arched toes

PUGGLE

WITH SUFFICIENT EXERCISE, THIS DOG MAKES AN IDEAL FAMILY COMPANION

Height range
25-38cm (10-15in)

Weight range
7-14kg (15-31lb)

Life span 10-13 years

Origin USA

Other colours

Red or tan

Lemon

Black

Developed in the 1990s, the Puggle is a cross between a Pug (see p.265) and a Beagle (see pp.152-53) that has become increasingly popular in recent years. It is good with people and with other dogs and easily adapts to living in a town apartment or on a farm. It needs daily walks, including games, to keep it happy.

Very pronounced stop

Square body

Short, dark muzzle

Drop ears with some black hairs

Fawn coat

Lighter-coloured chest and throat

Short, smooth double coat

Compact, round feet

RANDOM-BRED DOGS

THESE DOGS MAY LACK A PEDIGREE BUT THEY CAN PROVIDE LOVE, COMPANIONSHIP, AND FUN

Dogs with random breeding are usually of unknown ancestry, with the parents themselves likely to be the result of accidental mixings that may go back several generations. Choosing a random-bred puppy is a bit of a lottery for prospective owners as it is difficult to predict what the dog will look like at maturity. Many of the dogs available for adoption in rescue centres are random crossbreds; in the majority of cases they make excellent pets.

LONG AND SHAGGY
Puppies with soft, fluffy coats often grow up to have long, coarse coats, like this dog's, that require regular grooming to prevent matting.

Long hairs cover feet

SOFT AND SILKY
Many random-bred dogs resemble sheepdogs with soft coats and feathering on the chest, legs, and tail. This dog has sheepdog markings too.

LARGE DOG
Random-bred dogs can grow to any size or shape. This large dog may be the same size as one or other of its parents or somewhere in between the two.

Expressive, brown eyes

SHORT AND SMOOTH
The short coat and drop ears of this dog suggest a hound-like ancestor, but its merle colouring is less easy to explain.

Black, triangular, drop ears

MEDIUM-SIZED DOG
Many mixed-breed dogs are intermediate in size and sandy in colour, like this one.

SMALL DOG
This small dog has some distinctly terrier-like features, including semi-erect ears and a broad head.

Well-feathered tail

UNIQUE APPEARANCE
Unlike pedigree dogs, no two random-bred dogs are alike. This dog may resemble a terrier superficially but its offspring may look very different.

CARE AND TRAINING

PREPARING FOR ARRIVAL

Forward thinking and early preparation will help to make your puppy's introduction to his new home as stress free as possible. Before the newest member of the family arrives, check that the home environment, both indoors and outdoors, is safe for a young, inquisitive dog. Ensure too that you have all the basic equipment needed for his daily care and development, including his collar, bed, and toys.

A puppy is life-changing

Puppy-proofing your home

Start your safety checks by walking around your home and garden and trying to see everything as your puppy would see it. What looks like a tempting object to chew? Is that table in a prime position to be knocked over? Is there a small gap in the fence that he could squeeze through if he tried? Take preventive action now to avoid trouble later.

Safety indoors

Making your home safe for a dog is similar to making it safe for children. Dogs investigate a new object by chewing it, so place anything potentially hazardous well out of a puppy's reach. Toxic household chemicals are an obvious danger but your puppy could be poisoned by many other things, such as certain pot plants and some human foods, including chocolate. Remind children not to leave small toys lying around for your puppy to pick up and choke on. Watch out for electrical wires, remote controls, and anything else near the floor and small enough for a puppy to gnaw. Objects that you may think are

out of reach may be accidents waiting to happen; a washing basket is easy to knock over and its contents can create hours of fun for a destructive puppy. Consider keeping some doors closed or using a stair gate to limit the areas that your dog can access. Excitable dogs can suffer back and leg injuries from slips and falls on smooth or polished floors. Put down non-slip mats; if they are machine-washable, it will be easy to deal with dirt and stains.

Safety outdoors

Look for gaps in fences and underneath gates, even if you plan to supervise your dog outside. Puppies can disappear through the smallest holes and thickest hedges if they think there is something interesting on the other side. Keep garden chemicals out of the way. Slug pellets and other pesticides can look like tasty treats, but may be harmful if eaten. Do not let your puppy chew garden plants – many are poisonous. Avoid leaning tools or wheelbarrows against fences where a boisterous puppy could knock them over and cause injury.

HAZARDS FOR YOUR DOG TO AVOID

TOXIC PLANTS

HARMFUL CHEMICALS

LOOSE FLEX

GAPS UNDER GATE

SLUG PELLETS

TOP TIPS

- **Book a vet's appointment** to complete your puppy's vaccinations soon after you bring him home.

- **Microchipping your dog** improves the likelihood of finding him if he gets lost, and is compulsory in some countries.

- **Pet insurance** can provide peace of mind in an emergency.

- **Ask your breeder** for a towel or blanket that smells familiar to your puppy. It will help to reassure him for the first few nights.

Collars and leads

To begin with, you will need to buy a small, light puppy collar and replace it as your dog grows. The style of collar depends on what your dog finds most comfortable. For example, long-haired breeds will find a smooth, rolled leather collar more comfortable because it does not pull on their coat as much as a nylon collar. Greyhound-type breeds are happier with a wide, flat collar that is less likely to damage their sensitive necks. Whatever type of dog you have, make sure that the width of his collar exceeds the width of one of his neck vertebrae. When choosing a lead, simply handle a few to see which one feels most comfortable for you.

Harnesses and halters

A typical harness fits around the body with the lead attaching on the dog's back. This can be beneficial for some dogs, as it removes tension from around the neck, but harnesses can be fiddly to take on and off, especially with an exuberant or over-excited dog. The harness straps should be well fitted at all points, leaving enough room for you to slip two fingers easily between the harness and the dog's body. Contrary to popular belief, harnesses do not stop a dog from pulling on the lead; only training can do that. If you have a dog that is a determined puller, you may find a halter with a fixed noseband helps to restrain him.

Name tag

Address holder

NAME.................

TEL.....................

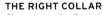

THE RIGHT COLLAR
Choose a collar for comfort, not fashionable appearance. Avoid collars that tighten when the dog pulls, such as check chains or half-check collars.

Nylon collar

Leather collar

ID TAGS
Include your name and emergency contact details so that people can get in touch with you easily if your dog is lost.

TYPES OF LEAD
Short leads are ideal when you need close control – for example, during training. Extending leads allow your dog more freedom to run.

Extending lead

Short lead

FITTING A COLLAR

A collar should fit securely around a dog's neck without being too tight. As a guide, you should be able to fit two fingers between the collar and the dog's neck. Check the fit regularly as your puppy grows and alter it as necessary. Replace the collar as soon as your puppy grows out of it.

Body harness

Fixed noseband halter

HARNESSES AND HALTERS
Instead of a collar, you may prefer to use a harness or halter. These must fit correctly and be introduced to a dog carefully. Some short legged dogs cannot wear harnesses and short muzzled dogs cannot wear halters.

Types of bed

Dog beds vary widely in price, and until your puppy is settled and fully house-trained it is not worth investing in anything expensive. A new dog may chew or soil his bed, so look for a cheap and washable option.

There are two main types of bed: hard and soft. Hard beds, made from moulded plastic, are easy to keep clean. They are also relatively difficult for a young puppy to chew, although a dog who has his adult teeth may inflict some damage. You can use disposable items such as old towels to make a plastic bed comfortable for your dog, safe in the knowledge that you can wash or discard bedding that gets chewed or soiled. These beds are also a good choice for an older dog who suffers from incontinence. Soft, foam-filled beds are more comfortable to sleep on, especially for an older dog who is beginning to experience stiffness in his joints. Although the cover may be washable, these beds are not suitable for young puppies because they like nothing better than pulling the bed's foam filling out, leaving you with the expense of a replacement bed.

STAIR GATE
Use a stair gate to keep your young dog safe in one room without making him feel trapped.

Cages and playpens

Until your new puppy is house-trained, use a cage or a playpen as his personal space. Never confine your dog as a punishment. A cage or playpen should be a place that your dog enjoys – you may even feed him there. A playpen also gives you peace of mind, safely containing your puppy away from trouble while you are in another room. If you introduce your puppy to a cage when he is young and only shut the door for short periods, he will be happy to use it should it be necessary if he is ill or when you are going on a long journey. However, do not restrict your dog to a cage for long periods as this can increase the risk of behavioural problems.

Moulded plastic bed

Keep the gate open unless you leave the room

Cage

Foam-filled bed

Playpens have open tops

Playpen

DOG BEDS
Plastic beds are hygienic and hard-wearing. Pad them with soft bedding to make your dog comfortable. Foam-filled beds and beanbags are cosy and attractive but are not suitable for young puppies until they are house-trained and have stopped chewing. Soft beds usually have washable covers that can be removed.

USING A CAGE
A cage or playpen allows you to leave your puppy unsupervised when you are busy. He will probably sleep some of the time, but give him plenty of toys to keep him amused. Do not leave him confined alone for long periods at a time.

TOYS FOR YOUNG PUPPIES
Soft toys are best for young puppies who have not yet grown a set of adult teeth. A puppy is likely to go through several toys, so don't buy expensive ones.

Soft toys

Rope tugger

Puppy with chewable rubber ring

Chewable rubber toys

Rubber and rope bone

TOYS FOR OLDER PUPPIES
As puppies get older, they will chew vigorously and need more durable toys. Thick rope tuggers, or toys with a combination of rope and chewable rubber, are a good choice and last a long time.

TOYS FOR ADULT DOGS
Adult dogs also love toys and appreciate those with a variety of textures and materials. Harder toys are best, as they will withstand chewing by a mature dog's full set of teeth.

Buying toys

Toys provide a dog with mental stimulation and something permissible to chew on. Used for games or during training sessions, they are great for encouraging a dog to interact with his owner. When buying toys, choose only those that are specially designed for dogs. Children's toys are a dangerous substitute as they may have small pieces that a dog can chew off and swallow. Never leave your dog alone with his toys for long periods; even playthings that are meant to be chewed, such as rawhide bones, can be a choking hazard.

Soft toys are best for young puppies while they still have their baby teeth. As puppies get older and begin teething, they are more likely to chew and at this stage stronger toys such as rope tuggers are the best choice. Once your dog is an adult, choose toys with a variety of textures and shapes. Toys that can be thrown or tugged are good as long as you are able to play with your dog, otherwise choose a toy that he can chew on. Some chewable toys have tasty flavours and there are also food-dispensing toys that release treats when played with. These can keep a dog entertained for a long

time, and are useful if you are too busy to play. Dogs that are dedicated chewers can often be kept out of mischief with rubber toys, which are very durable, or the ranges of rubber toys that are designed to be stuffed with food. Most dogs have favourite toys, and you will soon get to know which ones your dog likes best.

TOP TIPS

■ **Playing with a tug toy** is a great way to train a puppy not to mouth at your hand. Offer to play with him but end the game as soon as his teeth meet your hand.

■ **Use food-dispensing toys** to keep your dog entertained if you have to leave him alone for short periods.

■ **Keep a favourite toy** hidden out of your dog's reach and use it only as a prized reward during training sessions.

FOOD AND FEEDING

A puppy's dietary needs change as he matures

Keeping a dog healthy is largely a question of feeding him the right food in the right quantities. There are several options: complete, pre-prepared dried or wet foods; raw, uncooked foods; or a diet created from combination of these. Whatever you decide on, aim for a good nutritional balance and tailor the quantities to suit the size and age of your dog.

A balanced diet

Ready-prepared dog food is the choice of many owners as it is both quick and convenient. Reading the labels on processed foods will tell you what type of dog they are suitable for. Make sure you use a type that is appropriate for your dog's age. Some foods are available in puppy, junior, adult, and senior varieties, and buying the right formula is important. When in doubt about what quantities to feed, ask your vet for advice. If you decide to feed your dog a mixture of wet and dried food, be careful to halve the quantity of each so you are not over-feeding him.

A balanced diet consists of the right quantities of nutrients: proteins, carbohydrates, fat, vitamins, and minerals. Using processed foods ensures that you get the balance right; if you feed your dog fresh food, his diet needs a little more thought. A dog's nutritional requirements change as he ages. Puppies need high levels of protein and calcium to aid growth and development. Geriatric dogs, on the other hand, require particularly high-quality protein as well as increased levels of certain vitamins as their kidney function slows down. Reduced kidney function can lead to dehydration, due to too much water being excreted, so you may decide to feed an older dog a wet diet rather than dried food, to increase his water intake. The sort of food your dog eats will also

Stainless steel bowl

affect the care of his teeth. A dog that is fed exclusively on wet food is more likely to need to have his teeth cleaned regularly.

Your dog needs two bowls: one for food and one for water. Put the food bowl down only at mealtimes and remove it as soon as your dog has finished eating. The water bowl should be left in an accessible place at all times and should always be kept filled with fresh water. Of the various types of bowl available, the best are stainless steel, as they can be thoroughly cleaned after each use and, unlike plastic bowls, cannot be chewed. Bowls with sloping edges are a good choice as they are difficult for your dog to tip over.

Plastic bowl

TYPES OF FOOD
Dry food provides your dog with a complete, age-appropriate diet. Wet food alone may lead to dental problems. Raw food, such as meat and vegetables, takes a little longer to prepare.

Dry food for puppies

Senior food

Tinned food

Meat from a sachet

Raw food

FOOD OPTIONS AND AMOUNTS PER DAY

DOG WEIGHT	DRIED FOOD	TINNED FOOD 400G (14OZ)	MEAT FROM A SACHET	RAW FOOD
Pekingese 5kg (11lb)	75g (3oz)	1 tin	300g (11oz)	150g (5oz)
Beagle 10kg (22lb)	200g (7oz)	2 tins	600g (1lb 5oz)	300g (11oz)
Border Collie 20kg (44lb)	400g (14oz)	3 tins	1kg (2lb 3oz)	600g (1lb 5oz)
Dobermann 30kg (66lb)	500g (1lb)	4 tins	1.2kg (2lb 10oz)	900g (2lb)
Irish Wolfhound 40kg (88lb)	600g (1lb 5oz)	5 tins	1.8kg (4lb)	1.2kg (2lb 10oz)

TOP TIPS

■ **Opened packets** or tins of wet food will need to be sealed and refrigerated between uses. Dried dog food should also be kept in a sealed container, to keep it fresh and free from contamination.

■ **Puppies need** three or four small meals a day, but by the time they are mature will only require feeding morning and evening. Feeding your dog smaller meals twice a day as opposed to one big meal is preferable, as it puts less strain on their digestive systems.

■ **Introduce new foods** gradually over several days to avoid stomach upsets.

Treats and chews

If you use a lot of edible treats to reward your dog during training, you may risk over-feeding him. Consider the treats part of your dog's overall diet and slightly reduce the amount of food you give him at mealtimes. Alternatively, you can take part of your dog's main rations to give as treats throughout the day, especially if you use dried food.

Either buy ready-made dog treats from a pet shop or make your own at home by chopping up foods such as cheese, chicken or sausage. Dogs are particularly fond of treats that have a strong smell and taste.

Chews are a great way to keep your dog occupied for a while and provide something to take a puppy's mind off chewing your household possessions. They are also very effective at keeping a dog's teeth clean. Be careful what type of chew you give your dog. Canine teeth are extremely strong and can tear apart chews with ease; swallowing the loose parts can lead to choking or a blockage. Never leave a puppy or young dog alone while he has a chew.

PRACTICAL CHOICE
Hide chews not only keep your puppy entertained but also help to clean his teeth. Always supervise him when he is chewing and remove any small pieces he tears off in exchange for a treat.

TREAT VARIETIES
Using a variety of treats keeps your dog motivated during training and allows you to create a hierarchy of rewards. Knowing which treats appeal most to your dog will make training easier and more enjoyable.

Cubes of cheese

Bite-sized training treats

Meaty strips

Cooked sausage

FIRST DAYS

Your puppy's first days in his new home are important to the rest of his development. Start as you intend to go on and set the rules right from the beginning. Do not be tempted to be lenient while your dog settles in. He will feel at home much more quickly and easily if you set clear boundaries. The sooner you establish a routine the sooner you will succeed in training your dog.

It's never too early for a puppy to learn

Choosing a name

Family discussions about choosing a name that suits your new puppy are likely to be long and difficult. The name should be something that you feel comfortable calling out in public. It must also be clearly distinguishable from any commands you are likely to want to teach your dog. For example, a dog called "Kit" will find learning the command to "sit" very difficult. Overly long names make training problematic, so pick something with just one or two syllables. Remember that dogs do not understand language, only sounds. Giving your dog a long name that you shorten in some situations will only confuse him. Also to keep it simple for your dog, make sure that all members of your family use the same name to address him.

TRAINING | TEACHING YOUR DOG HIS NAME

1 When your puppy is nearby, crouch down and clearly call his name in a cheery, enthusiastic voice. Use your hands to guide his attention towards you.

3 Make sure you show your puppy how pleased you are to see him by giving him lots of warm attention. Never use your puppy's name to scold him.

2 As your puppy approaches, praise him in an excited tone of voice. Stroke and fuss him when he reaches you.

TRIP OUTSIDE
Your puppy must learn that outside is the place to go to the toilet. Take your puppy into the garden first thing in the morning and last thing at night as well as whenever he wakes from a nap. Also, go outside with him after each feed or after playing with him.

puppy appears to be clean. It may be simply that you have become better at predicting your puppy's toilet habits and not that he has learned to control himself indoors.

What to do at night

Inevitably, your new puppy will cry or whine at night-time. This is a natural response to being separated from his mother and litter mates and is unlikely to last for more than a few nights. Ignore him, unless he is being very noisy, in which case he may need to go to the toilet. If you can take him outside to relieve himself in the middle of the night, he will learn to be clean indoors much more quickly. Tiring your puppy out during the day is the best way of getting a peaceful night. Spending time playing with him and feeding him a warm evening meal will make him feel sleepy. Always give your puppy the opportunity to go to the toilet just before you settle him down in his bed.

House-training

Some dogs learn to be clean indoors sooner than others, but with all of them the most important factor in house-training is vigilance. Supervision is the key to success in the first few weeks. Your puppy may need to relieve himself at any time, so learn to spot the signs, such as sniffing the ground and circling. You can also try to predict the times when he is most likely to need the toilet. Even in the absence of any signs, take your puppy into the garden at regular intervals, no matter what the weather is like, and wait patiently. Stay with your puppy to make sure that he does not get distracted. When he does go to the toilet, give a command such as "hurry up" and praise him enthusiastically when he has finished.

The occasional house-training accident is inevitable and unless you catch your puppy in the act there is nothing you can do except clean up the mess. Never punish or scold a puppy for having an accident but if you are nearby and spot him squatting, interrupt him with a sharp noise such as clapping your hands. Your aim is to stop him in mid-flow, not to scare him. When he stops, encourage him into the garden and wait for him to perform, giving the command "hurry up" followed by praise as described above.

Continue to take your puppy on regular toilet trips to the garden even when he has stopped having accidents. You may be able to lengthen intervals between trips, but beware the common mistake of stopping house-training as soon as your

SECURE PLACE
A cage can be used at night as a way of keeping your puppy safe if there is no alternative, but confinement is not natural for a puppy and should not be used simply as a way of dog-proofing your home. A cardboard box is a cheap, disposable alternative.

HANDLING YOUR DOG

Accustom your puppy to regular handling

Getting your dog used to being handled early on will make his day-to-day care much more pleasurable. Teach him to accept being held without protest so that you can perform routine health checks or administer occasional treatments such as ear drops. A dog that is happy to be handled is a joy to groom, and tasks such as nail clipping and tooth brushing will not be a chore or turn into a struggle.

How to handle your dog

Make handling an opportunity for your dog to receive lots of attention, treats, and praise. Handling sessions should be frequent and fun, but keep them short so that your dog does not feel smothered. Begin by calling your dog to you and give him some gentle fuss and lots of praise when he approaches. Then practise handling him by examining his ears, eyes, mouth, paws, and tail. After each examination, reward your dog with a treat. When you have finished, spend some more time fussing him. In the early stages, handling sessions should be no more taxing than that. If your dog appears reluctant for any part of his body to be handled, do not force him.

PETTING
Pet your dog by crouching down to his level and talking to him in a gentle tone. Never lean into his space. If he is willing, slowly put your hand out and stroke his chest; avoid placing your hand directly over his head.

GOOD PRACTICE | EXAMINING YOUR DOG

LIFTING THE EARS
Get your dog used to having the inside of his ear handled. Check that the ear is its usual, dull, pink colour with no unpleasant odour or excessive wax.

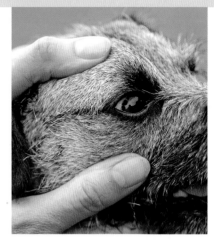

EXAMINING THE EYES
Handle the area around your dog's eyes with great care. If the eyes need cleaning, wipe them lightly using cotton wool moistened with warm water.

PLENTY OF SUPPORT
When lifting both large and small dogs, support them front and back and hold them close to your body.

support his front and back, praise your dog, and hold him without lifting him. Reward him with a treat for standing still. Gradually increase the length of time you hold him, before gently lifting him just off the ground. Immediately put him down and reward him with a treat.

Small breeds and puppies are relatively easy for one person to pick up. Larger breeds, however, should not be lifted by one person alone. Any dog over 15kg (33lb) requires two people to lift it, one at the front and one at the back. Dogs can move suddenly, causing strain to the person lifting them; they also risk being dropped, undoing hours of patient training and causing problems for the future. When you lift, bend from the knees to avoid back injury, and check that there are no obstacles on the path to your destination.

GENTLE SLOPE
If lifting your dog is impractical, a ramp is a good alternative, particularly to help older dogs to get into a car.

You may notice that he suddenly stiffens when you lift up his tail, for example, or growls when you try to pick up his paw. If this is the case, and on checking there is no sign he is hurt, use treats to gradually build up the amount of handling your dog will tolerate. Stiffening and growling are signs of aggression and, if they go unheeded, may result in a bite. Always get advice from a professional behaviour counsellor to help a reluctant dog accept being handled.

Lifting your dog

A dog that is not used to being lifted may panic and react aggressively if you pick him up, so it is worthwhile practising lifting your dog. To begin with, simply place your hands to

INSPECTING THE TEETH
Gently lift your dog's lips to check that the gums are pink and there are no signs of soreness. His teeth should be white and lack excessive tartar deposits.

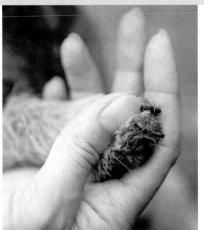

TOUCHING THE PAWS
Check the pads for sore or broken skin, and look in between the toes for injuries or swelling. Examine the nails and get them trimmed or clip them yourself if necessary.

LIFTING THE TAIL
Lift your dog's tail while you tickle his stomach with your other hand. Ensure that the area below the tail is clean and that there are no signs of redness or swelling.

GROOMING

Both dog and owner alike should find grooming an enjoyable experience. The contact encourages a strong bond to develop and is beneficial to your dog. Not only do dogs find being groomed relaxing, but it is also good for their skin and coat. You can check your dog for lumps and bumps, parasites, and minor injuries too, while you brush him.

A dog's coat needs regular grooming – more frequently if it is a show dog

Learning to be groomed

Grooming is really an extended period of handling. It should not be difficult if you have taken the time to teach your dog to accept being restrained. Approach grooming as a training session. Place a towel on the floor and encourage your dog to stand still on it, in return for a treat. Calmly stroke and praise him, but do not allow him to become over-excited. Introduce your dog to each piece of grooming equipment that you will be using regularly. Let him sniff each brush but do not allow him to chew it. Restrain him gently and move the brush through the coat on his back without pressing too hard. After a few strokes of the brush, stop and reward him with praise and a treat.

No matter what type of coat your dog has, spend time each day practising grooming and getting him used to the sensation. With a new dog, make grooming sessions very short and always reward him for standing still. Speak to him in a calm, reassuring tone and avoid tugging on tangles or knots, which may hurt him. Gradually increase the length of time you require him to stand still. Be firm from the start. If he tries to bite the brush, do not let him turn the session into a game. Instead, gently turn his head away from the brush. He should remain standing, unless you ask him to sit or lie down so that you can reach another part of his coat. Once he is used to standing still on the towel for an extended time, you can start a proper grooming routine.

DETANGLING
Some coat types, such as the silky coat of the Yorkshire Terrier, are particularly prone to tangles. Silky coats need regular grooming to manage any small knots, so that they do not form uncomfortable mats.

CLIPPING NAILS
Dogs that do not regularly walk on hard surfaces, or that have long hair around their paws, need their nails clipped regularly. Remove the pointed tip of the nail only and be careful to avoid cutting the quick.

GROOMING TOOLS

A rubber brush or glove removes shedding undercoat in smooth-coated breeds. For all other breeds, a slicker brush is the best general tool, although a bristle brush may be preferable for long coats. Use a comb on all coat types as a finishing tool.

Fine-toothed comb

Bristle brush

Slicker brush

Rubber grooming glove

HAVING A BATH

Brush any knots out of your dog's coat then wet him all over – avoid getting water into his eyes and ears. Massage dog shampoo into his coat; never use human shampoo, as it can cause painful skin problems. Rinse the shampoo out completely before drying him thoroughly, and finish off with a good brush.

Work your way round

Stick to a routine when you brush your dog to ensure that no areas are missed. Start at the foot of one of his hind legs and use an appropriate tool (see above) to brush from the bottom of the coat outwards. Keep tension on the skin with your other hand, to prevent the coat from pulling painfully as you brush. Whatever tool you use, make sure you work it right through the coat but be careful not to scrape it painfully on the skin. Work your way up the leg and along your dog's side, then down the front leg to the foot and across the chest. Repeat this process on the other side, then finally brush the tail and around your dog's head.

Mats can form in a dog's long coat when loose underhairs wrap together or when the coat tangles. Matting that occurs in movement spots, such as the armpits, can be very painful. To deal with mats, you need a de-matting comb to break up the clumps so that they can be removed with a brush. As well as being time consuming, de-matting can be a very uncomfortable experience for your dog and may make him resent grooming. It is far better to prevent the mats from forming in the first place by brushing your dog at least every other day.

COAT CLIPPING

Clipping the coat is the usual practice for many breeds. Find a professional dog groomer who can do this for you. A good groomer will not rush a new dog and will spend time getting him used to the sound and feel of the clippers, using treats to help him feel comfortable.

TEETH CLEANING

■ **Never use human toothpaste**, buy special dog toothpaste instead.

■ **Clean one tooth** per day to get your dog used to the sensation.

■ **Some dog chews** are designed to help clean your dog's teeth.

GOOD BEHAVIOUR

A well-mannered dog is not only a pleasure to live with but is also happier. If your dog understands the house rules, he will stay out of trouble and can take part in family activities and greet visitors. Preventing bad habits from forming is much easier than trying to undo them later on, so start teaching your new dog how to behave as soon as he arrives in your home.

Where to rest

Although it is tempting to allow a new puppy on to the furniture and into your bed when he is very small, you may not want this to happen when he is much bigger, hairier, and dirtier. Changing the rules as your puppy grows up is unfair, so it is best to decide at the start which rooms he can go in and whether he can sit on the sofa. Make sure that the whole family agrees and treats the puppy consistently.

It is very important to give your dog a private corner to relax in on his own, but he may need encouragement to use it. At the times in the day when your dog normally goes

QUIET CORNER
To encourage your dog to go to his bed, give him a treat or chew to take with him. When he goes to his bed, offer gentle praise and encouragement.

to sleep, coax him on to his bed with a gentle cue such as "go to bed". Spend some time there with him, gently stroking him and quietly praising him as he falls asleep. Should he take himself to his bed of his own accord, praise him quietly or toss a treat so that it lands just in front of his nose.

TRAINING | GETTING OFF THE FURNITURE

3 When your dog jumps off the furniture, clearly give the command "off" and praise him. Guide him to his bed and settle him there with praise and treats.

1 A light, long lead makes it easier to teach your dog to get off the furniture. Use this in the early stages of training when he does not yet understand the appropriate voice cue. If he sits on a forbidden chair or sofa, pick up the long lead and ask him to get off.

2 If encouragement and putting gentle pressure on the long lead fail to make him get down, do not use the lead to drag your dog off the furniture. If he does not jump off immediately, use a toy or a treat to encourage him further.

TRAINING | NO JUMPING UP

1 If your dog jumps up, remove all attention by turning your back and folding your arms. Avoid eye contact and do not speak to him until he stops.

2 When your dog has all four feet on the ground, reward him with lots of fuss in the form of praise, treats, and play. If he gets too excited and jumps up again, turn away immediately. He will quickly learn that keeping all four paws on the ground is the key to getting attention.

Good manners

Puppies often receive the most attention from people when they are jumping up or barking, so understandably they often continue to use the same technique as they get older, when such behaviour is less appealing. It is not wise to allow even the smallest dog to jump up at anyone, because a boisterous dog can scare people, especially young children, or even cause injuries.

For a dog to learn good manners, he must not receive any attention at all when he is jumping up or barking. This does not just mean withholding praise – to some dogs, being shouted at or pushed away counts as satisfactory attention. Ignore your dog completely to teach him that when he is sitting quietly, people come to him and lavish him with praise and treats.

GREETING VISITORS
Dogs can get over-excited when visitors call. Control your dog with a long lead to make sure that he is behaving politely before you let visitors say hello.

If your puppy is a persistent play-biter, keep a soft toy nearby to grab quickly whenever you spend time playing with him. Use a big toy so that you can hold on to it without needing to put your hands too close to your dog's teeth.

Teething troubles

Dogs investigate the world with their mouths. Young dogs, in particular, want to chew everything they come across to find out more about it. This habit often becomes more pronounced at around four months of age, when puppies begin to lose their first teeth. It is natural for puppies to play-bite their litter mates but they must learn never to use their teeth on humans in the same way. This lesson is an important part of teaching a young dog good manners. When your puppy play-bites at your hand, form a fist to make it harder for him to chew and offer him a soft toy instead. Engage him with the toy and have a good game with him, but stop if his teeth touch your hand. Either get up immediately and walk away to indicate the game has ended or keep your hand still and let out a yelp as another puppy would do.

TRAINING | TAKING FOOD GENTLY

1 Hold a tasty treat firmly in your fist and show it to your dog. Keep your fist still as he tries to get the treat, but do not open it if he is touching your hand or chewing or pawing it.

2 When your puppy moves away from your hand, even for a moment, open your fist and allow him to take the treat. This will teach him not to snatch food but to wait for it calmly.

TRAINING | GIVING UP CHEWS

1 When your dog has been enjoying a chew for a while, approach calmly with a really smelly treat. Get close enough for him to smell it and use it to lure him away from his chew.

3 Once he has eaten the treat, immediately give him back the chew. Repeat the lesson at intervals. It won't be long before your dog learns to give up his chews happily.

2 As he moves away from his chew, give him the smelly treat and at the same time calmly pick up the chew with your other hand. Use the treat to keep him distracted.

Preventing food aggression

Dogs can be very possessive about their food and many will guard it against anyone who approaches. Although perfectly normal canine behaviour, it is not tolerable in a pet dog and must be discouraged at a very early stage. Training a dog not to be aggressive about food is easy. Simply teach your puppy to expect that anyone who approaches him while he is eating will have something even tastier to offer. When you give your puppy his food, crouch down beside him and gently stroke and talk to him as he eats. Offer him some really tasty treats, such as cooked chicken or cheese, and allow him to take them from you. If he is comfortable with this, progress by putting your hand into his food bowl and letting him take the treat from there. Repeat this once or twice before leaving him to finish his meal. If you approach and your puppy looks up expectantly, lift up his bowl and place some tasty treats in it before returning it to him straight away. Once his response is absolutely predictable, get a variety of different people, including children, to repeat the procedure. As the puppy grows up, repeat this training less frequently but do not stop completely until your dog is fully mature. A dog that has already developed aggression around food poses a genuine risk and will bite anyone who gets too close. Do not attempt to treat this problem without the advice of a professional behaviour counsellor.

HANDOUT
Offering your dog a treat on the flat of your hand prevents him from accidentally catching you with his teeth. Make sure that friends and children offering him treats are taught this rule.

TUG-OF-WAR
Tug games are a great way to interact with your dog, as long as you can control when the game begins and when it ends.

THRILL OF THE CHASE
Many dogs love chasing toys that fly through the air. Keep your puppy on a long lead until he understands the rules.

Playtime

As highly social animals, dogs need interaction with both other dogs and people as much as they need physical and mental exercise. Play can offer this interaction and helps dogs to mature properly, so it is essential that they have as much of it as they need. However, it is during playtime that your dog is most likely to become over-excited and start misbehaving. Teach your puppy the rules of play, both with you and with other dogs. He must also learn to stop playing when you tell him to.

Use toys to help your dog learn that play with people is different from play-fighting with other dogs. Playtime should begin and end with a display of good manners, such as a sit. If your puppy gets over-excited, call a halt to the fun until he calms down. Don't restrain him with your hands during play as he will probably try to mouth you or jump up. It may be useful to keep a puppy on a light, long lead during playtime. This allows you to calm him down without offering the temptation of your hands. If this does not work, simply walk away from your puppy, making it clear that the game is over.

TOP TIPS

■ **Your dog should be taught** from an early age not to be possessive of his toys. It is understandable that any dog would want to guard a prized possession from human hands, but this can lead to snapping and biting. Spend time trading toys for treats until your dog learns that allowing people to pick up his toys leads to a tasty reward. Teach children that snatching something quickly away from a dog may startle him and possibly arouse aggression.

GOOD PRACTICE | PLAYING

RESPONDING TO A NEW TOY
Allow your puppy to nibble a new toy to find out whether it tastes nice and to check whether it will bite back.

PLAYFULNESS
Do not be alarmed if your puppy growls – he is simply treating the toy like another puppy. This is normal playfulness, not aggression.

GIVING UP A TOY
Occasionally take the toy away from your puppy and praise him before returning it. If he is reluctant to give it up, swap it for a treat.

Barking

Often puppies will "find their voice" at around six months of age. Puppy-yapping can be amusing and although it is tempting to encourage this new behaviour, it is not advisable. As your puppy matures, both you and your neighbours will become weary of persistent barking. If your puppy is prone to barking at certain moments of high excitement – for example, during a game – then use a lead to control his behaviour. Give him what he wants only when he is quiet. If your puppy tends to bark excitedly when you are about to do something, such as prepare his dinner or get ready for a walk, stop what you are doing until he is quiet. If necessary, sit down calmly on the sofa until he has stopped barking completely. It is worth spending a few extra minutes getting your puppy calm before going out of the door for a walk. Your puppy will realize quickly that barking is completely counter-productive when it comes to getting what he wants, whereas waiting quietly is always rewarded.

OVER-EXCITEMENT
If your puppy barks when you are about to go for a walk, ignore it and he will learn that staying quiet is a quicker way to get what he wants.

ON GUARD
Your dog may use barking as an alert signal when the post arrives. He should not be told off for this, but do not let alarm barking continue for long.

ATTENTION SEEKING
Barking to gain attention should not be rewarded. Ignore your dog until he is silent or walk away from him, returning with lavish praise when he is quiet.

SOCIALIZATION

Whatever your young puppy experiences will affect the way he responds to the world as an adult dog. At an early age, introduce him to everything he is likely to encounter, from different people and other dogs, to cars and vacuum cleaners. This process, called socialization, is the single most important task you can undertake to ensure that your puppy grows into a friendly family pet.

Everyone's friend

Understanding your dog

Socialization must begin with an understanding of how dogs interact with their surroundings. A puppy views the world very differently from humans. Whereas we rely on our eyes to get information about the world, dogs place much more reliance on their sense of smell. A new puppy learns about things more quickly by smelling and chewing them than by looking at them. In fact, dogs cannot see the same amount of detail as humans or distinguish red from green, but their night vision is far superior to ours. Dogs have a much more acute sense of hearing than humans. This means a noise that is seemingly inconsequential to us may sound loud and scary to a dog.

Puppies go through a series of developmental stages as they mature. These stages are windows of opportunity for socialization, and positive experiences during such times will help to shape your puppy into a happy and balanced adult dog. In his first weeks your puppy is still inquisitive,

PAT ON THE HEAD
A well-intentioned pat on the head can be frightening for your puppy. Crouch down and stroke his chest instead.

DOG'S EYE VIEW
People appear huge to a young dog with little experience of the human world. Try not to overwhelm your puppy by looming above him.

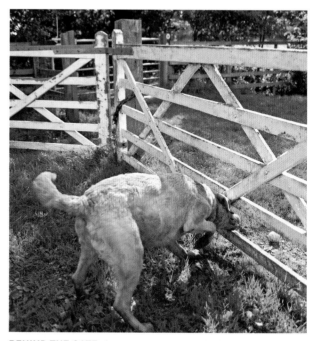

BEHIND THE GATE
Your dog will need help to figure out how things work in a human world. His thought processes are different from ours, and to begin with he may not understand things like gates.

full of play, eager to please, and also less inclined to be wary of new and unusual things than he will be later on. Some socialization may have happened while your puppy was with the breeder. This is important as the period at which socialization becomes most critical is, broadly speaking, between 8-12 weeks of age, and you may not pick your puppy up until he is about that age. Once you have brought your puppy home, socialization must continue. Anything that he does not come across during his formative period and make a positive association with, will be looked upon with distrust or fear if he meets it as an adult. It is important not to miss this deadline, so introduce your puppy to your friends and their children. Having contact with toddlers and older people is particularly important. Once fully vaccinated, take him out to meet other animals, go for a bus ride, and visit the park to look at the ducks. Socialize your puppy early and socialize him well; you will find it a rewarding and joyful experience.

Getting used to other dogs

Dogs need to learn how to interact with other dogs at the earliest opportunity. A puppy that is not socialized correctly will grow up becoming more and more fearful of other dogs, and this usually leads to aggression. Puppies learn best about getting on with other dogs by playing with puppies

MAKING NEW FRIENDS
Meeting a variety of other animals, both large and small, will give your puppy confidence.

of their own age. During play, dogs discover how to read each other's body language and how to respond appropriately. They also learn how to display friendliness as well as how to judge whether another dog is friendly.

Adult dogs can also be very good at teaching puppies how to behave. Make sure that all the adult dogs your puppy meets are friendly and well socialized themselves. It can be difficult to stick to this rule if you take your puppy into public spaces, so stay vigilant and move away quickly from potential trouble. A negative experience at this tender age could be enough to make your puppy wary of other dogs for life. A good puppy class should include interactions with "safe" adult dogs. By taking care that all your puppy's experiences with other dogs are positive, you ensure that he has no reason to be afraid in later life.

HIGHLY PERCEPTIVE
Dogs do not have our acute vision but they are good at detecting movement, however slight. This allows them to predict our movements, sometimes before we are conscious of them ourselves.

PUPPY CLASS
A well-organized puppy class will be of great benefit to your puppy. Look for classes that use only reward-based methods and have only a few puppies playing together at any one time.

Meeting the family

If your puppy is to become a polite and confident dog, you must introduce him to a variety of different people. Puppies soon make friends with all the members of their family but some of them are shy with strangers. Invite visitors of all ages, male and female, to your home, to meet your puppy. Show your visitors how to interact with your puppy but do not let them overwhelm him. Instead, ask them to wait for the puppy to make the first approach before greeting him. When the puppy does come to them, make sure that your visitors give him plenty of treats and gentle attention.

Give your puppy plenty of experiences with children early on so that he becomes used to them, and teach your children how to behave around dogs. Interactions between your dog and children should always be supervised, as children's sudden movements and noises can sometimes startle young puppies. However, do not shy away from such encounters – taking a new puppy to the school gate when you drop off and pick up your children is a great way to socialize him with children of all ages. Using lots of praise and tasty treats on these visits will guarantee that your puppy remembers the experiences fondly.

Take the time to meet and greet all kinds of different people when you are outside the house with your puppy. Ask joggers and cyclists to stop and say hello to your puppy if he seems to be alarmed by their fast movement. If people are willing and able, get them to crouch down with a treat and wait for him to approach for his reward.

YOUNG PLAYMATE
Children and dogs can become the best of friends, but they need time to get used to one another.

NEW ARRIVAL
Introduce babies and dogs gradually and never leave them alone together. Begin by getting your dog used to the smell of your baby's clothes.

FELINE INTRODUCTION
Introduce a cat by holding your dog to prevent him from chasing it. The cat must be free to escape if it feels threatened.

STRANGE SOUNDS
Introduce noisy objects like vacuum cleaners slowly and with lots of treats. Get your dog used to the movement of the vacuum before turning it on.

New sights and sounds

In addition to other dogs and people, puppies need to get used to the many strange objects they will encounter during their lifetime. Washing machines, coffee grinders, lawnmowers, vacuum cleaners, tumble dryers, and cars are all examples of objects that are big, loud, and scary to a young puppy. It is important to take the time to actively seek out these things and allow your puppy to get accustomed to them at his own pace. Do not force him to investigate them – instead, set up situations where he can observe the object from a distance and allow him to approach when he feels more confident. Take treats with you wherever you go; make each new experience fun by playing games with your puppy, and rewarding him generously. Watch your puppy closely. If certain objects or experiences disturb him, don't avoid them but gradually familiarize him with them so that he learns not to react negatively. During these more stressful situations distract him with a toy and talk to him until he forgets his nerves. Once he relaxes, you can encourage him to move closer.

ONCOMING VEHICLE
Allow your puppy to get used to cars at his own pace, using treats to reinforce calm behaviour. He will lose fear once he accepts they are background objects.

GAME OF CHASE
If your puppy chases vehicles or livestock he may get injured, so discourage this behaviour from the start and get professional guidance if needed.

TROUBLE AHEAD
When you see a cyclist or jogger approaching, encourage your puppy to sit quietly. Once they have passed reward him with treats.

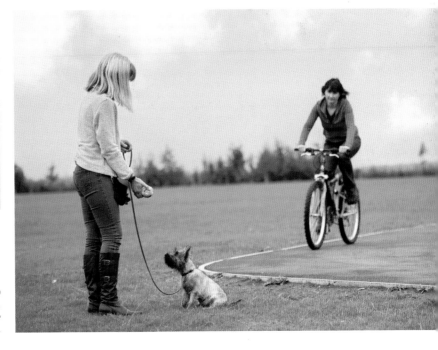

Car travel

For a young dog, car travel is a very strange experience at first and he needs time to get used to it. Puppies are usually wary of car rides because the first two trips they go on are when they are taken away from their mother and their first visit to the vet. Neither are very pleasant occasions and can leave many dogs with negative feelings about cars. Spending time rebalancing the way your puppy views the car will prevent travelling problems in the future.

Encourage your dog to investigate the car when the engine is turned off. Get him used to the sound of car doors opening and closing and to the feeling of being in a car. Spend time simply sitting in the car with your dog, or leave him there to sleep, so that he begins to see it as a great place to be. Put him in the place where he will be travelling in the future. For example, if you plan to travel with your dog in a car crate, that is where he should be placed from the start.

When you take your dog on a car journey, make sure he relieves himself before you set off. To begin with, go on lots of short trips that end with something enjoyable like a walk in the woods. By associating car journeys with positive endings, your puppy will soon forget the earlier trips that caused such distress. Over time, gradually increase the length of the journeys as your dog becomes happier and more relaxed in the car.

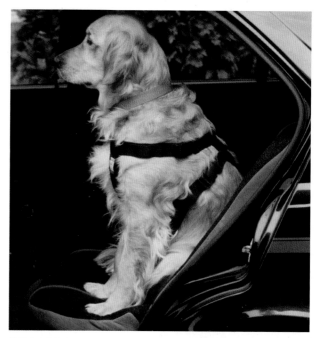

STRAPPED IN
Restraining your dog while he is in the car is essential. It stops him from interfering with the driver or other passengers and prevents him from being thrown around in the car during the journey.

TRAINING | SUCCESSFUL JOURNEYS

1 Before your dog does any travelling, he should learn that cars are fun. Take time to play with him in and around the car and even feed him his dinner in the car.

2 Until your dog is big enough to jump into the car without hurting himself, lift him in and be ready to prevent him from trying to jump out again. Settle him in the car by staying with him, praising him, and giving him lots of treats.

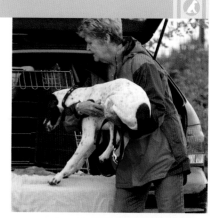

3 A travelling crate is a good way of keeping your dog contained and feeling secure. Dogs that are already used to sleeping in a cage or crate will find this particularly reassuring.

Travel sickness

Many dogs suffer from travel sickness as they find it difficult to adjust to the unnatural movement of a car journey. In fact, many problems experienced while travelling with a dog, such as excessive barking or panting, are due to underlying travel sickness making the dog restless. It is possible for many dogs to get over this with time. However, there may also be a psychological element involved, so think about whether your dog has good or bad feelings about the car. If you have a rescue dog, his previous experiences with cars may be unknown so stopping him from being sick may be more difficult. Treat a dog that is habitually travel-sick in the same way you would a dog who has never travelled before. Spend

SAFETY FIRST

Insist that your dog waits until he is asked to get out of the car. He should never jump out as soon as the door opens, as one day he may jump into the road. Restrain him if necessary and praise him for waiting calmly. Teach him to wait for just a few moments at first, gradually extending the length of time.

time with him, making a positive association with the car. Keep the engine off, play games around the car, and use lots of treats. When your dog is relaxed in the car, turn the engine on briefly and then play with him. For your first journey with your dog, just go to the end of the road before stopping for more games and treats. In extreme cases, consult your vet.

THIRSTY PASSENGER

The car is one of the few places where your dog may not have free access to water. Be sure to stop regularly to offer him a drink and to relieve himself; he may be more thirsty than usual due to the heat inside the car.

TOP TIPS

■ **Help prevent car sickness** by making sure your dog has a non-slip surface if he stands up in the car. Take corners slowly and accelerate smoothly.

■ **Even on a cool day**, dogs can quickly overheat in a car, so never leave your dog alone in the car for very long.

CONTENTED DOG
Take your dog for a walk before
leaving him. If he is tired and
content, he is likely to accept
being left alone and will curl
up and go to sleep.

Learning to be left alone

Everyone wants to spend a great deal of time with a new puppy in the first few weeks after his arrival. The general fuss and attention, combined with socialization, usually mean that the puppy is never alone for more than a few of his waking moments. As he gets older and stops receiving such constant attention, he may become anxious at being left alone. Part of his socialization should include teaching him to accept being on his own.

Choose a time when your puppy is ready for sleep. Take him outside to relieve himself before guiding him to his bed and calmly leaving the room. Shut the door behind you and ignore whining and barking until he gives up and falls asleep. This exercise should be repeated until the puppy has learned to settle quietly on his own for a few hours.

Puppies should be discouraged from following their owners around everywhere they go. Make a point of shutting doors behind you as you move around the house so that your puppy cannot always come with you. At first, go back to him quickly and reassure him, so that he knows he has not been abandoned and that you never stay away for long. He will soon learn that there is no need to become worried or nervous at being left alone.

Never tell your dog off for something that has happened in your absence. If you leave your puppy for half an hour and return to find he has chewed his blanket, do not punish him. Dogs associate events that occur very close together: scolding your puppy will teach him to be afraid of you coming home, not that chewing a blanket is wrong.

SEPARATION ANXIETY
When dogs are really worried they can work out their anxiety by chewing whatever is nearby, including furniture and other possessions. This is a sign that your dog is not coping with being left alone for long periods.

TOP TIPS
■ **Early on in your puppy's** training, get him comfortable with being alone. Set aside periods during the day where you leave him for a short time. He will rapidly gain confidence.

GRADUAL SEPARATION
Use a stair gate to help an anxious dog build up to full separation. He will be reassured by seeing and hearing you, even if he cannot follow.

Anxiety in the older dog

A mature dog that has never been acclimatized to being left alone may become extremely anxious on his own. Scratching at doorways, panting and pacing, howling, and lapses in toilet training are all signs of a dog that is struggling to cope with being left alone. The damage caused by an anxious dog can be expensive to repair, and there is also a danger that the dog may injure himself.

Deep-rooted separation anxiety can be tricky to overcome. Some dogs are so anxious that they panic at the mere sight of their owner picking up the keys. Long-standing cases may require assistance from a professional behaviour counsellor and, in the short term, possibly medication to calm the dog down enough to concentrate on learning new lessons.

Socialization consists of patiently going back to basics and, to begin with, getting your dog used to being left alone for a few seconds at a time. You can then gradually build up to longer periods of separation.

TRAINING YOUR DOG

To enjoy spending time with your dog, both in the house and outdoors, you need to train him to be well behaved. Training strengthens the bond between the two of you, and provides your dog with some of the mental stimulation he craves. If you learn how to communicate with your dog and read his body language, it will make teaching him much easier and more satisfying.

Communicating with your dog

Dogs and people have very different ways of communicating with each other. Although dogs become quite good at interpreting what people mean, successful training depends on people learning to "talk dog".

A dog does not understand language; he merely responds to different sounds. "Lie" and "down" may mean the same thing to humans but they sound quite different to dogs. So you should choose a simple verbal cue for each command and stick to it. Tone of voice also matters; puppies learn quickly that a low, growly voice means they are doing something

INVITING GESTURE
Facing your dog and crouching down with open arms is a positive signal. Any time you face your dog directly, you are inviting interaction.

wrong and that treats and fuss usually follow a cheery tone. Most important of all is body language. Eye contact is a vital part of communicating with your dog, but remember that a prolonged stare can be seen as a threat. Dogs do not immediately understand hand movements, such as pointing; they have to learn to make an association between what your hand does and what they must do to earn a reward.

HAND SIGNALS
Your dog will probably recognize your hand signals before he learns what the voice cue means. It is important to be as consistent with your hand signals as with your voice cues.

VOICE CUES
With repetition, your dog learns that certain words mean he should perform certain behaviours. A good test to see if your dog has learned the voice cue properly is to see if he will respond to your voice, even if you turn your back to him.

Reading a dog's body language

Being able to interpret your dog's body language means you will have a clearer idea of what he is feeling. You cannot train a dog effectively until you have learned to read the signs that tell you when he is happy or when he is scared. When dogs are stressed, it is impossible for them to concentrate on learning. If your dog is not responding well to training, it is important to stop the session straight away and try to analyse what is going wrong.

A relaxed dog shows no signs of tension and will hold his tail roughly level with his back and gently swinging. The ears will most likely be forward and the expression calm. A frightened or anxious dog tucks his tail in between his back legs and pulls his ears back. You may also notice that the dog is tensing his body or cowering. Other signs of fear or anxiety include excessive panting, pacing, or a sudden disinterest in food. A scared dog needs help to work through his worries and should never be punished, as this will only increase his anxiety.

You can also learn a lot about canine body language by observing what happens when your dog meets another. If your dog raises his hackles along his back and carries his tail straight up in the air, it means that he is worried and is trying to make himself appear as large as possible. This body language normally changes as the dogs exchange greetings and, if the other dog is friendly, the initial tension passes. However, raised hackles may also be the prelude to trouble if both dogs decide they do not like one another.

RELAXED DOG
A happy, confident dog will move in a relaxed manner. Any sign of tension, evident in a stiffening of the body, is a warning that he feels uncomfortable. Pay attention to his tail carriage. A tail held erect may suggest over-excitement or aggression, while a tucked-under tail suggests fear and anxiety.

YAWNING
Dogs have many subtle ways of showing that they are feeling anxious or afraid. Signs include yawning or acting sleepy when the dog has no reason to be tired.

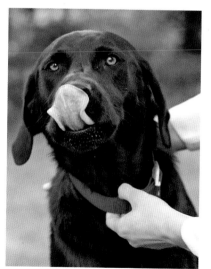

LICKING NOSE
A dog that repeatedly licks his nose or lips, even though there is no tempting food nearby, may be trying to communicate fear, anxiety, or stress.

TURNING HEAD AWAY
Dogs sometimes indicate unease by turning their head or whole body away, to break eye contact and distance themselves from what they perceive as a threat.

Rewards-based training

There has been a great deal of research into the best methods for training dogs. The results show that resorting to harsh punishments for disobedience, such as using a choke chain, shouting and hitting a dog, or pinning him down, is simply not effective. Such treatment is likely to cause more problem behaviours, including aggression and anxiety. The most successful way to train a dog is to find out what motivates him and use that to reward him for behaving in the way you want.

To do this, you need to find out what works with your own dog. All dogs are individuals and react differently to rewards, but there are some common motivators that can be used as training aids for the majority of dogs. Simple praise is a very effective reward for a young puppy. Dogs are sociable animals and find positive contact with people in their family unit deeply rewarding. Most dogs will happily do what you ask of them in return for praise.

However, for some dogs the situation in which they find themselves can be so distracting that the desire to please may temporarily be taken over by more impelling urges.

FAVOURITE TOY
Many dogs are motivated by toys. If your dog loves to play, keep his favourite toy aside and bring it out only as a reward during training.

For instance, your dog may choose to ignore your calls when he is running after a rabbit. This is not because he no longer loves or respects you; it is simply that for a few thrilling moments he finds the unusual excitement of the chase more rewarding than your praise, which is always on offer. To overcome such distractions during training, you must find other things that are particularly rewarding to your dog. The most powerful motivators used in dog training are toys and food. Use something that your dog really loves and will therefore be strongly motivated to receive.

USING PRAISE
One of the best forms of reward is praise. This requires no training aids – you simply have to make a big fuss of your dog. Talk to him in a friendly tone and stroke him.

MOTIVATING FOOD
All dogs find food motivating. Treats used for training should be small, bite-sized pieces of a food that is particularly tasty to your dog. Go for healthy choices such as cooked chicken or cheese.

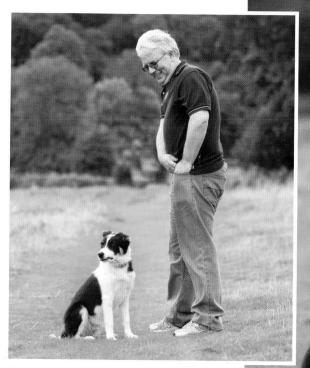

TIMING REWARDS
Giving rewards too slowly may make your dog learn the wrong thing. If his attention is distracted, by the time he receives the reward, he may not make the connection between it and adopting the desired "sit" position (see above). Be prepared to give your dog his reward as soon as he follows your command (see right), and he will learn very quickly.

The importance of timing

Probably the most important skill for you to master as a dog trainer is good timing. Dogs learn exclusively by association. This means that if they do something and immediately receive a reward, they are more likely to repeat that behaviour. Of course, this also causes some behaviour problems. For example, if a dog that wants attention jumps up and gets pushed off or shouted at, he has received the attention he wants. Effectively, he has been rewarded for jumping up and is therefore more likely to jump up again. If this is repeated, jumping up becomes a learned behaviour - one that is repeated frequently.

Nevertheless, the way that dogs make associations is also extremely useful in teaching them how they should behave. If every time your dog sits he receives a food treat immediately afterwards, he will start sitting more frequently. An association has been made between the behaviour of sitting and a reward. It is then fairly simple to insert a voice cue as he folds into a sit, creating a learned behaviour that your dog will produce on command. However, if you keep your food treats in your pocket and take a few moments to get them out, your dog will have sat, got bored, and jumped up at you by the time he gets the treat. Again, he learns that jumping up is a rewarding behaviour and will therefore repeat it more often.

SLEEP TIME
Your puppy will learn better if he sleeps between lessons. A young puppy tires easily, so keep training sessions short with frequent breaks.

Basic commands

Sitting is a behaviour that comes quite naturally to puppies and is therefore a good place to start formal training. It is a very easy command for a puppy to learn and gives him a guaranteed way of earning a reward. Because of this, most puppies will offer a sit as the first option, when there is a reward available. As your dog gets older and a sit becomes less exceptional, the behaviour is less likely to be rewarded, so he will try other methods to get noticed, such as jumping up or barking. Keep rewarding your dog whenever he offers a sit, to reinforce the calm behaviour you want from him.

Teaching a puppy to lie down can be more difficult than getting him to sit, but this is probably the most useful of all the basic positions for your dog to learn. Lying down is a more stable position than sitting, meaning that a dog is less likely to move again immediately afterwards. Having a reliable "down" command can be vital in emergencies when you need to stop your dog on the spot – for example, if he is running towards a road. Lying down also reinforces a relaxed state of mind and can help to calm a puppy in an exciting situation. Make it one of your puppy's earliest lessons, as the "down" command comes in handy if he becomes distracted during a training session and stops paying attention.

AT THE ROADSIDE

Put the sit command into practice whenever you need control over your dog. For example, asking a puppy to sit at every roadside will teach him not to walk straight into traffic (it is not always possible to shorten a lead in time to prevent mishap). Remember to practise sitting at every roadside you come to – not just at main roads. Your puppy cannot tell what type of road he is approaching.

Start teaching your puppy to lie down when he is highly motivated. For example, if you carry out a training session just before a meal, when he is hungry, he will be more receptive to what you ask because he will be eager for food treats. Encourage him by starting on a soft surface, such as carpet or grass, before moving on to harder, less comfortable surfaces. As with all your commands, be very precise about the meaning of each word. If your command to lie down is "down", then do not use the word "down" to ask your puppy to get off your furniture.

TRAINING | SIT

1 With your dog standing in front of you, hold a treat right in front of his nose and slowly move your hand up and backwards, close over his head. Do not let go of the treat immediately.

2 As your dog's nose moves up to follow the treat, he will have to place his bottom on the floor. Ask him to "sit" and as soon as his bottom is down, let him take the treat and praise him. Continue to praise him for as long as he is sitting.

3 Once your puppy is reliably performing a sit every time food is lured over his head, move on to giving a clear hand signal while asking him to "sit". Then bend down and lure him into position as before.

TRAINING | DOWN

1 In a distraction-free environment, such as your back garden, attract your dog's attention by showing him that you have a tasty treat. Use the treat to lure your dog into a sitting position but do not let him take it from you.

2 Move the treat from his nose in a straight line to the ground. Do this slowly so that your dog's nose follows your hand, but still hold on to the treat. Let him nibble at the treat so that he does not lose interest.

Alternative If your puppy is reluctant to lie down, another method can be used. Make a bridge with your legs and lure him underneath. Use lots of treats and keep your legs positioned over him until he is lying down.

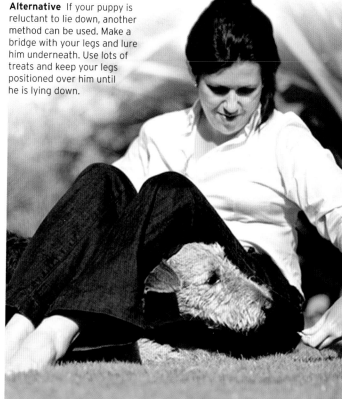

3 As your dog follows the treat, he will gradually fold into a lying position. Once he is fully down, let go of the treat and praise him. Give the command "down" as his elbows touch the ground.

More advanced commands

Teaching your dog a command that means "stay there and wait for me to come back to you" is useful in any number of situations. This command works well for everyday use, both in the house and on walks, but it can also be helpful in other more difficult situations. For example, if your dog escapes and runs across a road, you will want him to wait where he is, rather than recrossing the road and putting himself in danger again. Your dog's natural instinct is to follow you, so when you want him to stay in a particular position, it will make training easier if you turn sideways to him and avoid eye contact. By doing this he doesn't think you are communicating with him and will therefore be less likely to move towards you.

All dogs need to learn to walk on a lead, and must do so without pulling, if going for walks is to be an enjoyable experience and not a constant battle. Puppies do not instantly understand what a lead is for and it is natural for them to pull in an attempt to reach an exciting destination sooner. If they learn from the start that pulling on the lead is never successful, they will soon stop trying. Make sure that whenever your puppy pulls, you either stop and wait until he stops, or call him back to the correct heel position.

RESISTING TEMPTATION
The "stay" command can be used to teach your dog to ignore food and other temptations. Reward your dog for staying away from human food by giving him a more suitable treat.

TRAINING | WALK ON A LEAD

1 Start your session in an area where there are few distractions. Keeping your dog on a long lead, lure him into the correct position next to your left leg by offering a food treat. Praise him when he is in the correct position by letting him take the treat.

2 Before your dog starts to lose interest and attempts to wander off, show him that you have another treat but hold it out of his reach. Use his name to keep his attention and do not allow the lead to tighten as you get ready to move.

3 Take a step forward and give your dog the command "heel". Immediately bend down and give him a treat. Repeat this exercise, taking single steps, stopping, and quickly pulling out another treat so that your dog does not get distracted.

TRAINING | STAY

1 Ask your dog to "sit". Stand up straight, then immediately bend down to reward him with a food treat. Next time, stand up straight and count to two before rewarding him. Gradually extend the amount of time between the sit and the reward.

2 When your dog will stay in front of you for some time, take a step away from him before rewarding him. Repeat, gradually extending the time before the reward. Once he is confident with you one pace away, increase the distance.

4 As your dog becomes more confident and attentive, begin increasing the number of steps before he receives a treat. Do this very gradually, praising him all the time. As soon as the lead tightens, stop and lure him back into position before starting off again.

WALKING TO HEEL

It may not be necessary for your dog to walk precisely to heel at all times, as long as he does not pull on his lead. However, sometimes it is useful to keep your dog close – for example, when walking past people on the pavement. Use a similar method to that used to teach long-lead walking (left), keeping your dog in position by using a treat. Once your dog is reliably walking close to you, gradually phase out the treat.

Returning on cue

All dogs love being able to go to the park or out into the country where they can run free, really stretching their legs and playing with toys or other dogs. However, until your dog has learned to return when you call, it is not safe to let him off his lead. You may come across someone who is nervous around dogs, or perhaps encounter another dog that is not friendly. Your dog may catch sight of a rabbit or squirrel and run after it towards a road. No matter what the distraction, part of responsible dog-ownership is keeping your dog under control – even when he is off-lead. Teaching your dog to come when he is called is imperative.

Puppies are born with a natural instinct to follow, and they never want to be far from you. This makes it easy to get your puppy used to the meaning of the word "come" at an early age. When your puppy is a short distance away from you, crouch down and throw your arms wide, calling his name. As he hurtles towards you, tell him he is a good boy and insert your cue "come". Always reward him with an extra special treat for coming when he is called, so that he knows it is worthwhile. As he gets older and more independent, he will be less keen to run straight to you and more likely to continue investigating whatever else has caught his attention. On your first walks with your dog, teach him on a lead to come when called, until you are confident he will respond every time.

TOP TIPS

■ **Always praise your dog** for coming when called, no matter how long it has taken him. Resist the urge to tell him off for taking his time; it will only make him reluctant to return in future.

■ **Using a whistle** as your recall command can be useful as it is a very clear noise that travels a long way.

When he responds well on the lead, switch to an extending lead and practise the command before letting him off completely. Find a safe place to experiment with this stage.

Teaching your dog to fetch a toy is a great way to reinforce the command "come" through play. When your dog has reached a toy you have thrown, he will want to bring it back to you so that you can throw it for him again. Asking him to "come" as he naturally returns to you helps him learn this command. Teaching your dog to fetch properly will also prevent him from developing problem behaviours, such as stealing items and running off.

TRAINING | COME WHEN CALLED

1 Show your dog that you have a really tasty treat in your hand before moving a short distance away. If your dog will not wait, ask someone else to gently hold on to the end of his lead.

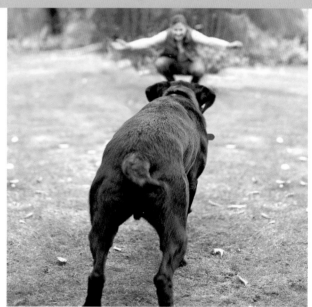

2 Turn and face your dog, crouch down, and spread your arms wide. In a loud, cheery voice call your dog's name and ask him to "come". Keep calling until he responds.

TRAINING | FETCH

1 Get your dog excited by playing with him and his favourite toy. When he is fully focused on the toy, throw it a short distance away.

2 As he heads to his toy, ask him to "fetch". When he reaches it, praise him before immediately calling him in a cheery tone.

3 As soon as your dog moves towards you, encourage him by crouching down and praising him. Exchange his toy for a treat and repeat the process.

4 If your dog drops the toy, run over to it with him and move it to catch his interest. As he grabs it, walk backwards a few paces before taking the toy from him.

4 When he is right next to you, prevent him from immediately running off again by gently taking hold of his collar before giving him the treat and lots of praise.

3 As soon as your dog moves towards you, praise him lavishly and keep praising him as he returns. Show him the treat and use it to lure him close to you.

HEALTH

It is your responsibility to keep your dog as fit and healthy as possible throughout his life. You should learn the basic facts about health care and how to recognize when a trip to the vet is necessary. Make sure that your puppy is happy and relaxed at the vet's surgery from an early age – this is important preparation for stress-free visits later on.

If your puppy scratches, check him for fleas

Meeting the vet

Even before you bring a new puppy home you should register with a local veterinary surgery. Visit several surgeries to ask questions and make comparisons, and ask other dog owners, who are likely to be a good source of recommendations. Once you have your new puppy, it is advisable to take him to the vet as soon as possible for a full health check and vaccinations.

This is also a good opportunity to seek advice on such matters as feeding and local puppy classes.

Although veterinary surgeries are strange places, full of unusual smells and noises, puppies are not born fearful of vets. If your puppy's first few visits to the vet's surgery are largely pleasant experiences, full of treats and cuddles, he is less likely to object to the occasional injection and won't become stressed when later visits are necessary. The surgery may allow you to make a social visit with your puppy even if you don't have an appointment. Ask a nurse or receptionist to give your puppy some treats so that he makes a positive association with both the building and the people in it.

On your first official visit to the vet, arrive early having given your puppy the chance to relieve himself before leaving home. When you enter the surgery, be aware of other animals, and do not assume that all dogs will be pleased to see a puppy. However, there will

EARLY ENCOUNTER
Your puppy's first visit to the vet is as much about socialization as it is about getting a health check. Try to ensure that it is a pleasant experience.

VACCINATIONS
Typically, puppies have their first vaccinations with the breeder and will need a second vaccination shortly after moving to a new home. Routine vaccinations protect against a number of potentially lethal diseases such as distemper, hepatitis, and parainfluenza.

NEUTERED DOGS
Most owners have their pet dogs neutered to prevent accidental matings and unwanted puppies. Your vet can advise you on the best time to get this done.

be many people keen to take an interest in your puppy, so ask them to make a fuss of him, but don't put him down on the floor unless he has been fully vaccinated.

During the consultation, your vet will want to examine your puppy all over and give him an injection. Take the process slowly, speak reassuringly to your puppy, and provide him with lots of treats throughout the examination, both from your hand and the vet's.

Preventative measures

If your puppy has not already been microchipped by the breeder, ask your vet to do this for you. Although your puppy should wear a collar and tag at all times, having a microchip means he is identifiable even if he loses his collar. Get your vet to check the microchip's location every year when your dog gets his booster vaccinations.

In between routine visits to your vet you need to take steps to protect your dog against common parasites. There are a variety of highly effective worming and flea treatments available; your vet will advise which are best for your puppy.

Unless you intend to breed from your dog you may want to discuss neutering on one of your early visits. Apart from unwanted pregnancies, female dogs benefit from a reduced risk of life-threatening conditions, such as mammary cancer and pyometra (pus in the womb). Neutered males are less likely to be aggressive and to go wandering. Your vet will fully explain the advantages and disadvantages of the procedure and recommend when to have it done if you decide to go ahead. Neutering is carried out under anaesthetic, so ask about post-operative care of your dog (see p.333).

Microchip

Syringe used to implant microchip

Microchip injected into fold of skin

CHIPPING YOUR DOG
Microchipping is a quick and painless procedure to insert a small chip under the skin. It enables your dog to be identified at all times and returned to you if he is lost.

Identifying when your dog is ill

Different dogs react to illness in different ways. As an owner, you know how your dog behaves day to day and are in the best position to recognize any changes away from this norm as soon as they occur. If health problems are recognized and diagnosed early, treatment can start without delay and is more likely to have a successful outcome.

If your dog is in pain, he will probably make this immediately obvious by limping, or yelping when he moves or is handled. Other physical signs of ill health include breathing difficulties, such as coughing or heavy panting, for no apparent reason. Unusual discharges from the eyes or nose are also signs to be noted, as are excessive scratching, hair loss other than normal shedding, an unwillingness to exercise, or a sudden change in eating or drinking habits. However, not all indicators of ill health are physical signs. Changes in temperament or behaviour can also mean that your dog is not well. For example, if your dog becomes unusually aggressive, this may be a protective mechanism because he is uncomfortable or in pain.

It is also wise to keep track of your dog's toilet habits so that you learn what is normal for him. Any sudden change in amount, appearance, or frequency of production of urine or faeces can indicate a health problem. Similarly, vomiting may be a sign of ill health. Remember, however, that as natural scavengers, dogs have a very active vomit reflex to protect them from anything toxic they may have eaten.

SECURITY BLANKET
A warm blanket can be beneficial in treating many conditions, including shock or hypothermia. It also comforts your dog if you need to leave him at your veterinary surgery. The scent of the blanket will remind him of home and help to reassure him until you return.

Minor injuries and first aid

Your first response when dealing with any injury should be to take your dog to the vet. However, in some situations you may be able to administer first aid before having to move the dog. In the case of severe injury, call for veterinary help and then put your dog in the recovery position. Lay him on his right side and straighten his head and neck to keep the airway free. Pull his tongue forward and to one side of the mouth so that the airway is open. Monitor his breathing and pulse until help arrives.

If there is extensive bleeding from a wound, this must be controlled until a vet can take over. Apply a piece of clean, absorbent material, such as gauze, to the site of the injury

EMERGENCY EAR BANDAGE
To protect an ear wound and prevent your dog from scratching it, bandage the ear flap flat against the top of the head. A pair of old tights can make a suitable bandage that goes around the neck and is not too constricting.

TOP TIPS

■ **Check for dehydration**
Gently pinch the loose skin on your dog's back, lift it slightly then let go. In a well-hydrated dog the skin springs back quickly into position. A dehydrated dog's skin returns more slowly.

■ **Check gum colour** Pale gums can indicate shock or internal bleeding, and very red gums can be caused by heat stroke or fever. Blue gums suggest a shortage of oxygen in body tissues.

and cover this with bandaging to hold it in place. Take care not to apply too much pressure if you suspect that there is debris in the wound, as you may push it in deeper and cause more damage. Do not attempt to pull any large foreign body, such as broken glass or metal, out of a wound as you could cause severe bleeding.

Home care after surgery

A dog that has had surgery needs plenty of affection and care when he comes home from the vet. He may be very lethargic if he is still recovering from the anaesthetic. On the other hand, he may act as if he is perfectly fine and try to behave as normal, to the detriment of his recovery. Jumping up may pull out stitches or displace broken bones, so encourage your convalescent dog to remain calm by settling him on a blanket in a quiet area of the house, perhaps with a toy to chew, if his vet allows. Make sure children in the household understand that their playmate cannot romp energetically or be allowed to exercise off-lead until he is fully recovered.

After surgery, a dog will almost certainly be given some sort of medication and probably have bandages or stitches. He may have to wear a special collar, called an Elizabethan collar, to prevent him from touching the wound. If your dog was well handled as a puppy, you are unlikely to have difficulty in giving him any prescribed treatment. There is a good chance that he will just enjoy the extra attention.

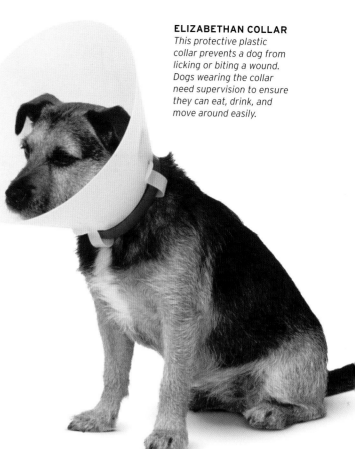

ELIZABETHAN COLLAR
This protective plastic collar prevents a dog from licking or biting a wound. Dogs wearing the collar need supervision to ensure they can eat, drink, and move around easily.

CONCEALED TABLET
The easiest way to give your dog a tablet is to hide it in his food. Watch your dog while he eats, and check the bowl afterwards to make sure the "hidden" tablet has been eaten.

GIVING YOUR DOG MEDICINE
Liquid medicines are best given using a syringe. Gently holding your dog's mouth shut with one hand, insert the syringe under the side of his lip and slowly squirt the medicine into his mouth.

Breed-specific problems

Since humans first started breeding dogs, they have been tailoring them for different purposes. As a result, there is huge diversity among dogs, each breed having its own special qualities and traits. However, in some breeds particular characteristics have been greatly exaggerated, and you will need to take these into consideration if they apply to your chosen pet, because they can cause health problems. For example, dogs that have been bred to have excess, wrinkly skin are very prone to skin infections and require their wrinkles to be cleaned regularly. Similarly, dogs with very thick coats designed to cope with extremes of cold can develop uncomfortable skin conditions when placed in a relatively temperate climate. Hairless breeds feel the cold, but are also at risk of sunburn and need to have their skin protected before they go outside. Long-backed dogs may be very good at disappearing down holes after small mammals, but have problems when faced with going up and down stairs and jumping on to sofas. Dogs bred to have a short, flat face are prone to breathing disorders and also heatstroke, because although they pant, the short muzzle does not give them the means to keep cool effectively.

Weight issues

Dogs are scavengers and tend to eat whatever is placed in front of them, because they do not know when they might next find food. For pet dogs with regular access to plentiful food, this natural trait has led to a high incidence of excess weight gain. Overweight dogs, like overweight humans, are at increased risk of serious health problems. Changes in your dog's waistline are hard to spot from day to day, so it's advisable to weigh him regularly as a routine health check. Owners of very large dogs may need to visit the veterinary surgery to use their scales. If you find your dog is becoming too heavy, aim to reduce his weight gradually by increasing his exercise levels and cutting down his food intake. For a dog that is obese, a vet may recommend a low-fat diet.

OVERWEIGHT
There are many health problems associated with excess weight gain in dogs. Recent studies have shown that the stress placed on a dog's body can shorten his life span by as much as two years.

SKIN PROBLEMS
Deep wrinkles like those of the Shar Pei provide a breeding ground for bacteria and need regular cleaning to prevent infections.

UNDERSHOT JAW
Dogs with undershot jaws, such as the Bulldog, also tend to have short muzzles. In warm environments, air passing through these shorter nasal passages does not have time to cool down properly, and as a result these dogs tend to warm up quickly. They must pant to cool down and need to do so for longer than other dogs.

CHECKING YOUR DOG
As your dog gets older, it becomes more important to make regular checks for any new lumps or bumps that may appear. Signs of pain or discomfort should be reported promptly to your vet.

EXTRA REST
Older dogs need increasing amounts of rest and tend to sleep more deeply. Allow them to lie undisturbed whenever possible and to wake up in their own time.

Elderly dogs

Senior dogs often do very well for many years but, as with humans, old age brings the need for changes. If your ageing dog loses a few teeth and finds it difficult to eat, ensure that he gets the correct level of nutrients for his age by switching to a specific senior diet, usually softer food that is easier to chew. Senior foods also contain nutrients aimed at easing joint pain, which is common in older dogs. Keep brushing your dog's teeth, because plaque build-up tends to increase in older dogs.

An elderly dog will not require the same amount of exercise as before, but a daily walk improves his circulation and provides much-needed stimulation from sights and smells. As your dog spends more time lying down, he may be at risk of developing pressure sores, so pay extra attention to vulnerable areas like elbows. If you own a long-coated breed, check that his coat is not becoming matted.

Keep an eye on your dog's general comfort and make sure that he can still access everything he needs. For example, he may begin to find stairs more challenging, or find it difficult to reach down to a water bowl to drink adequately.

FAILING SIGHT
Many elderly dogs begin to lose their sight, and rely on previous knowledge of their surroundings to get around the house. Think before you start moving furniture and confuse your dog with unexpected new obstacles.

Inherited diseases

An inherited disease or disorder is one that is passed from one generation to the next. Such a disease can mean that an individual is born with a medical condition or is genetically predisposed to developing one in later life. In the case of dogs, there are conditions common to each breed that are known to be inherited. These include joint disorders, blindness, and deafness. Responsible breeders do all they can to make sure that dogs affected by these disorders are neutered to prevent them passing on their genes to the next generation. Nevertheless, the nature of inheritance means that these conditions can never be eliminated completely, because some dogs are carriers (see box below).

Many inherited disorders can be traced through a pedigree and therefore breeders can take steps to reduce the chances of breeding an affected puppy by choosing their bloodlines

for breeding carefully. Good breeders will be able to go back through several generations to tell you whether any of the dogs in their breeding lines have had medical problems. They will also know what, if any, conditions remain a potential source of concern in the puppy of your choice.

For many conditions, especially those with a simple recessive inheritance pattern (see box below), screening tests can be carried out. Ask your breeder to show you the results of any tests that are relevant to your puppy or his parents. If one of the parents is a carrier, then their puppies may be too, so it would be unwise to breed from your dog without screening it first. If both parents are carriers, your puppy is at risk of being affected by the condition. Before you visit a breeder, learn all you can about the screening tests that apply to your chosen dog and his likely conditions, and make sure you know what results to look out for.

GENETICS AND INHERITED DISEASE

A common way for hereditary disorders to be passed on to offspring is through recessive inheritance. In the example of congenital blindness, dogs will be blind if they inherit a recessive gene (r) from both parents. The diagram shows how this can happen.

In cross 1, a sighted dog (RR) is crossed with a sighted carrier (Rr). All the offspring possess at least one dominant gene, and as a result are sighted. However, two of the puppies are carriers of the recessive gene for blindness.

In cross 2, both parents are carriers of the recessive gene. This means that there is a one in four chance that one of the puppies (rr) will inherit the recessive gene from both parents and be born blind; two puppies will be carriers (Rr); and one puppy (RR) will have normal sight.

CROSS 1

CROSS 2

Key
R = Dominant gene for normal sight
r = Recessive gene for blindness

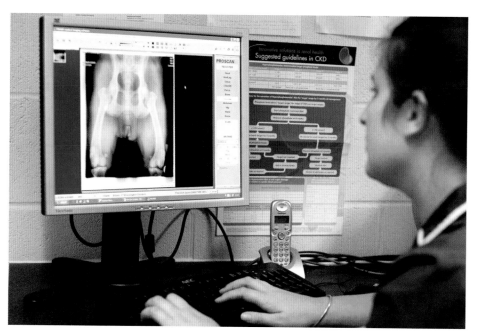

SCREENING
The likelihood of breeding puppies that develop the joint disorder hip dysplasia can be reduced by checking whether the parents are affected. This is done by assessing an X-ray of their hip joints and giving each a score that is compared to the average for the breed.

CONGENITAL DEAFNESS
Some breeds can inherit deafness, either complete or partial. There is a link between pigmentation and inherited deafness, and breeds with white variation, such as the Dalmatian, are often more at risk. Deafness should be tested for in all susceptible litters and any affected dogs neutered.

Even an ideal screening result is no guarantee that your puppy will not develop a chronic disorder. If you do have a problem, contact your vet but also be sure to report back to your breeder, who may choose not to repeat the mating that led to your puppy in future.

Think about the future
When you have decided what type of dog you are going to have, it is important to research which hereditary disorders are common problems within that particular breed. Read about each condition and be aware of the implications of taking on a puppy with a problem. Some disorders can be managed relatively easily and do not significantly affect the dog's general well-being and natural lifespan, although some adaptations may have to be made. A deaf dog, for example, needs to be trained using sign language and will not be able to run safely off-lead the majority of the time. Other disorders are potentially life-threatening and may require dedicated day-to-day, long-term management.

Consider also the increased cost of caring for a dog with a chronic condition. You could be faced with many years of vet's bills, regular medication, and special diets – and the expenses will soon add up. Work out what you can realistically cope with before going to visit a litter of puppies. It is all too easy to be persuaded to take on a cute puppy, but you may not have the skills, experience, time, or money to care for him adequately.

INHERITED DISORDERS

DISEASE	DESCRIPTION	CAN IT BE SCREENED FOR?	MANAGING THE DISEASE	TYPES OF DOG AFFECTED
Intervertebral disc disease	Similar to a prolapsed ("slipped") disc in humans; can cause intense pain and even paralysis.	No. The genetics of the condition are not fully understood.	Can be managed with rest and anti-inflammatory drugs; surgery may be necessary in severe cases.	Achondroplastic (dwarf) breeds that originated from a genetic mutation for short limbs.
Hip dysplasia	A condition in which the hip joint develops incorrectly.	Yes. An X-ray can be analysed and then measured against the breed average.	Careful management and pain relief is normally sufficient; surgery is available but relatively uncommon.	Heavy-bodied breeds, such as the mastiffs.
Elbow dysplasia	Abnormal development of the elbow joint.	Yes. X-rays of each elbow are analysed and given a numeric score. The overall grade is the higher of the two figures.	Affected dogs often benefit from exercise management and pain relief.	Large breeds. More prevalent in males than females. Rapid growth and weight gain exacerbate the symptoms.
Luxating patella	A congenital condition in which the patella (kneecap) slips out of its groove.	No. Affected dogs should not be used for breeding.	Controlled exercise and diet are the main treatments, with pain relief if necessary; surgery is indicated only in younger dogs or those with extreme mobility difficulties.	Most prevalent in toy breeds.
Aortic stenosis	A congenital disorder in which narrowing of the aortic valve reduces blood flow from the heart. Symptoms include breathlessness.	No. Affected dogs should not be used for breeding.	Exercise management may help dogs that become breathless on exertion.	Most prevalent in large breeds.
Von Willebrand disease	The most common inherited bleeding disorder in dogs. Varies in severity but can be lethal.	Yes. By blood and DNA tests.	Lifestyle adjustments and the use of blood-clotting drugs.	Not breed or group specific.
Progressive retinal atrophy (PRA)	Deterioration of the retina, leading to blindness.	Yes. A simple test categorizes dogs as affected, carriers, or unaffected.	Lifestyle management.	Occurs in most breeds but inheritance of the condition differs. Genes may be dominant or recessive. Symptoms usually apparent by three years of age.
Cataracts	Clouding of the lens of the eye, causing impaired vision.	Yes. For some breeds there is a DNA test. Affected dogs should not be used for breeding.	Cataracts are removed surgically; the operation is relatively simple.	Not breed or group specific and may occur at any age.
Entropion	Inward turning of the eyelids, causing damage to the surface of the eyeball.	No. Affected dogs should not be used for breeding.	Can be corrected surgically.	Common in brachycephalic breeds (flat-faced with short muzzle) and breeds with heavy, folded skin on the head.
Ectropion	Outward turning of the lower eyelid; may lead to dry eyes and infection.	No. Affected dogs should not be used for breeding.	Can be corrected surgically.	Most prevalent in breeds with loose facial skin, as seen in spaniels and some breeds of hound.

DISEASE	DESCRIPTION	CAN IT BE SCREENED FOR?	MANAGING THE DISEASE	TYPES OF DOG AFFECTED
Distichiasis	Abnormal growth of the eyelashes. May cause pain and discomfort.	No. Affected dogs should not be used for breeding.	A vet may remove the abnormal hairs by plucking.	May occur in any breed but is more common in those with moderate to heavy skin folds on the head.
Deafness	Complete or partial loss of hearing; can occur from birth or over the course of the dog's life.	Yes. A non-invasive, painless test can be carried out by a specialist vet.	A dog completely deaf from birth is not recommended for a pet. Partially deaf dogs often have normal lives.	Most common in dogs with white, spotted, dappled, or merle coats. Some dogs also have blue eyes.
Abnormal dentition	In most breeds, the teeth normally meet in a scissor bite. Deviation from this can result in an overshot or undershot jaw.	No. Affected dogs should not be used for breeding.	Most dogs experience no problems. Occasionally, surgical intervention is called for if the dog has trouble eating or drinking.	An undershot jaw is acceptable in some brachycephalic breeds. In others, it is considered a fault.
Elongated palate	A condition in which the soft palate at the back of the mouth abnormally overlaps the airway, obstructing breathing.	No. Affected dogs should not be used for breeding.	Serious cases can be corrected with surgery to remove excess tissue on the palate.	Most prevalent in brachycephalic breeds.
Hypothyroidism	A deficiency in thyroid hormone that causes slow metabolism.	Yes. A blood test is available. Affected dogs should not be used for breeding.	Typical symptoms such as weight gain, lethargy, and hair loss can be controlled with medication.	Occurs in medium- and large-sized dogs. Symptoms tend to appear when dogs reach middle age.
Diabetes mellitus	A condition in which the dog's ability to metabolize blood sugar is impaired.	Yes. A DNA test is possible but not routinely carried out. Affected dogs should not be used for breeding.	Dogs who eat or drink unusually large amounts may be suffering from diabetes; the condition can be controlled with medication.	Not breed or group specific. More common in females. Symptoms tend to appear when dogs reach middle age.
Cleft palate	The roof of the mouth does not join correctly in the middle, preventing puppies from suckling properly.	No. Any dog that has produced puppies with cleft palates should not be used for further breeding.	Most vets recommend euthanizing affected puppies. Occasionally, it may be possible to hand rear a puppy until it is old enough to undergo corrective surgery.	May occur in any breed or cross-bred dog but most common in brachycephalic breeds.
Megaoesophagus	An enlarged oesophagus that lacks muscle tone and cannot convey swallowed food down to the stomach. An affected dog constantly regurgitates.	No. Any dog that has produced puppies with megaoesophagus should not be used for further breeding.	Depending on the severity of the condition, changes such as feeding small amounts from a raised bowl can have a positive impact.	Not breed or group specific. If condition is congenital, symptoms appear in the first few weeks or months of life.
Epilepsy	A neurological disorder causing characteristic fits or seizures.	Yes. DNA test. Affected dogs should not be used for breeding.	Epilepsy is not curable, but drug therapy can greatly reduce the likelihood of seizures.	Not breed or group specific. If congenital, symptoms appear between six months and five years of age.

GLOSSARY

Achondroplasia - A form of dwarfism that affects the long bones of the limbs, causing them to bow outwards. It is a genetic mutation that has been selectively bred for, resulting in short-legged breeds such as the Dachshund.

Almond-shaped eyes - Oval eyes with slightly flattened corners that are present in breeds such as the Kooikerhondje and the English Springer Spaniel.

Beard - Thick, sometimes coarse and bushy hair around the lower facial area. Often seen in wire-haired breeds.

Belton - A coat pattern that is a mix of white and coloured hairs (roan) that may have a flecked or ticked appearance.

Bicolour - Any colour combined with white patches.

Black and tan - A coat colour with clearly defined areas of black and tan. The black colour is usually found on the body and the tan colour on the underparts, muzzle, and perhaps as spots above the eyes. This pattern also occurs in liver and tan and blue and tan coats.

Blanket, blanket markings - Large areas of colour over the back and sides of the body; commonly used to describe hound markings.

Blaze - Broad, white marking running from near the top of the head to the muzzle.

Brachycephalic head - A head that is almost as wide as it is long due to shortening of the muzzle. The Bulldog and Boston Terrier are examples of breeds with this head shape.

Bracke - A term used for continental hounds that specialize in running down small game such as rabbit or fox.

Breeches - Fringing of longer hair on the thighs, which is Iso known as culottes or trousers.

Breed - Domestic dogs that have been selectively bred to have the same distinctive appearance. They conform to a breed standard drawn up by a breed club and approved by an internationally

recognized body, such as the Kennel Club, FCI, or American Kennel Club.

Breed Standard - The detailed description of a breed that specifies exactly how the dog should look, the acceptable colours and markings, and the range of height and/or weight measurements.

Brindle - A colour mix in which dark hairs form a striped pattern on lighter background of tan, gold, grey, or brown.

Brisket - The breastbone.

Button ears - Semi-erect ears in which the top part folds down towards the eye covering the ear opening. They are seen on breeds such as the Fox Terrier.

Candleflame ears - Long, narrow, erect ears that are shaped like a candleflame. They are seen on breeds such as the English Toy Terrier.

Cape - Thick hair covering the shoulders.

Carnassial teeth - Cheek teeth (upper fourth premolar and lower first molar) that are used, rather like a pair of scissors, to slice through meat, hide, and bone.

Cat-like feet - Round, compact feet with the toes grouped closely together.

Conformation - The general appearance of a dog that is determined by the development of individual features and their relationship to one another.

Croup - An area of the back just above the base of the tail.

Cropped ears - Ears that are erect and pointed due to surgical removal of part of the ear cartilage. The procedure, which is illegal in many countries, including the UK, is normally carried out when puppies are about 10–16 weeks old.

Dander - Small scales of dead skin shed from the body.

Dapple - A spotted coat of darker markings on a lighter background. Usually used as a description for short-haired breeds only; merle is used to describe the same colouring in long-haired dogs.

Dewclaw - A non-weight-bearing toe on the inner side of the lower foreleg (pastern). Some breeds, such as the Schipperke, may also have dewclaws on the hindlegs, while others, such as the Norwegian Lundehund, have double dewclaws.

Dewlap - Loose, hanging skin that falls in folds on the chin, throat, and neck of some breeds: for example, the Bloodhound.

Docked tail - A tail cut to a specific length in accordance with the breed standard. The procedure is normally carried out when puppies are only a few days old. The practice is now illegal in the UK and parts of Europe except for the tails of working dogs such as the German Pointer.

Dolichocephalic head - A long, narrow head with an imperceptible stop, as seen in the Borzoi, for example.

Double coat - Coat consisting of a thick, warm underlayer and a weatherproof top layer.

Drop ears - Ears that hang down from their base. Pendant ears are a more extreme form of drop ears, being longer and heavier.

Erect ears - Upright or pricked ears with pointed or rounded tips. Candleflame ears are an extreme type of erect ears.

Feathers, feathering - Fringes of hair that may be found on the ear margins, belly, backs of legs, and the underside of the tail.

Flews - The lips of a dog. Most commonly used to describe the fleshy, hanging upper lips in dogs of the mastiff type.

Forelock - Lock of hair on the forehead that falls forward between the ears.

Furrow - A shallow groove, visible in some breeds, that runs from the top of the head down to the stop.

Gait - Movement or action.

Griffon - (Fr.) Referring to a coarse or wire coat.

Grizzle - Usually a mixture of black and white hairs, which gives a blue-grey or iron-grey shading to the coat. It is seen in some breeds of terrier.

Group - Dog breeds are classified into various groups by the Kennel Club, FCI, and American Kennel Club. The groups are loosely based on function but no two systems agree. The number and names of the groups differ, as do the breeds that are recognized and included in them.

Hackney gait - Dogs with this type of action, such as the Miniature Pinscher, raise the lower part of the leg particularly high as they walk.

Harlequin - A colour pattern comprising irregular-sized patches of black on white; seen only in the Great Dane.

Hock - Joint on the hind leg; equivalent to the human heel; in dogs this is elevated because they walk on their toes.

Isabella - A fawn colour found in some breeds, including the Bergamasco and Dobermann.

Mask - Dark coloration on the face, usually around the muzzle and eyes.

Merle - A marbled coat with darker patches or spots. Blue merle (black on a bluish-grey background) is the most common variation.

Mesaticephalic head - Head shape in which the base and width are of medium proportions. The Labrador Retriever and Border Collie are examples of breeds with this type of head shape.

Neutering - A surgical procedure that prevents dogs from breeding.

Oestrus - A period of about three weeks in the reproductive cycle during which a female dog can be mated. Primitive breeds tend to come into oestrus once a year (as do wolves); in other breeds it is usually twice a year.

Otter tail - A thickly furred, rounded tail that has a broad base and tapers to the tip; the hair on the underside is parted. It is seen in breeds such as the Labrador Retriever and Chesapeake Bay Retriever.

Pack - Usually used to describe a group of scent or sight hounds that hunt together.

Pastern - Lower part of the leg, below the carpals (wrist bones) of the foreleg or the hock on the hind leg.

Pendant ears - Ears that hang down from their base; an extreme form of drop ears.

Pendulous lips - Full, loosely hanging upper or lower lips.

Rose ears - Small, drop ears that fold outwards and backwards so that part of the ear canal is exposed. This type of ear is seen in Whippets.

Ruff - A long, thick collar of stand-out hair around the neck.

Sable - A coat colour in which hairs tipped with black overlay a lighter background colour.

Saddle - A darker coloured area that extends over the back.

Scissors bite - The normal bite of dogs with mesaticephalic and dolichocephalic heads. The upper incisors (front teeth) are slightly in front of but in contact with the lower incisors when the mouth is closed. The other teeth interlock with no gaps and form the cutting edge of the "scissors".

Semi-erect ears - Erect ears in which only the tip is inclined forwards, as seen in breeds such as the Rough Collie (right).

Sesame - A coat colour comprising an equal mixture of black and white hairs. In black sesame, there are more black hairs than white; red sesame is a mixture of red and black hairs.

Sickle tail - Tail that is carried in a half circle over the back.

Spoon-like feet - Similar to cat-like feet but more oval in shape because the middle toes are longer than the outer toes.

Stop - The indentation between the muzzle and the top of the head, in between the eyes. The stop is almost absent in dolichocephalic breeds, such as the Borzoi, and very pronounced in brachycephalic and dome-headed breeds, such as the American Cocker Spaniel and the Chihuahua.

Temperament - The character of a dog.

Topcoat - Outer coat of guard hairs.

Topknot - Long tuft of hair on the top of the head.

Topline - The outline of the dog's upper body from ears to tail.

Tricolour - A coat of three colours in well-defined patches, usually black, tan, and white.

Tucked up - Referring to the belly, an upward curve to the abdomen towards the hind quarters, typically seen in breeds such as the Greyhound and the Whippet.

Undercoat - Underlayer of hair, usually short, thick, and sometimes woolly, that provides insulation between the topcoat and the skin.

Undershot - Facial conformation in which the lower jaw protrudes beyond the upper jaw, seen in breeds such as the Bulldog.

Undershot bite - The normal bite of brachycephalic breeds such as the Bulldog. Because the lower jaw is longer than the upper jaw, the incisor teeth do not meet and the lower incisors are in front of the upper ones.

Withers - The highest point of the shoulder, where the neck meets the back. A dog's height is measured vertically from the ground to the withers.

INDEX

The dog breeds listed in this index may be followed by any combination of the initials KC (Kennel Club), FCI (Federation Cynologique Internationale - the World Canine Organisation), and AKC (American Kennel Club). The initials indicate which of these three international organizations recognize the breed. Occasionally the KC, FCI, and AKC recognize the same breed but use a different name to the one used in this book. This alternative name is also listed along with the initials of the organization that uses it. Some breeds have been granted provisional acceptance by the FCI and these are indicated here as FCI*. Other breeds have no initials following their name but may be recognized by other kennel clubs in their country of origin, and be in the approval process of one of the organizations listed here.

INDEX *continued*

INDEX *continued*

M

Magyar Agar FCI
 see Hungarian Greyhound 127
Majorca Shepherd Dog 80
Malinois KC 39
Mallorca Mastiff 83
Mal-Shi 287
Maltese KC, FCI, AKC 11, 17, 269
Manchester Terrier KC, FCI,AKC 60, 211
Maremma Sheepdog KC 15, 33, 63
Mastiff KC, FCI, AKC 84, 93, 95, 159
Mastín Espagnol FCI
 see Spanish Mastiff 16, 87
Mastín del Pirineo FCI
 see Pyrenean Mastiff 76
Mastino Napoletano FCI
 see Neapolitan Mastiff 16, 33, 91
Mexican Hairless
 see Xoloitzcuintle 31
Miniature American Shepherd 280
Miniature Black and Tan Terrier
 see English Toy Terrier 17,
  208, 210, 270
Miniature Bull Terrier KC, FCI, AKC 198
Miniature Pinscher KC, AKC 17,
 187, 217
Miniature Schnauzer KC, AKC
 16, 218
Mioritic Shepherd Dog FCI
 see Romanian Shepherd Dogs 65
Modder Rhu
 see Irish Setter 15, 241
Monkey Dog
 see Portuguese Sheepdog 46
Montenegrin Mountain Hound 182
Mountain Cur 184
Mudi FCI 40

N

Neapolitan Mastiff KC, AKC 16, 33, 91
Nederlandse Kooikerhondje FCI, AKC
 see Kooikerhondje 238
Nederlandse Schapendoes FCI
 see Dutch Schapendoes 15, 54
New Guinea Singing Dog 23, 24
New Zealand Huntaway 15, 58
Newfoundland KC, FCI, AKC 16, 71, 74

Nihon Supittsu FCI
 see Japanese Spitz 116
Nihon Teria FCI
 see Japanese Terrier 208
Nihon Terrier
 see Japanese Terrier 208
Nippon Terrier
 see Japanese Terrier 208
Norrbottenspets FCI
 see Nordic Spitz 16, 121
Nordic Spitz 16, 121
Norfolk Spaniel
 see English Springer Spaniel 220,
  221, 226-27
Norfolk Terrier KC, FCI, AKC
 16, 191, 287
Norsk Buhund FCI
 see Norwegian Buhund 121
Norsk Elghund Gra FCI
 see Norwegian Elkhound 110
Norsk Elghund Sort FCI
 see Black Norwegian
  Elkhound 110
Norsk Lundehund FCI
 see Norwegian Lundehund 120
Norwegian Buhund KC, AKC 121
Norwegian Elkhound KC, AKC 110
Norwegian Hound 156
Norwegian Lundehund AKC 120
Norwich Terrier KC, FCI, AKC 187,
 197
Nova Scotia Duck Tolling Retriever
 KC, FCI, AKC 243

O

Ogar Polski FCI
 see Polish Hound 180
Old Danish Pointer 255
Old English Sheepdog KC, FCI,
 AKC 15, 49
Olde English Bulldogge 263
Österreichischer Pinscher FCI
 see Austrian Pinscher 219
Otterhound KC, FCI, AKC 137,
 140-41, 142
Ovtcharka
 see South Russian Shepherd
  Dog 55

P

Papillon KC, AKC 17, 122
Parson Russell Terrier KC, FCI,
 AKC 195
Patterdale Terrier 15, 212
Peintingen Hound
 see Styrian Coarse-haired
  Mountain Hound 15, 147
Pekingese KC, FCI, AKC 11, 17, 261,
 264, 266
Pembroke Welsh Corgi KC, AKC
 16, 33, 56, 60
Perdigueiro Português FCI
 see Portuguese Pointer 248
Perdiguero de Burgos FCI
 see Spanish Pointer 255
Perro de Agua Español FCI
 see Spanish Water
  Dog 230
Perro Dogo Mallorquín FCI
 see Mallorca Mastiff 83
Perro sin Pelo del Perú FCI
 see Peruvian Hairless 30
Peruvian Hairless 30
Peruvian Inca Orchid 29
Petit Anglo-Française
 see Anglo-Française de Petite
  Vénerie 151
Petit Basset Griffon Vendéen
 KC, FCI, AKC 143
Petit Bleu de Gascogne FCI 166
Petit Brabançon FCI
 see Griffon Bruxellois 17, 262
Petit Chien Lion FCI
 see Löwchen 17, 268
Phalene see Papillon 17, 122
Pharaoh Hound KC, FCI, AKC 23, 25
Picardy Sheepdog KC 36
Picardy Spaniel 16, 239
Piccolo Levriero Italiano FCI
 see Italian Greyhound 127
pinschers
 Doberman Pinscher AKC see
  Dobermann 179
 other varieties see under
  terriers
Plott AKC
 see Plott Hound 159

Plott Hound 159
Podenco Canario FCI
 see Canarian Warren Hound 26
Podenco Ibecenco FCI
 see Ibizan Hound 23, 27
Podengo Português FCI
 see Portuguese Podengo 28
Pointer AKC
 see English Pointer 15, 221,
  254
pointers see under gundogs
Poitevin FCI 15, 168, 170
Polish Greyhound 15, 131
Polish Hound 180
Polish Lowland Sheepdog KC,
 AKC 15, 54
Polski Owczarek Nizinny FCI
 see Polish Lowland
  Sheepdog 15, 54
Polski Owczarek Podhalanski FCI
 see Tatra Shepherd Dog 73
Pomeranian KC, AKC 17, 97, 123
Pont-Audemer Spaniel 235
Poodle AKC
 see Standard Poodle 16, 231, 233,
  261, 271
Poodle KC, AKC 11, 251, 267, 271,
 284, 285, 288
Porcelaine FCI 151
Portuguese Cattle Dog
 see Castro Laboreiro Dog 45
Portuguese Podengo KC, AKC
 28
Portuguese Pointer KC 248
Portuguese Pointing Dog FCI
 see Portuguese Pointer 248
Portuguese Sheepdog 46
Portuguese Warren Hound
 see Portuguese Podengo 28
Portuguese Watchdog 45
Portuguese Water Dog KC,
 AKC 16, 231
Posavaz Hound 181
Posavski Gonic FCI
 see Posavaz Hound 181
Powderpuff Chinese Crested
 see Chinese Crested 11, 17, 261,
  274-75
Presa Canario FCI 16, 84

INDEX *continued*

INDEX *continued*

ACKNOWLEDGMENTS

First Edition

DK UK

Senior Editor Kathryn Hennessy
Design Manager Amanda Lunn
Editors Cressida Tuson, Nicola Hodgson, Jemima Dunne
Designer Steve Woosnam Savage
Design Assistant Kirsty Tizzard
Art Worker Philip Fitzgerald
Picture Researcher Kate Lockley
DK Picture Library Claire Bowers, Emma Shepherd
Database Peter Cook, David Roberts
Deputy Production Editorial Manager Luca Frassinetti
Senior Production Controller Angela Graef
Managing Editor Esther Ripley
Managing Art Editor Karen Self
Publisher Laura Buller

Art Director Phil Ormerod
Associate Publishing Director Liz Wheeler
Publishing Director Jonathan Metcalf

DK INDIA

Deputy Managing Editor Pakshalika Jayaprakash
Senior Editor Garima Sharma
Editor Antara Moitra
Assistant Editor Archana Ramachandran
Managing Art Editor Arunesh Talapatra
Deputy Managing Art Editor Priyabrata Roy Chowdhury
Senior Art Editor Chhaya Sajwan
Project Art Editor Anjana Nair
Art Editors Shruti Soharia Singh, Priyanka Singh
Assistant Art Editors Nidhi Mehra, Vidit Vashisht, Payal Rosalind Malik, Aastha Tiwari, Mansi Nagdev

DTP Manager Balwant Singh
Senior DTP Designers Dheeraj Arora, Jagtar Singh
DTP Designers Bimlesh Tiwari, Nand Kishor Acharya, Mohammad Usman, Arjinder Singh, Tanveer Abbas
Production Manager Pankaj Sharma

The publisher would like to thank the following people for their assistance with book:

Lez Graham for text; Johnny Pau for design assistance; Monica Saigal, Gaurav Joshi, Suparna Sengupta, and Sreshtha Bhattacharya for editorial assistance; Caroline Hunt for proofreading; Margaret McCormack for the index; The Kennel Club; Jean-Baptiste for help with the Saint Germain Pointers at the Paris Dog Show; John Wilesmith and Stewart Comely from the Three Counties Showground, Malvern; Project Manager Afa Yahiaoui for her help at the World Dog Show, Paris; All committee members and show

organisers of the International Dog Show, Genk, Belgium with special thanks to Chairman Willem Vervloet and Deputy Secretary Patricia Claes; Special thanks to the dog handlers and photographer's assistants Hilary Wilkinson, Stella Carpenter, Stephanie Carpenter, and Kim Davies, and photographer Tracy Morgan

The publisher would like to thank the following owners for letting us photograph their dogs:
Breed name (owner's name/dog's name) Airedale Terrier (Graulus Francois/Hurbie Van'tasbroek); Akita (D and J Killilea and A Clure/ Ch Redwitch What Goes Around); Alaskan Malamute (Sian and David Luker/Anubis); American Cocker Spaniel (Wilma Weymans/ Chicomy's Midnight Special); American Staffordshire Terrier (Kim Hahn/Beauty Power Pride Justify); American Water Spaniel (Sanna Kytöjoki and Tiina Närhi-Jääskeläinen/ Afire's Chocolate Robber "Aapo"); Appenzell Cattle Dog (Claas Wentzler/C-Mexx vom Markgrund); Australian Shepherd (Jens Goessens/

ACKNOWLEDGMENTS *continued*

Leading Angels Diamond Shock Factor); Australian Silky Terrier (I Leino, shown by Mr and Mrs De Bondt/Bombix Moren par Noster); Australian Terrier (Iris Coppée/Ch Cidan von den Grauen Anfurten); Beagle (M Cherevko/Valsi Imagemaker for Bravo Vista Maxim; Peter Lakatos/Black Magic of Celestina's Garden); Belgian Griffon (Mr Nikulins and Patricia Blacky/ Harpersband Aleksandra); Blue Picardy Spaniel (Nichael Chayentien/ Defi de la Ferme de la Conduene; Richard Floquet/Fangio); Boston Terrier (R Lutz/Macho Tex Mex); Bourbonnais Pointing Dog (Irma Širmeniene/Canine Dawenasti); Bouvier des Flandres (Peter Aerts/ Hero von Gewdraa Oel; Nadine and Johan Schoonackers/Juno Black Mystic Legend); Boxer (Mr and Mrs Cobb/Topauly Wizard Apprentice); Bracco Italiano (Mr and Mrs M E Wilson/Braccorions Cruz); Braque d'Auvergne (Peteris Zvaigzne/ Khyannes Fata Morgana); Broholmer (Peeraer Alfons/Hugin); Bulldog (Mr and Mrs P W Davies/Quintic Doris at Kismond JW and Flash Zach Kismond); Caucasian Shepherd Dog (Patrick Juilla/Cal); Chinese Crested (D Rich and J and B Long/Champion Sole Splash Russian Dancer Rudy); Clumber Spaniel (Sandra Queen/ Tweedsmuir Makaya; Mrs Monaghan/ Tweedsmuir Dambuster; Susan Boden/Tweedsmuir Beautiful Dream Among Suelynda and Tweedsmuir Klassic Edition Among Sueynda); Corded Poodle (Françoise and Nadége Baillargeaux/Amazone de Cybele des Can'Tzu and Alaska de Cybele des Can'Tzu); Cursinu (Gilles Cano/T'Ribellu); Dalmatian (R and H Tingey/Hoderness Hillbilly by Dallyador JW); Dogo Argentino (PHC Bakkereren/Intl Paradero del Montero and PHC Bakkereren/Jomilito Paradero del Montero); Drentsche Partridge Dog (Niels Peter Jakobsen/ Fog's Lucca); English Cocker Spaniel (Luise and Peta Doppelreiter-Baines/ JW Riondel Riddick's Cronical from Furians); English Pointer (Mrs Siddle/ Wilchrimane Ice Maiden); English Springer Spaniel (C Woodbridge and T Dunsdon/Seaspring Shipwrecked "Eddie"); Entlebucher Mountain Dog (Dog's Name: Kazanova iz Blagorodnogo Domh); Field Spaniel (CH and J Holgate/Ewtor McEwan at Nadavin); Flat Coated Retriever (Steve Hammersley/Stranfaer Doctor Foster); French Bulldog (Jack Meerten/Usm u.d Mestreechteneerkes); French Pyrenean Pointer (Mr and Mrs Jacques Brain/Elfy de Bois le Bon; Maria Fernelius/Farin de la Balingue); German Hunting Terrier (W.F.D (Fred) Amiabel/Faita vom Eichblatt); German Pointer - Short-haired (Shelley Fisher/Will I Am Of Ankherwood JW); German Pointer

- Wire-haired (Karel Brusten/Hans); Giant Schnauzer (Marie-France Seewald/Gloris Gaia); Glen of Imaal Terrier (Marc Vande Wiele/Fiddlers Green Bel-Ami); Goldendoodle (James Harrison/Elsie); Great Swiss Mountain Dog (Astrid and Oliver Thomas/Aljosha vom Muckenbruch); Greyhound (Uwe and Cordelia Schmidt/Artefakt Demigodat Resch Wind); Griffon Fauve de Bretagne (Michel Imbert and Daniel Carrat/Carlos); Hungarian Kuvasz (Jeanette De Jong/Grada-Merieno A Gázdaság Rol); Hungarian Vizsla - Smooth-haired (Jessie Claire Van Brederode/INT LUX NL CH Bink V D Achtoevenslag; Irma Sirmeniene/ Malomkozi); Hungarian Vizsla (Mrs Jane Delf/Tragus Kashka); Irish Terrier (Nanna Pesola/Karamell-in Kuutar); Italian Corso Dog (Wendy van den Berg/Estilo Bettino Del Montagna Oro); Italian Spinone (M D Wellman and A J Cook/IR SH CH NL ch Jaspins Be My Sweetheart JW); Jack Russell Terrier - Wire-haired (Agnes Polleunis/Suzan's Pride Houplapoum); Korthals Griffon – Wire-haired (Reisa Antila/D'Wicca Dubois Du Onzion); Labradinger (Jemima Dunne/Winston); Labrador Retriever (Jenny King/Rollo and Sky); Lakeland Terrier (Mr and Mrs Friedrich-Wilhelm Schöneberg/Nujax Rising Sun At Saredon); Mallorca Mastiff (Noelle Lecoeur/Cave Canem de la Tour Gelee); Miniature Pinscher (Yvan Hulpiau/A Dreams Black Y Cha); Miniature Schnauzer (D L and M May/ By God Sir Maybe A Rumour); Norfolk Terrier (Theo and Sophie Braam/R U Kidding Me John Owen); Norwegian Buhund (M E Leoehoorn/Yrsa-Yitze Fra Den Norske); Norwich Terrier (Mr and Mrs Souply Philippe/Antares Du Taillis De La Grange Au Rouge); Old English Sheepdog (E S and C J Jones/ Wenallt Wonder Why); Otterhound (Rae Ganna/Champion, French Champion, World Champion Keepcott Connoisseur); Parson Russell Terrier – Wire-haired (Katinka Stotyn/ Jenny and Coldy); Pembroke Welsh Corgi (J Whitehead/Wharrytons Golden Legacy; L A Weedall/CH Bronabay Cherish The Moment JW; L A Weedall and N A Bogue/Bronabay Troopin The Colour; M Fairall, handled by Emma/Bertley Harvester); Petit Brabançon (Olga Gordienko and Patricia Blacky/Zerkalo Dushi Eminem); Pont-Audemer Spaniel (Mr and Mrs Stalter/Divora des Marais de la Risle); Poodle - Miniature (A Corish and J Rowland/Dechine It's A Secret At Tinkersdale); Poodle - Toy (S É Martin/Philora Silver Thomas and Philora Vanilla Ice); Pyrenean Sheepdog (Per Toie Romstad/ Quidam); Romanian Shepherd Dog - Carpatin (Marian Crisan/ Cronos and Dog's Name: Gorun de Ovican); Romanian Shepherd

Dog - Mioritic (Anne Lasti/Agada and Boss Nordic Delight); Rottweiler (Yvonne Bekkers/Munanis Enjoy); Rough Collie (J Margetts/Libby); Russian Black Terrier (Kristiane van den Driesch and Elena Graf/Christo Russkaya 12 Chigasovo); Russian Toy - Long-haired (Anna Bogdanova/ Stempfor Beatrix); Russian Toy - Short-haired (Dog's Name: Malenkaya Makiya Detomaspantera); Saint Germain Pointer (Brigitte Turmel/ Diwan de Rosa Bonheur; Corinne Mercier/Divine de la Noue des Aulnes); Samoyed (Chris Brookes/ Kyia); Schipperke (Mrs Lefort/Buffy; Mrs Oreal/Frambois); Sealyham Terrier (owned by A Klimeshova bred by Olga Ivanova/Olbori Missis Marpl); Slovakian Pointer - Rough-haired (L A H and A J H van Heynsbergen/1X Yvka Van De Merlin Hoeve); Smooth Collie (Jane Evans/Southcombe Starman); Smooth Fox Terrier (Mr and Mrs Pitel/Clara); Soft-coated Wheaten Terrier (Ammette Buscher and Alima Lammering/Duke-Camillo Vombelker-Bad); Spanish Water Dog (Dawn Galbraith/Valentisimo Neuschocoa); Standard Poodle (L Woods and J Lynn/Afterglow Tough Luck); St Miguel Cattle Dog (Noelle Lecoeur/Dolce Querida da Casa de Praia); Sussex Spaniel (Mr and Mrs J C Shankland/Jubilwell Mars At Nyrrela); Swedish Vallhund (A W M Muys/Stenrikas Ivriga IDA); Vizsla (Gillian Ellis/Finch); Weimaraner - Short-haired (C Mutlow/Risinglark Hawk Wing JW); Weimaraner - Long-haired (Kimberley Harman/ Lassemista Tango); Welsh Springer Spaniel (Karolien Kemerlincke/ Precious; Loyal Jada and Marian Smolenaers/Mastermind From Kind Of Magic); Welsh Terrier (PMJ Krautscheid/Nagant From Michel); Whippet (E C Walker/Shoalingam Silver Willow); White Swiss Shepherd Dog (Andre Maryse/C'Keops and Doumo); Wire Fox Terrier (Veronique Gehan/Legend of Crudy Zapphir); Xoloitzcuintle (Dog's Name: Fernando du Coeur Des Tenebres); Yorkshire Terrier (S T Carruthers/Champion Frasermera Tempting Kisses JW; Margaret Comrie-Bryant/Roxanne)

Second Edition

DK Delhi would like to thank:
Shipra Jain and Sampda Mago for design assistance; Rishi Bryan and Janashree Singha for editorial assistance; Harish Aggarwal for DTP design assistance; Priyanka Sharma for jackets editorial coordination; and Saloni Singh, Managing Jackets Editor.

Picture credits

The publisher would like to thank the following for their kind permission to reproduce their photographs:

Picture Key: a-above; b-below/bottom; c-centre; f-far; l-left; r-right; t-top

6-7 Fotolia: lunamarina. 8 Dorling Kindersley: Jerry Young (br). 20-21 Alamy Images: Juniors Bildarchiv. 22 Corbis: Cheryl Ertelt / Visuals Unlimited (c). 23 Alamy Images: FLPA (bl). 32 Getty Images: AFP (c). 59 Animal Photography: Tetsu Yamazaki (br). 69 Alamy Stock Photo: Arco Images GmbH / Steimer, C. (cra). 70 Animal Photography: Eva-Maria Kramer (b, tr). 77 Dreamstime.com: Biserko (br). 83 Flickr.com: Yugan Talovich (tr). 84 Animal Photography: Eva-Maria Kramer (t). 85 Courtesy of Jessica Snäcka: Sanna Södergren (b). 87 Animal Photography: Eva-Maria Kramer (t). 96 Getty Images: Zero Creatives (c). 108 Alamy Images: imagebroker (br). Photoshot: imagebroker (bl). 112 Dreamstime.com: Isselee (br); Photovova (bc). 113 123RF.com: rottoro (bl). Dreamstime.com: Gitamaluo Kemkon (br). 115 Getty Images: Mitsuaki Iwago (bl). NHPA / Photoshot: Biosphoto / J.-L. Klein & M (br). 124 Getty Images: (c). 136 Getty Images: Jupiterimages (c). 148 Alamy Images: imagebroker (t). 149 Alamy Stock Photo: Ricant Images (br). Dreamstime.com: Elisa Bistocchi (bl). 172 Animal Photography: Eva-Maria Kramer (b). Photoshot: NHPA (t). 173 Animal Photography: Eva-Maria Kramer (tr, cl). 175 Animal Photography: Sally Anne Thompson (tr, cl). 186 Alamy Images: Juniors Bildarchiv (c). 194 Alamy Stock Photo: Iuliia Mashkova (cla). Shutterstock: yykkaa (tr). 215 Getty Images: Mark Raycroft (br). 220 Getty Images: David Tipling (c). 224 Pamela O. Kadlec: (t). 247 SuperStock: Jean-Michel Labat / Pantheon (bc). 260 Alamy Images: RJT Photography (c). 263 Alamy Images: Farlap (tr). 280 123RF.com: Erik Lam (tr). Alamy Stock Photo: Erik Lam Boats (cla). 282 Getty Images: Steve Dueck (c). 285 Dreamstime.com: Ian Mcglasham (bl, br). 287 Alamy Stock Photo: Bill Bachman (br). Warren Photographic Limited: (clb). 292-293 Corbis: Ben Welsh / Design Pics

All other images © Dorling Kindersley
For further information see:

www.dkimages.com